GUTS

John Lyons

amacom

AMERICAN MANAGEMENT ASSOCIATION

This book is available at a special
discount when ordered in bulk quantities.
For information, contact Special Sales Department,
AMACOM, a division of American Management Association,
135 West 50th Street, New York, NY 10020.

Library of Congress Cataloging-in-Publication Data

Lyons, John, 1940–
     Guts: advertising from the inside out.

     Bibliography: p.
     1. Advertising.   I. Title.
HF5823.L92   1987   659.1   86-47816
ISBN 0-8144-5537-9

Printing number

10 9 8 7 6 5 4 3 2 1

PREFACE

Once upon a time I was a spunky little boy who wanted to grow up to be Pete Rose.

Rolaids, a fire would break out in a man's stomach, suck in
Clorets, modulating mouth beepers would broadcast bad breath.) I can't tell you that this style of selling didn't work. I can only say that life at Bates never pretended to imitate art.

I saw advertising then as a stop-gap measure, a diverting way to make money doing what I loved to do: write.

Now, 20 years later, here I am, having just finished the fourth draft of a book on the subject. Psyched by the merger craze and the immense realignment of money, power, priorities, and talent, I remain steadfast in my belief that we cannot only do far better but win and have a lot more fun playing the game.

To understand how to play, one needs to establish the rules. Agencies win when they create superior advertising. Agencies lose when they put their own interests ahead of their clients' interests. Yet we all know what the priorities of many agencies are. The things they consider important and how they spend their time are a matter of record. Which may explain why we don't feel like gifted golden boys playing and loving the game anymore.

Are we all a bunch of "talented chumps," as one hard-working art director friend of mine suggests? And why is Pete Rose still having all the fun? I needed an answer.

I went to Roger Angell, one of our best reporters, who is as fascinated with the art of hitting as I am with the art of persuasion. Here's what he says about Rose: "He has been able to maintain a kid-like innocence motivated by a simple love for the game." A beguiling thought. And a rather angelic premise for a book about advertising—that is, we lose our innocent belief in fun and fire for our work every time we compromise an idea we love.

While Pete Rose runs the bases in heat, we often work in a cold sweat. We create out of fear. Fear of the creative director. Fear of clients. Fear of the network. Fear of lawyers. Fear of Burke. The result is a loss of participation, presence, and passion.

This book examines ways to get us out of what Oliver Hardy refers to as "a fine mess." It presents our predicament and offers specifics. Some practical, some outrageous, on how to play the game without playing it scared. And how to win for your agency, your client, yourself. If you're young, raw, and ambitious, I'll show you how to stop hiding behind your business degree and get where you want to get in half the time. If you're a woman, I'll let you in on your single most powerful equalizer. If you're a writer/art director, I'll tell you why a management supervisor can't make you do bad work. If you're a client, I'll let you in on some of the most damning revelations you can make about yourself.

Finally, I know that Pete Rose is an exception. Advertising has its exceptions, too. Agencies whose fiery personalities show through in the work they do, typifying the rage and passion for winning that inspires this book.

Hear this from Amil Gargano, as president and chief executive of Ally Gargano: "Everyone wants to hire winners. A lot of agencies have trouble identifying them. We look for several qualities. First, there's no substitute for talent. Second, a desire to do something constructive. Third, a fire inside drives them to excellence."

Fire in the belly. How do we get it? How do we keep it? How do we get it back when it's lost?

There are at least two ways. One is a Russell Baker invention: an abdominal fire stoker. The other is to remember that our talent resides in our craft. When we give it that edge, that little one-up, when we present the truth in an unexpected way. That's the fun and the glory of the game.

This book doesn't claim that advertising is easy. It may even be impossible. Still, it's the only game in town that lets you prove to yourself, every day, whether or not you're a coward.

ACKNOWLEDGMENTS AND
AUTHOR'S NOTE

To Carolyn and Barbara, a great audience.
To Nora Slattery and Inez Sanchez at Ketchum.
To Holly Ricci, my researcher, interview-getter, and sanity.
To all of you who ever asked, "How's the book coming?"

Author's Note: I would like to point out to readers that throughout *Guts* I have frequently used the pronoun *he* to connote men and women. It should be emphasized that this has been done solely in the interests of avoiding awkwardness and that such passages are of course intended to apply equally to both genders.

CONTENTS

1.	On Intangibles	**1**
9.	Making the Near-Blind See	**178**
10.	Television and Radio	**213**
11.	Techniques	**241**
12.	On Responsibility	**289**
13.	Heroes	**297**
14.	Starting Out	**307**
	Afterword	**317**

Chapter One

On Intangibles

It's enthusiasm that helps mark the great ones. Sometimes it takes a form like Phil Dusenberry's passion "to be a star, to be the best, to push for perfection." Other times, it's more like the quiet resilience of the late Bob Miller, creative director of Warwick, Welsh, & Miller, describing his own career: "A superstar I'm not. I've never won a Gold Key or an ANDY Award. I was never interviewed on the decline and fall of creativity. What I think I am, and always have been, is a clear-thinking, hard-working, nuts and bolts, nose-to-the-grindstone copywriter." Without exception, though, the great ones share the quality of having advertising in their blood.

Maybe that's why all the great ones willingly paid their dues and paid them early. As a young photographer, Richard Avedon took I.D. shots of merchant marines during World War II as part of his training. Visual intelligence or any exceptional gift, however innate, has to be honed to be great. The lesson here is that the learning of craft takes time—and there are no shortcuts, even for an Avedon.

SOME DAMN TALENTED PEOPLE

What makes the great players in advertising great? As part of my search for the answer to this question, I went to Jim Johnston, compulsive truth-teller, chairman of Jim Johnston Advertising, and creator of the famed *Wall Street Journal* series of ads featuring "some damn talented people who are great at what they do."

Everyone is there: Helmut Krone (see Figure 1-1), Bob Gage, Amil Gargano, Burt Manning, Jay Chiat, Bill Backer, John O'Toole, Ed McCabe, Hal Riney, Norman Berry—"egos that would not easily park in Giant Stadium," quipped Johnston. He described this amiable series as not so much interviews but therapy: "All I wanted to do was understand them."

1

Figure 1-1

What did Johnston learn? "The truly talented people in our business are craft oriented. It's not money or awards that make them do it. It's their personal vows to their craft. That's what makes them members of the priesthood. They have no choice. They can't turn their back on their vows."

Take Helmut Krone, who Johnston described as "the most gigantic talent in

would be just as happy making $25,000 more as making a name for

As a practicing member of the advertising "priesthood," you will never find me without a religious article on my person: specifically, a well-creased wallet copy of Bill Bernbach's obituary in *Ad Age,* hailing him as the creative leader who gave much-needed class and distinction to a profession often attacked as vulgar. Bernbach exemplified the most telling parts of advertising: the artistic value of *doing it right* . . . of having it in your head first—the idea, the vision of what it should be . . . the performance itself, when the execution exceeds that vision . . . the intuitive sense that it IS right . . . the determination not to be deflected from our original purpose and passion. These are the points in advertising where the deepest choices are made.

JOY AS COMPENSATION

When I think about advertising as "the priesthood," the connections go beyond accomplishments. We are attached to a much larger structure rooted in our founders, warriors, and war stories that illuminate our history and make our prodigies visible.

Leaping to mind with crazy clarity is the tale of a young art director named George Lois clinging to his roughs high on a ledge of a noodle factory in Brooklyn, pledging to jump unless a terrified Mr. Goodman bought his Passover ad for matzos (see Figure 1-2).

This George Lois story is typical of why this game is great. Because it isn't really a game of deflection, defection, or adjustments to keep committees happy; it's a game of passions, fun, even joy. As Keith Reinhard, CEO of Needham, Harper, Steers put it: "If I am seen as having fun at my work, the rest of the agency will understand that making advertising is supposed to be fun. Thus, the pop slogan which expresses our corporate mission: 'To make the world's best advertising and have a glorious time doing it.' "

Figure 1-2

Taking a cue from Eric Leinsdorf, who said, "The most important decision a conductor makes is choosing the tempo," Reinhard adds, "We have chosen to perform our duties *allegro con brio.*" (Now that the Doyle, Dane, Bernbach/Needham merger has been consummated, Reinhard's orchestral skills will be severely tested. How will he handle the cultural differences between the shops—Needham's bent toward heartland advertising and DDB's ethnicity and hard sell via humor, power, and drama? Reinhard would probably say these cultures aren't different at all.)

Compare the Reinhard vision with this from a CEO of a megasized, sedate New York agency describing his shop after a recent merger: "Our board oversees not just an ad agency, but a diversified international communications company whose board members [a body including not one practicing creative person] have to reflect other elements as well."

This CEO was describing, without a trace of playfulness, one of the agency deals of the century. But who can savor "a network of communication technology"? Was he describing an agency or an electrician stringing wire between poles? Some may think of me as a lunk for not caring to understand the current merger craze, but I'll forever hold to my belief that an agency's only assets are its people and its only calling card is its work.

If you are working in the advertising trenches, there's only one question to ask: How much fun are you having? Fun here doesn't mean that advertising is paradise. It doesn't mean that you don't take the problem at hand seriously. It means that fun is an appropriate goal. It means that you don't take *yourself* seriously.

No other business can offer more opportunities for fun. What could be

where freedom, imagery, and possibility reign, is endless.

THE PRIESTHOOD

All advertising people are connected with each other through the usual—lists of business successes, billings, profit centers, accounts won and lost—but to me they seem connected as well through the personalities themselves: the invaluable, the indestructible, the famous, and not-so-famous, many possessing uncommon talent.

Is there a common trait shared by those uncommon talents? Is it toughness, resolution, independence, pride, careless energy, noisy joy in one's own accomplishments, or just plain ego?

Perhaps, surprisingly, the answers, like the best in human nature, are fairly simple, unswanky, and, in many cases, changeless.

The garrulous Jim Johnston, one of advertising's more cheerful and well-integrated curmudgeons, unhesitatingly pointed to "an astounding lack of confidence in our creative giants who aren't quite sure they ever did the best ads they could."

Bob Levenson, in 1986 crowned creative chieftain at Saatchi & Saatchi Compton mentioned "fear . . . not the nail-biting kind, but an internal fear that, yet again, commands you to be great."

On the other hand: "If I thought about fear," says Roy Grace of Grace, Rothschild, "I'd be too scared to do anything." Grace equated the sensation of having the perfect idea to the boyhood experience of diving off a high board into shallow water. "As a kid, I never thought about fear, because the jump gave me such a great sensation."

Keith Reinhard spoke of insecurity. "The kind which drives creative people forward in endless pursuit of accomplishments which prove that there is no basis for the insecurity. Ironically, if that insecurity should ever disappear, the creative flame would go out."

Don Just, president of the Martin Agency in Richmond, explained advertising people this way: "Bankers talk banking. Advertising people can talk anything. They're more complete people, they contend better, they have a capacity for empathy."

Amil Gargano, president and creative leader of Ally Gargano/MCA, spoke of "a need to place our imprimatur on our profession." Not one to stand at a philosophical intersection very long, Gargano added, "the great ones have the ability and guts to put things down, universal truths, that allow the consumer to say, That's so true, or Yes, that's me."

John Chervokos, managing editor of *Madison Avenue,* cited "the capacity for lateral thinking as opposed to syllogistic strategy stuff.

"It amazes me," he said, "from how many totally different angles a creator can come at a problem." As an example, he cited a golf ball ad he saw in a young writer's portfolio. "It showed some golfers in the woods with a headline that said 'Let's us keep looking, it's an Acushnet.' While every other golf ball ad is talking about distance, this writer jerked my head by being *different.*"

For Ed McCabe, there's not that much uncommon talent around. "I know dozens of people who call themselves creative when in reality they've never done anything but McCall's patterns: stamped-out stuff."

Continued McCabe, "If, on the other hand, you are uncommon, you will be impatient with the norm."

"Abnormal" is McCabe's definition of "creative." "If it isn't unfamiliar, keep it away from me," added a pleading McCabe.

Joining the tribe of independent types was Helmut Krone, who knew only a handful of people with uncommon talent: "They had aptitude, will, and knew how to dream. Lamenting their departure from DDB, he said: "I wish I had one of them here now but they've all gone from here."

I end this line of thought with these words from an ex-copywriter describing his six-year career: "It certainly helped me write *Catch-22.* Much of the book's comic structure, the changes of pace, the surprises and the use of language are very much like the kind of writing you find in advertising."

Would Joseph Heller like to get back into advertising today? "No. I enjoyed my time in the business, mainly because I always thought of it as a temporary job. . . ."

Lacking any sweeping conclusions of my own regarding the truly talented people in advertising—many of whom make their feelings accessible on these pages—I associate them with perseverance, independence, nonconformity, intensity, flexibility, and dreaming (the kind not reserved for sleeping). Hardly marks of the neurotic.

Personally, the best bit of luck I ever had was being bounced from St. Vincent's Seminary, out of one priesthood into another. In both cases, I always felt I was in good company.

Chapter Two

My Favorite Things

always got into the same fixes as his readers. He was also the very best at the "snapper" (the withholding of a wonderful twist until the end).

Steinbeck, because he knew his territory—the Monterey Peninsula—and because his language was passionate and colorful and matched so well the people he wrote about.

But the most important influence was Hemingway because his style was uniquely his own—stripped-down, unimpressed, economical. By reading Hemingway, my style was hopelessly set. It seemed to me then (and it seems to me now) that for a writer with average talent, his example would be the best to follow.

THE HEMINGWAY OF AD WRITERS

Here's a favorite campaign of mine that Hemingway could have written and Edward Hopper could have art directed. This campaign for Horn & Hardart by Ed McCabe demonstrates the rigorous art of compressive power (see Figure 2-1).

This campaign knows who it's talking to, and it's not all the little old ladies who used to inhabit Schrafft's. It's people who count their nickels. (Remember the automat? A slice of coconut cream pie, perched behind a bulletproof—or so it seemed—glass door, required a total of seven nickels.) The campaign keeps the reader alternately delighted, surprised, and finally sold. Stark visuals and cryptic headlines are unmistakably consistent (see Figure 2-2).

At the heart of this campaign are the consumers themselves—Hooperesque types lingering over the last bite of strudel. (You can still see them there in the big glass windows at the corner of 42nd and Third.)

Today when New Yorkers chow down alfresco at uncomfortable sidewalk tables amid the ambiance of diesel fumes and acid rain, and when the price of

7

Figure 2-1

Figure 2-2

mediocre food has outdistanced cultivated judgment, I look at this campaign and conclude that the most dependable things in life are usually the simplest.

Admitting that this campaign is one of his favorites, too, McCabe was quick to add, "I may sound arrogant, but if this was my only favorite, I'd think of myself as a failure."

Does the strategy have one objective, or is it cluttered with secondary goals because your brand group and agency couldn't make up their minds?

Is your strategy focused or open-ended and vague?

Are there any executional elements in the language? If not, why not?

Is the language alive or stiff, predictable, boring?

Does the strategy make your product unique or interchangeable with the rest of the category?

Does the strategy define a real issue of concern to a real consumer in the real world?

Is it confrontational and feisty?

With the help of my friend Woody Wiedenhofer, defensive coordinator for the four-time Super Bowl Champion Pittsburgh Steelers and the head coach at the University of Missouri, allow me to put down a working definition of a good strategy: "It's when you button up your chin straps and level the other guy."

To understand why I admire the "Never had it, never will" campaign for 7-UP should be an easy jump. This is a strategy that's willing to take the gloves off and come out fighting.

While Coke and Pepsi were engaged in their version of Star Wars (Michael Jackson for Pepsi, Julio Iglesias for Coke), 7-UP was out listening to consumers. What they heard was a real concern about additives and the potential health hazards of caffeine, an ingredient that innocent-sounding sodas like Mountain Dew and Mello Yello are loaded with. And so was born "the uncaffeine" 7-UP strategy. 7-UP's succession of ad campaigns reflects a very clear, agreed-to, premeditated strategy about where this brand is going.

All this strategy did was create a whole new segment in the one-billion-dollar soft drink category. While Coke and Pepsi were crying in their colas, shouting "foul," "shame," and "dirty pool," 7-UP was experiencing a sales gain of more than 10 percent, the biggest in the industry. At the time it didn't take long for

Coke and Pepsi and every other soft drink manufacturer to join the game with their own caffeine-free sodas. The leaders were now the followers. The entire category was put on the defensive.

What Coca-Cola had labeled "detrimental to the industry," was, in fact, healthy for the consumer. This campaign demonstrates what advertising does best: it gives information and helps to eliminate consumer confusion. Today the no-caffeine, no-additive segment amounts to 7 percent of all soda consumed. This is a remarkable strategic achievement.

The TV commercials featured Tony-Award-winning director and actor Geoffrey Holder.

They were visual extensions of the strategy "cool, crisp, and clean" with nothing added except perhaps a little Holder charm (see Figure 2-3).

I hope this example will help you to rewrite a few of your own strategies. Remember, don't be too gentlemanly or ladylike when you do.

RESEARCH: A RETORT AND APPEAL

I am not a friend of research. Particularly when it is asked to do what it was never intended to do: predict the future. Research can't tell us whether an ad is going to succeed any more than a critic can tell us whether a movie will succeed.

Intuition is much more helpful. Not half-baked intuition. Intuition springing from information that triggers the idea.

Research properly used gives me the right information. But I need it *before* the idea in order to trigger the idea in the first place. And to get the right idea I need research that talks to the right people so I know what they need and feel. For example, did you know that only 20 percent of the beer-drinking population consumes 80 percent of the beer? I can be friendly to research that gives me a fact like this, because now I can put my talent to work and if I'm lucky I can come up with the best beer campaign ever written: *Schaefer is the one beer to have when you're having more than one.* What a campaign, and what a story to go with it!

Here it is as author Jim Jordan, then of B.B.D.O., related it. "I'll grudgingly admit research was helpful. But there was a single key interview with a mechanic. He was describing what he did when he got home from work. He said, 'I take off my greasy clothes, jump into the shower, but you know I never open my mouth in the shower.' When I probed 'Why,' he said, 'I save my mouth for that first cold beer.' The mechanic then went on to say, 'The only trouble is, as the evening wears on, *most beers lose something along the way.*' "

So was born a campaign that claims "a taste that doesn't fade" and that demonstrates the benefit in its execution by showing a deserving, hard-working man building a more-than-one-beer thirst.

As Jordan says, the research sought out the right consumer and the advertising verified the fact that Schaefer was the one who really knew him. This

Figure 2-3

campaign ran for 13 years. In that time, Schaefer became New York City's number-one beer and the fastest-selling regional brand in the country.

"This is the only way to use research," adds Jordan. More about that later.

BUSTER KEATON AND ME

His obituary on the front page of *The New York Times* noted that he "looked like the kind of man that dogs kick."

This mournful little man, with bassett-hound eyes, a saucer-brimmed hat, a Salvation Army suit, and a floppy tie stood with Charlie Chaplin and Harold Lloyd as among the greatest comedians of the silent screen. In an appraisal of Keaton's work, Bosley Crowther wrote, "There are still plenty [of reviewers] who are inclined to rate him as the greatest of the great comedians."

This was Buster Keaton. My recollections of him as our stone-faced spokesman for the Ford Econoline van are some of the fondest of my career (see Figure 2-4).

In the early 60s, Ford made a wise and timely decision to rethink its conventional panel truck. The changes were drastic: they pushed back the front axle, chopped off the end, stretched the windshield, cut holes in both sides and replaced them with double doors, eliminated 1,000 pounds of dead weight, shrank the tires, and slimmed the engine. The result was the Econoline van.

My partner Tony Perone and I got the advertising assignment. These were the days when Lee Iacocca was Ford's general manager. Even then, in the call reports we got from our Detroit office, Iacocca was insisting on continuity in Ford's advertising. "I want something to tie our advertising together, a string through it. We need consistency throughout all media," he said.

Whatever we did, we knew we had to find that thread—something people could point to and recognize every time they saw an Econoline commercial.

We also knew that a boring nuts-and-bolts recitation of the facts wouldn't do it either. Words alone didn't seem to capture the dramatic changes Ford engineering had accomplished or the fun that the Econoline offered to a whole new breed of truck owners.

"Let's not do it with words," Tony said, "Let's do it with movement. Buster Keaton," he said. "He'll be our thread. He'll demonstrate it without saying a word."

Well, if you work solving problems, you know the feeling when you get hold of an idea that's really great. You can't wait to bring it to life.

Bring it to life we did, and in a little over a month and a half we had a commercial you can still see on the Museum of Modern Art's Commercial Reel of Classics, the first of four commercials Keaton did for us.

Keaton deadpanned Ford's covered van into unit sales equaling the com-

Figure 2-4

bined total of Chevrolet and Dodge. He also taught me some important advertising lessons. Keaton had a special way of arriving at things: Start with an idea or storyline, work up a strong ending, and kind of let the middle take care of itself.

Keaton taught me nuance and timing. In one commercial, he was to be a lonely hitchhiker. Hidden behind a billboard were his life possessions. An Econoline van would stop, and Keaton would load the van with an assortment of oddities and props. On the day of the shoot, Keaton showed up with a basket of fried chicken.

"You don't like our caterer, Buster?" I asked.

"This is for the driver to eat during the commercial while I fill up the van."

This suggestion not only made the premise more believable (that anyone would really wait for the entire van to fill up), but it gave us a "cutaway" point in the editing room.

The hitchhiker's last possession was a shaggy dog. As Keaton put the dog on the seat next to the driver, his hat fell off. As he bent down to pick it up, the van pulled away. Keaton turned and did a pratfall onto the hard pavement. For an instant, everyone on the set thought he had misjudged the fall and cracked his head. The next second he was up, running after the van.

All through his life, Keaton was up and down, but never out.

Keaton's appearance in these Ford commercials served to introduce young people, especially students of film, to this granite-faced clown, master in the art of exquisite frustration. This began a renaissance for Buster. His films began to reappear at festivals all over the world.

He once told me how much satisfaction he got from the knowledge that a new generation was finding his films funnier than ever. Although he never smiled once in any of our commercials, he had to admit that he wasn't doing badly. "I can't feel sorry for myself. It all goes to show that if you stay on the merry-go-round long enough, you'll get another chance at the brass ring. Luckily, I stayed on."

Buster Keaton taught me something else: you can't spot the bums if you haven't seen the great ones first.

Lines I Wish I'd Written and Why

By the time you finish this book, I'll hope you'll have gained some admiration for the writers and art directors who are courageous enough to expose their work and their talents to the judges and juries and the committees, where, according to E.B. White, "the moistened finger in the wind reigns."

Writers are resilient cusses. They can and they will continue to sit down at the typewriter and write what Eudora Welty has called "that ever miraculous thing, the opening sentence." For copywriters who still keep trying, this section is for you.

A while back, I gave a copy workshop for 22 assistant brand managers from Procter & Gamble. After the presentation, I got several requests for this ad (see Figure 2-5). I gladly complied. A few days later, I got a note in the mail: "Thank you for the ad. It is permanently displayed on my wall at Procter & Gamble as an example of an ad that wasn't picked to death by a committee of guppies." This is the reason I continue to teach. You never know how much of an influence you'll be or how far that influence will go.

In the same workshop, another brand assistant, when asked if he would approve this ad—Figure 2-6—said, "No, I wouldn't, because you have to draw the line of good taste somewhere." His brand was Crest. "When you have 38 million dollars to spend like Crest, you can afford to be arrogant," I retorted.

Figure 2-5

Figure 2-6

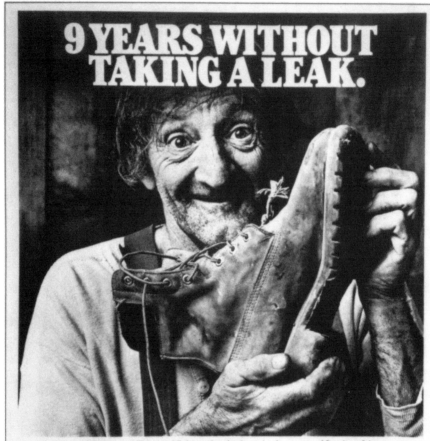

There is one kind of client who would look at this ad (Figure 2-7) and say: "I don't think it's funny. Getting hit in the balls is serious stuff." Then there is the other kind of client, the kind who approved this ad. He'd say: "Hey, it's only a jock strap. Let's try talking to jocks the way they talk to each other."

The impact of this campaign (Figure 2-8) is well documented. It made Talon

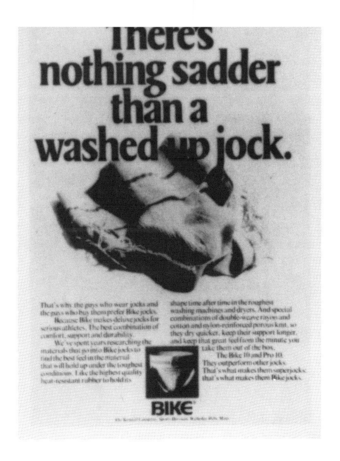

Figure 2-8

everybody, including Anita Baron, whose name and work are memorialized in this ad. Her comment on the ad:

> In order to do outstanding advertising, you have to work for an agency that is willing to stick its neck out and support you. You also have to have a client who trusts the agency's judgment and professionalism. When Ron Becker and I worked on the Talon account, Delahanty Kernit Geller was that kind of agency. And Talon was that kind of client. The campaign focused on the problems of broken zippers, with Talon, of course, being the solution. But the headline never mentioned the product or its benefits. All that was buried in the body copy. Most clients would consider that an enormous risk. But Talon had the courage to take it. And it paid off.

I think I know what some of you are thinking. All these ads could have been

18

written another way. Yes, and Abraham Lincoln could have begun the Gettysburg Address with this: "Eighty-seven years ago, in 1776 . . ."

The point is: A great headline is usually written by an anarchist. Anarchists aren't much interested in the democratic process; they don't take votes and run the winners.

Chapter Three

Early Lessons

The 1960s. It was the decade of revolution: on campuses, in the cities, and on Madison Avenue. The conflict was fundamental. "Reality-based advertising" championed by the creative forces versus fantasy-land advertising championed by the slice-of-life crowd. Agencies traditionally dominated by Ivy Leaguers (the I-can-prove-it's-right school) were now clamoring for the new creatives (the I-can-feel-it's-right school).

Much of the credit for the "creative revolution" of the 1960s goes to Bill Bernbach and, to a lesser extent, David Ogilvy. These men didn't set out to create a revolution. They set out to create environments—agencies with air to breathe based on creative freedom.

"I always ran my own show," said Phyllis Robinson, the first woman hired by Bernbach. "I loved my work. I never had to filter it through the Ivy Leaguers."

Work, she explained, was not so much work as it was a challenge, which is the difference between energy and ennui. Robinson continued, "The challenge was the presence of Bernbach. He never put a pencil to anything. But Bill sharpened our work, he gave it a kind of elegant sassiness."

Influenced by Bernbach, the small creative shops evolved, headed by Doyle, Dane expatriates Fred Papert and George Lois, Ron Rosenfeld and Lenny Sirowitz, Paula Green. Firms founded by brash young ethnics, firms like Della Femina Travisano with the street smarts to communicate to the young, cynical consumers of the day, joined the list.

CURIOSITY NEVER KILLED THE COPYWRITER

I wasn't a son of the city's pavement. I'm not Greek or Italian. I came to Madison Avenue from Pittsburgh (off the boat, as it were) and I was quite happy to take the first writing job that was offered—at J. Walter Thompson in the Ford group. Those people became my first professional family.

In spite of the kind of mind I was given at birth (I would describe it as first rate, second class), I've always needed to feel that I was working in a quality environment where people cared about what they did.

In this respect, Thompson couldn't have been a better place for me. In the cubicle to my left was the quiet, hermitic Gene Case, who later joined Helmut Krone to form Case-Krone. Behind me was a secretary named Regina Ryan, who became the first female editor-in-chief at Macmillan. Our music director was Sid Woloshin, one of the most respected and prolific "hit" men in the industry (more about Sid later). Around the corner was an assistant producer named Tim Newman, today one of the most demanded (and demanding) commercial directors in New York. And my first copy chief was Bill Muyskins, who today runs his own production company in the Connecticut Berkshires.

Bill had just come over from Young & Rubicam and he was unpacking his

can use to make life a little easier, better, more fun.

If Levi's is a legend, it's because the advertising takes the time to explain that a Levi's button and a Levi's stitch stay in place forever.

If Charmin is perceived as the softest toilet paper, it's because the advertising leverages the fact that Charmin is a two-ply tissue and a one-million-dollar machine puffs softness in between every tissue.

Look again at the Young & Rubicam ad. If you take its message to heart, you will never be a prima donna. You will never refuse a copy assignment because you think it's beneath you. You will never have an excuse to get lazy or blame your own lack of imagination on the product.

Apply this message to everything you do in advertising and you will always succeed in solving the problem. You'll be adept at taking a product nobody else wants and doing something with it nobody ever conceived of before.

Twenty years after seeing that ad I'm applying the same lesson.

In 1985, I was assigned to work on Bounce, the fabric softener from Procter & Gamble. Within the agency, working on Bounce was considered the equivalent of joining the Bataan Death March. It meant spending your creative life in badly lit subterranean laundries where one neighbor would burst in on another saying, "Don't mind me, Marge, I just came over to stare at your static cling."

In a little less than a year, the account group was smiling, the brand group had become heroes at Procter, and the whole creative department was killing to work on the business. All thanks to the new advertising we were running for Bounce.

Needless to say, the "nail ad" has been the most durable lesson of my career.

RESISTING THE USUAL

When I called Y&R and said that I'd like the story behind the nail ad, I was introduced to the delightfully genuine Mark Strook, the firm's historian-at-large. He reminisced about the Ray Rubicam days when a whole series of house

Figure 3-1

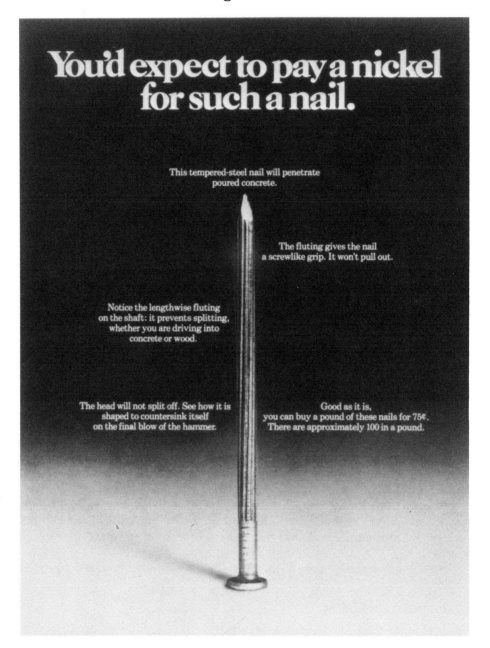

ads (including the nail ad) was created. "Ray Rubicam had one guiding principle," said Strook. *"Always resist the usual.* These ads were done in the thirties, and there is a movement here right now at Young & Rubicam to bring them all back."

As Strook went on to say, "That ad is 50 years old, but we apply it every day."

HIGH VITRIOL

There are few geniuses in this business. I work long hours making up for the fact that I'm not one of them. But I didn't always feel that way. I was often guilty of the worst kind of creative arrogance in believing that the only worthwhile ideas were my own. I have learned to respect divergent ideas, wherever they come from. Often they come from clients. You'll find classic examples later in this book. And regardless of what some of you might think, account executives often have big creative ideas of their own. A truth that's also illustrated later in the book.

There was a time when I thought the only important voice was my own. At meetings I was terrible at listening. I got a bigger kick out of "wowing" the client than selling him. I betrayed more cleverness than insight.

This was my little prayer: "Lord, give me humility, but not yet."

I didn't change overnight. My act is still a bit too ferocious. I'm working on polishing the edges (as opposed to rounding them off) so that what comes out is passion and caring for what I do.

The person most responsible for this turn was Herb Vitriol, an intelligent friend at Sullivan, Stauffer, Cowell & Bayles. Herb was the kind of person who always got his point across in a quiet yet firm way. Little things made me acutely aware of what Herb really was: a killer. (After meetings, for example, he would shake hands with me and try to crush my fingers.) But Herb saw something worthwhile in me—enough to give me a folded note one day after a meeting. He had covered one side with "I" written over and over, the other side with "we."

I won't tell you that this was a watershed experience (that only happens in advertising when you walk in to get a raise and the creative director fires you), but it was the best lesson in personal style that I ever took away from an agency.

Real quick, it gave me a clear picture of how I came across to other people. And, frankly, how I came across to me. The lesson of "we" helped me to understand the spirit of partnership.

"We" reminds me that we're all in the same foxhole together. "We" gives everybody a stake in the business. It helps me to regard the client's business as my own. The question asked most by creative people today is: why doesn't the client trust us? The answer is: because you haven't demonstrated that you really know his business, much less care. So, why should he trust you?

"We" means sitting down with the client and finding out his innermost thoughts, his frustrations, his vision.

"We" means involving the client *early* in the creative process. I always show clients tissues, roughs, work in progress. The last thing a client should see first is a finished storyboard.

"We" helps in the decision-making process because it never becomes a question of who's right. It becomes a question of what's right. Understand, I'm not saying that I think advertising is a democracy and that copy decisions are voted on. "We" here is intended to mean that agency people must care collectively. Thoreau had an expression for it: "a corporation with conscience."

What Goes on the Truck

In these audiovisual days, nine out of ten creative assignments begin with a TV commercial. Now, I'm not too crazy about things that move. I am especially wary of a storyboard that someone wants to "flash by me." I'd rather take a closer look. If it goes by too fast, I could miss the small details, like, Is it interesting and relevant? After I look at a storyboard that has been fleetingly presented, the first question I always ask is: "What goes on the truck?" Put another way, "What's the idea in five words or less?"

This was another early lesson, inspired by Bill Golden's dictum: "Nothing is not important."

Bill Golden, who designed the CBS eye logo, was corporate art director of CBS in the late 1930s. He believed that the visual environment of advertising improves every time a designer produces a good design. If our "useful little craft" is to be perfect and honest, then everything a consumer sees should reflect that.

If what goes on the truck is important enough to Bill Golden, it's important enough to me.

Accordingly, for every TV commercial I have to approve, I require that a print ad or poster adaptation go with it to the presentation. This really works, in at least four ways:

1. It requires every selling line to take a compelling visual form.
2. The result is something you can own—a look that is "trademarkable."
3. It forces you to make the idea simple and telegraphic.
4. Your design or word solution isn't subject to fashion. It should be able to stay on the side of the truck a long time.

Chapter Four

The Players

AGENCIES

If I were job hunting, or if I were a client looking for an agency with the right chemistry, I would ask this question first: If your agency were a person, what kind of person would it be?

The answers vary.

To chairman Jerry Della Femina, the Della Femina Travisano Agency is a person with good vibrations. "If I were a client, I'd want an agency where the vibrations suggest I'm going to get more for my money, more energy in every ad. That's what we try to achieve. I think we have."

To creative leader Jerry Siano, the N.W. Ayer Agency would be a person blessed with a good family: "I've always been part of a good family. The best families have fights. But in the crunch, they stick together."

To the caustic Ed McCabe, the Scali, McCabe Agency would be a person who is hard-working and diligent: "A person who wants to be exuberant in everything they do, who is willing to make that kind of commitment to this business of advertising." (See Figure 4-1, a typical Scali twist celebrating Miss Liberty.)

When I spoke to Amil Gargano of Ally Gargano/MCA, he gave me an admittedly "glib" answer: "We're a combination of Lenny Bruce, who struggled with the truth, and Jake LaMotta, who is fiery and angry." (Now that Gargano has merged with MCA, it'll be interesting to see if Lenny and Jake survive.)

When I caught Bob Gage, he offered this description of the Doyle, Dane, Bernbach agency: "A talented rebel with the strength to get it down on paper."

Creative honcho Tom McElligott of Fallon McElligott said, "We would be passionate perfectionists."

To CEO Bill Genge, Ketchum would be "the ultimate likable salesman."

To Dan Weiden, the Weiden, Kennedy agency is "John Belushi without the drugs, working always on the edge."

To Bill Backer, the Backer, Spielvogel agency personifies " 'the magnificent seven'—a bunch of professionals who act together against the crunch of deadlines to attack a problem."

And when I asked Phil Dusenberry to personify BBDO, he said, "You know who Laurence Taylor is, don't you?"

In my own search for the keys to agency personalities, I've come up with a little game called Match-Up. I've taken 15 first-rate agencies and matched them with 15 first-rate professional sports teams. These match-ups are based on a

Figure 4-1

TWO

SAM SCALI
Inducted into the Art Director's
Hall of Fame, 1984

ED McCABE
Inducted into the Copy Hall of Fame,
1974

MARVIN SLOVES

All of us at Scali, McCabe, Sloves would like to congratulate Sam Scali on his induction into the Art Director's Hall of Fame.

We're very proud.

We're also proud of the fact that Sam is not alone. He joins his partner, Ed McCabe, who entered the Copy Hall of Fame in 1974.

And that makes Scali, McCabe, Sloves something very rare indeed: an advertising agency with two founding partners in the Hall of Fame.

Both of these men are advertising legends for good reason. Together, they have created some of the most renowned advertising of all time.

If you're interested in talking to a great art director or a great copywriter about your advertising, Sam and Ed aren't hard to find. They still come to work every day.

Or, if you'd like to talk to the person who does most of the talking for Sam and Ed, call Marvin.

There is, unfortunately, no such thing as a Management Hall of Fame.

But Marvin Sloves is a great reason for creating one.

SCALI, McCABE, SLOVES, INC.

800 Third Avenue, New York, N.Y. 10022 (212) 421-5050 Offices in Houston, Melbourne, Montreal, Toronto, London, Düsseldorf, Mexico City

combination of things: first hand experience, rumor, affection, and out-and-out bias.

Ally Gargano—The Boston Celtics: competitive, fiery, lots of banners hanging.

Doyle, Dane, Bernbach—The "old" New York Yankees: domination, a star-studded cast, quality leadership.

Scali McCabe Sloves—The University of Indiana basketball team: what Bobby Knight is to the bench, McCabe is to the creative department.

Ketchum—"The Stars and Stripes" America's Cup sailing team: steady course, deep-keeled culture, unity, fiercely independent.

Ogilvy & Mather—The Dallas Cowboys: straight arrows, a class act, and in their view, the only place to play.

BBDO—The New York Giants: it's about time.

Ammirati & Puris—The Miami Dolphins: disciplined, balanced attack, success not short-lived, solid leadership, demands that players be accountable.

N.W. Ayer—The Pittsburgh Pirates of the 1970s: "we are family."

Hal Riney—The U.S. Olympic hockey team: baby-faced upstarts from out of nowhere; "a nursery for new ideas and new techniques," according to Riney himself.

Leo Burnett (not a team but a person)—Larry Bird: how can a hayseed be so great? (See worn photo of youthful Leo in Figure 4-2.)

J. W. Thompson—U.C.L.A. in the John Wooden days: top product year after year.

Young & Rubicam—The Pittsburgh Steelers: no tricks, heavy hitters, lots of diamond rings.

Della Femina Travisano & Partners—a pickup basketball team from Far Rockaway with Al McGuire as point guard, players are extensions of coach, arrogant and obnoxious.

Jordan, Manning, Case, Taylor, McGrath—The New York Mets: a tiger at the gates, the one to watch.

Fallon McElligott—The Oakland A's in their Billy Ball days: rebels with talent and the courage to take risks.

Note: On paper, some of these agencies resemble holding companies, boneyards of disintegrating culture. While their identities seem submerged, the spirit of the agency is still present in their leaders.

As you can see, an advertising agency is a subject of some complexity. Some you love. Some you love to hate. And most of the things that are generally quoted about agencies are unsuccessful attempts to say something else.

Figure 4-2

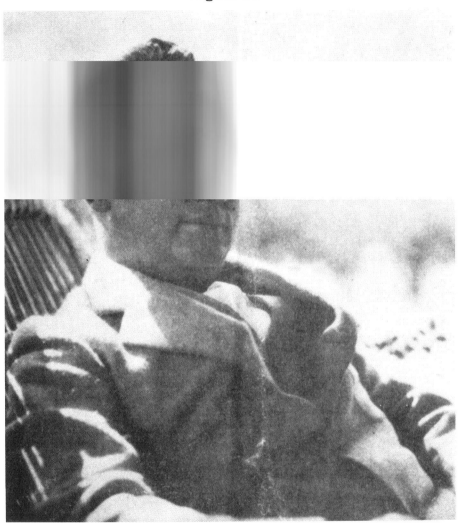

And what kind of person would I want my agency to be?

I would want a restless person, one with a state of mind that forces him to find a better way, when he already has a good way.

I would want a lonely person. An account executive alone at her desk on a sunny Sunday in June fine-tuning a recommendation. An art director alone at his board still trying to top himself long after his writer has gone home.

A person who would encourage failures and court the abnormal.

A person who would follow the advice of Keith Reinhard and make sure everybody knew that the minute they started turning out advertising that makes people yawn, their jobs were in jeopardy.

This is not a description of your standard-issue hero. But inarguably a person who would make agency life—and advertising—better for all of us.

What Makes Them Tick

Ask any advertising man why some agencies are of the first rank. Some will point to the work they produce. Some to the strategic thinking. Some to global expertise.

Some cite ambiance: "They let me pick out my own furniture." Some location: "We're only two blocks from P.J.'s, four blocks from Bloomie's, and five blocks from Grand Central."

Others resort to figures of speech: "They run a tight ship." "It's like being in an F. Scott Fitzgerald novel."

Ask again, and you might hear about "the quality of our people" or "the depth of our service."

On the other side, there are also "principles of failure" that mark the second-rate agencies. There are dozens of these: "They're more interested in making profits than making ads." "They'd rather make meetings than make it perfect." "They sink all their profits into glitz, not people." "They're expeditors and order takers." "They keep rewarding unremarkable people." "The client sneezes—the agency catches a cold."

But every agency needs an operating philosophy either stated or only felt. Preferably stated. Why? Because the troops have to know what's expected. Sounds obvious, but that *is* the answer.

Seldom does a client admit that an agency's philosophy influenced his choice. Yet, it's important for a client to have some understanding of his agency's guiding principles.

And those principles can never be based simply on size or service. "Full service" sounds good, but that heading usually means duplicating and xeroxing capabilities, P&L's, figure juggling, creative reviews, fancy organizational charts, and booklets in spiral binders printed in the agency's colors.

Full service is a good position for a prostitute or a gas station, not for an advertising agency.

I talked with many clients about what they want in an agency relationship. Four key ideas emerged:

1. The agency must contribute to the client's business with thought/idea leadership.
2. The agency and the client must have compatible values.

3. A long-term relationship is necessary to achieve long-term success.
4. Both sides have to work at it.

Further, these clients were candid about their likes, dislikes, and frustrations.

One client decried his agency's lack of responsiveness. "It takes a beer

On the positive side, one client said: "I feel that my agency is constantly putting out the little fires. That's good. It's the problems that keep smoldering that make me smolder."

Another client appreciated agency thoroughness: "I judge my agency on its ability to completely immerse itself and to penetrate my problem."

"Ideas I never ask for," said another. "My agency is always doing that."

For yet another, trust was the key: "Most agencies just don't understand that we don't go in as trusting, respectful souls. We've been burnt too many times by some bullshitter. It's the feeling the agency transmits, meeting after meeting, that they really know my problem and product that builds trust."

The most telling remark I heard from a client was this: "I can lose faith in my agency and they still have a chance. It's when I lose hope that they're gone."

The soul of many great agencies was a shining example—a single individual who was felt to be irreplaceable, who couldn't be fired, who was there as an outspoken ally for the creative product: a Rubicam, a Strouse, a Bernbach, a Burnett, an Ogilvy, a Reeves, an Ally, a Hal Riney. All quite different in personality, but each prepared to go to the wall for what he believed. These people weren't managers carrying policy manuals or stock reports. They were leaders with vision. Each had a profound effect on his agency and by his very example comes closest to defining the "kind of person I want my agency to be."

Have a Nice $5,000,000 Day

In the last several years, a new kind of agency has emerged: the advertising conglomerate. Its position is addressed to the stock market, not the client. Obsessed with the importance of image and reputation, these Brontasaurian bureaucracies actually position themselves as brands.

In their annual reports, these agencies will make strong cases for growth, global capacity, synergy, and the idea that with bigness comes greatness. Yet, in a

31

business that prides itself on originality, the duplication of mega-agencies is redundant. The effect along Madison Avenue among the rank-and-file ad makers is depression, low morale, fear for job security, and anger. As of this writing, New York City is probably the least creative spot in Adland.

If America is in a debt crisis, advertising is in an asset crisis. The result of merger-mania is creative default, endless realignment of products and people, eternal conflicts, and shaky client security. Everybody gets hurt. Priorities and pride get lost.

The flip and positive side is the emergence of the smart, small shops, still devoted to thought and idea leadership.

The ones determined to remain within their area of expertise: marketing and advertising.

The ones who like to beat their competition, not buy them out.

The ones who employ senior people who believe in deep involvement, not distance.

Ammirati & Puris, Fallon McElligott, Ketchum, Tatham, Laird and Kudner, Chiat Day: mid-size independents built with people drilled in marketing discipline. They left the big agencies to do great creative work. It's never been better for these kinds of agencies because they represent a client's best chance to produce what agencies are supposed to produce—advertising that contributes to marketplace success. Their guiding principle is: Big isn't better, better is better.

In a conversation marked by directness, listen to Ralph Ammirati as he describes life at Ammirati & Puris:

> I feel uncomfortable because you've heard it a hundred times, but we're a bunch of people who care passionately about being solid. The fact that Marty [Puris] and I are from creative side, well, we've had to live that down with some clients. We go out of our way to apply different disciplines, including marketing smarts. Our solutions aren't lopsided or short-lived. People know what they're supposed to do here because we have enough high quality people with the same objectives. The better work we do, the more you attract. Headhunters around town will attest to that—we rarely use them. That way we avoid people bringing in their own bad habits. There's communication here, there's an intelligent process. I know you've heard it, John. One-hundred percent of the agencies say the same thing but it's lip service—only about 2 percent really apply the discipline. You have to remember things don't go up, they go down—if you apply a morality about your work you can keep it up there.

COPYWRITERS

My editor, Karl Weber, suggested that I begin this section by explaining what copywriters are and what they do.

Basically, copywriters are people who grow up desperate. As kids in kindergarten, they were desperate to write stories or draw with crayons and magic markers. By puberty, they had a dream of actually getting paid and getting published.

Ad writing is the closest most of them will ever come. That's plenty close

Getting It Down in Black and White

A copywriter learns and earns by writing. Then rewriting. Then rewriting the rewrites. Writing *is* rewriting. Constant revisits to the typewriter often result in joyful revisions of your work. Bernard Malamud calls these revisions "the gems of afterthought."

Probably the most apt bit of advice ever recorded on the subject of writing was this from E.B. White: "I always write a thing first and think about it afterwards, which is not a bad procedure because the easiest way to have successive thoughts is to start putting them down."

Dig We Must

As a copywriter you write dozens, even hundreds of headlines until you make certain you've got the right idea and that it comes directly out of the product. These revelations aren't accidental or even incidental. They emerge from digging.

Webster's New Collegiate Dictionary, which has blond hair, a class pipe, and green pants, defines digging in three ways: "to turn up, to uncover, to work hard." All three processes are part of a copywriter's work.

The Rustle of Words

Let us assume that you have done your digging and have uncovered a gem—an idea you know you can use to sell the product. It is at this point that the copywriter learns something about himself, and that is, does he know the difference between what is compelling and what is not? Only the copywriter who can trust his writing knows. And a copywriter can trust his writing when his words have the authentic sound of the person he is *and* the person he wants to reach.

Nothing says lovin' like something from the oven, and Pillsbury says it best. This has the sound of the Midwest, and it comes from that barefoot agency in the Midwest, Leo Burnett.

Alan Kent was a copywriter I met at Grey Advertising who got more kicks out of a right-sounding line than anyone I ever met. Alan was working at Burnett when this line was written. "The minute we heard the line, well, the fire bell rang. It was the kind of line that reflected life and didn't hide from it. Leo was always after this. It's an honest sounding line, and how often honesty is missed."

I have been asked more than once, can copywriting be taught?

If you are in tune with human nature, if you keep it loose, and if at the bottom you are a storyteller with endless curiosity, you are 90 percent there. The rest can be taught.

You Gotta Have Kishkes

Kishkes is a Yiddish expression courtesy of Ron Rosenfeld. It means putting your ass on the table. The gentile equivalent would be guts. It takes guts to put it down on paper.

Many copywriters I know were at one time steamfitters, hod carriers, cabbies, minor league ballplayers, and mechanics. The sound of *Pay me now or pay me later,* for Fram oil filters, assures me that at least one of these working-class heroes is still at it.

There are lines that are simple music to my ears (and note the accompanying ad in Figure 4-3):

Figure 4-3

Now you see it/Now you don't/
Here you have it/ Here you won't/
Oh Diet Pepsi/One small calorie/
Now you see it/Now you don't/
That great Pepsi taste/Diet Pepsi
Won't go to your waist/So now
you see it/Now you don't.

~~And the sound of argued~~

New York Coalition.

At a time when the whole world seems to be hanging loose, the tightness of these lines has a definite charm.

Such charm does not come without a copywriter's quirks. BBDO's Phil Dusenberry cannot begin to write without utter quiet and a blank yellow pad.

Wells, Rich, and Green's Charlie Moss writes his "best stuff under the influence of sheer terror."

Before Alan Kent would begin typing, he would spit on his fingers as if anticipating a long day with an axe and a large pile of wood.

Jim Durfee, ex-Carl Ally man now residing at Durfee Solow, "does excessive walking around the hall."

A creative director who has sworn me to secrecy insists: "I get my best ideas on the throne. It's quiet, warm and peaceful—they haven't installed phones in there yet." For those of you suffering from copywriter's block, this is certainly a candidate for the ecstasy sweepstakes.

You Can See Them Coming

As I see it, either you're a copywriter or you're not. The copywriter who really wants to be writing the Great American Novel is not usually a great copywriter. To build a great agency, you need talent to build it around. If you are a real copywriter, your advertising career is something you like and are proud of and you keep asking for more.

Born copywriters are easy to spot. Their talent and ambition are so great you can see them coming.

Here are ads by three young writers named Kroll (Figure 4-4), Backer (Figure 4-5), and Wells (Figure 4-6), respectively.

Of this breed, John Noble is among the noblest. Others are richer and more illustrious, but they had to "drop what they were doing"—they had to do other

Figure 4-4

...and Spalding made them all

things to get there. But John Noble? Writing is the only thing he ever *had* to do. "I'm just not as good at meetings as I am at the typewriter," he says. Of all John's ads, here's his favorite (Figure 4-7).

John's in charge of all the writers at Doyle, Dane, Bernbach. And when I asked him what he looks for in young talent he gave me this wonderful example: "Not ten minutes ago I was looking at a kid's book. The first thing in his book was a double-page spread. It was for a plant vitamin. Both pages overflowed with healthy plants. He wrote this headline for it: *Seven weeks ago this was a single page ad.*"

Figure 4-5

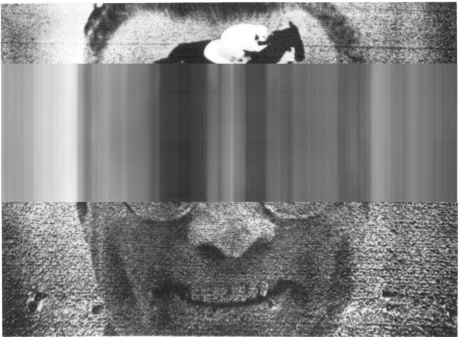

maybe you need a nice relaxing hobby out in the sun Big A

"Either you're a copywriter or you're not," John said. "This kid is and I'm hiring him."

Much at home on the subject of copywriters were the art directors I spoke with. The best and juiciest comment of all came from ex-Scali, ex-Ally, now DMB&B art director Peter Kingman:

> First of all, a copywriter has to listen to account people only so long. Second, he can't do what these people are expecting to see. And most important, a copywriter has to have a touch of anger—a Ralph Nader kind of zeal, to dig for a shining piece of information, a truth about the product that will kill the competition.

Talent in any business is always in short supply. And one can only encourage talented people to go on. Never dilute your standards. If you do, it exacts a toll. You will blame the business for what it did to your talent. You will demean

Figure 4-6

Where else can you see the greatest show on earth for the price of a cup of coffee?

copywriting as a legitimate calling. As opposed to what *you* permitted along the way.

I'll let Ed McCabe sum it up: "A copywriter has to construct his own freedom from the system. A truly great copywriter extends it for others."

THE ART DIRECTOR

The art director's main responsibility is to make simple order out of many elements. When it works, his craft is distinguished, original, and subtle.

White Space

One of the art director's most effective tools is the use of white space. White space acts as a relief, eliminates accessorized copy, and is both riveting and inviting to the reader. To the untutored eye, the urge to "one up" blank space is contagious. But as can be seen in Figure 4-8, the purity of white space is not to be violated. It is not the proper place for reviewers to practice their doodles.

Figure 4-7

"It was the only thing to do after the mule died."

Three years back, the Hinsleys of Dora, Missouri, had a tough decision to make.

To buy a new mule.

Or invest in a used bug.

They weighed the two possibilities.

First there was the problem of the bitter Ozark winters. Tough on a warm-blooded mule. Not so tough on an air-cooled VW.

Then, what about the eating habits of the two contenders? Hay vs. gasoline.

As Mr. Hinsley puts it: "I get over eighty miles out of a dollar's worth of gas and I get where I want to go a lot quicker."

Then there's the road leading to their cabin. Many a mule pulling a wagon and many a conventional automobile has spent many an hour stuck in the mud.

Also, a mule needs a barn. A bug doesn't.

"It sets out there all day and the paint looks near as good as the day we got it."

Finally, there was maintenance to think about. When a mule breaks down, there's only one thing to do: Shoot it.

But if and when their bug breaks down, the Hinsleys have a Volkswagen dealer only two gallons away.

Figure 4-8

Standing Still versus Standing Out

Every time an art director produces a good design, he not only raises the stature of paper but improves our visual environment. A striking visual presentation is the difference between a page that stands still and a page that stands out (see Figure 4-9).

Knowing When to Stop

A good art director can make even a small idea look big and important. But the real test is to make a big idea, which is usually simple, look as though it hasn't been art directed at all. Consider this statement from an artist of some renown: "When you start from a portrait and try by successive eliminations to get down to pure form, to clean unbroken volume, you inevitably end up with an egg and in the opposite direction you can arrive at the portrait.

"But art, I think, escapes from that oversimplified motion, which consists in going from one extreme to the other. One has to be able to stop in time."

Not every art director has a touch of Picasso in him (see Figure 4-10). But I can't emphasize enough how much we need understatement like this today in commercial art. Being beautifully believable is so much better than just being beautiful. Following are two examples of understated design that is logical, tasteful, and executed with brilliant simplicity.

Figure 4-9

As Bold As a Zebra.

Introducing the Citizen Nobl
Crisp designs. Brilliant techn
Like delicate herringbone b
styles. All for a look as rar
Noblia (No-blee-a) breed's
ultrathin (1.2 mm.) quartz
among the world's thinnest
Noblia. F

Once you see the Noblia itself, you'll know what making this breed so unique.
It's the richly textured bracelets that move with amazing grace. Because every link is so finely
aligned. Even the dials—in gold or ivory—complement this interwoven elegance.
What's more, Citizen has overseen technology with all this style. So you can not only rely
on Noblia to look beautiful. You can rely on Noblia, beyond
Noblia. By Citizen Each watch shown priced at $139.

A Unique Breed of Watch.

Figure 4-10

Owl, drawing. 1946

This gold medal winner (Figure 4-11) is the original "rough" of art director Charles Piccirillo. As the story goes, it was literally ripped from his sketch pad, rushed to the client, plated, and run off before he could make it better.

That is the hard and unromantic school of art direction. But look closely at Figure 4-12. With this design, no copywriter could slip in a vague thought. Or a careless statement. Or an awkward word.

Figure 4-11

Or buy a Volkswagen.

Figure 4-12

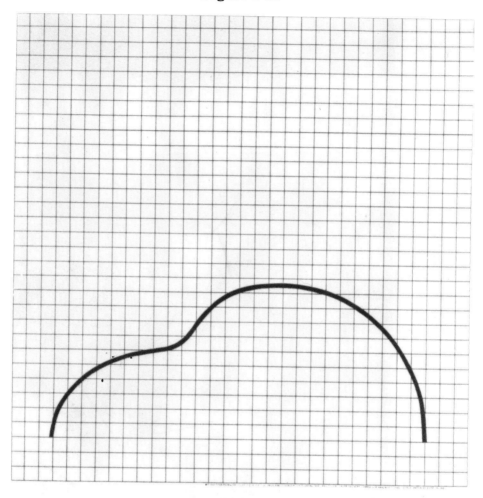

Is the economy trying to tell you something?

If you've hesitated about buying a new car because of the economy, maybe you should look into the economy of buying a new Volkswagen.

To begin with, while the average new car sells for about $3185, a new VW sells for only $1839*

That saves you about $1300.

Then, while the average car costs 10.9 cents a mile to run, a Volkswagen costs only 5 cents.

That saves you about another $700

every year (or 12,000 miles) you drive

And in just one year, it can bring your total savings to $2000.
In two years, $2700.
In three, $3400.
Happy days are here again.

A successful ad does one thing well. It usually happens when both writer and art director apply Picasso's simple yet demanding guideline: Know when to stop.

Product as a Page

If your product offers alternatives to confusion, the page should reflect a reverence for order (see Figure 4-15). Reflecting on the uncluttered page is art director of the year Nancy Rice, who, with copywriter Bill Miller, created this well-documented campaign (ad spending up 30 percent) for *Rolling Stone*: "It's the thought that should come through. If you have to decorate, decorate with the elegance of the idea. If that's not enough, you have got a dull idea."

Every client should demand more for his money. One way is to make the product a page (see Figure 4-16).

The question for every art director is not so much whether you can draw better or design better or even arrange elements better, but can your art persuade better? No other kind of art requires this cause-and-effect connection (see Figure 4-17).

An Art Director's/Writer's Manifesto

As a writer, I have always had a special kinship with art directors. If I could describe my ideal working relationship, it would come down to reciprocity—equal status, equal exchange, equal accountability. It is the mutual right to disagree, but with affection—affection that stems from the understanding that we're both after the same standard.

If my headlines fall to puns and double entendres, if my copy lacks meat, I fully expect my art director to remind me that I still have it in me. Every art director should know how idiotic writers become over flattery.

On the other hand, if my art director resorts to tricks like computer typeface underscoring a word in a headline or is tempted to change typeface in the same ad, I will find him guilty of bad taste and will sentence him to 72 months at Eliott Unger and Eliott conforming video tape.

If I, the writer, am feeling insecure, if nothing I'm doing is turning out right

Figure 4-13

Figure 4-14

Figure 4-15

or it's not what I expected, I need to hear from my art director: "It's all right, what you're trying is new." If, on the other hand, the art director is basically a quiet, reserved person, a recluse, and unable to express himself, I will insist that he get on the plane, come to the meeting, and present the work. Invariably, he will learn that being articulate in meetings isn't something an art director can't do, it's something an art director either chooses to do or is too lazy to do.

Finally, the most essential gift for a good copywriter is to have an art director with what Hemingway might call a built-in, shockproof shit detector.

The Account Executive

There is little love lost between account people and the creative department. Love, however, is not the issue. Dealing in good faith is.

Promises

To account executives and assistant account executives who may be reading this book, I offer the following promises about this chapter:

Figure 4-16

I will not take cheap shots.

If I resort to calling you names, you will get to call me names back.

I will never use the word *anal* or *overanalysis* in describing you.

I will not bury Easter eggs. You won't have to dig for a missing meaning.

I promise a chapter for your ultimate safekeeping—a collection of "valuables" that you might want to revisit from time to time.

What Does an Account Executive Do?

Of all the starting jobs in advertising, this is the toughest. An AE or an assistant is expected to be an instant whiz at numbers and an astute analyzer of

Figure 4-17

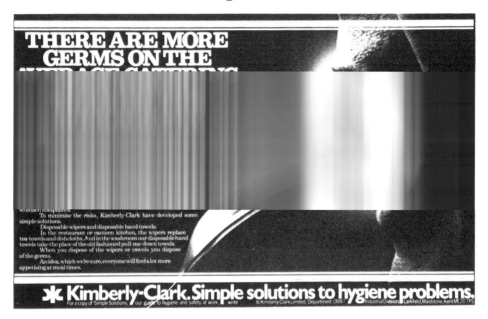

budgets, media weights, share of market, share of voice, research, and research conclusions.

An AE is expected to be vigilant in tracking the competition—what the competition is running, where, and at what levels.

An AE must spot competitive leaks via store checks—sniffing out new test markets, new products, and product improvements.

An AE is expected to be a keen evaluator of competitive advertising. And, at the same time, an AE must plus that evaluation with strategic and tactical thinking.

In addition, an AE is expected to write call reports, agency recommendations, and accounts of his or her personal perspective on events. An AE must not only write well but write with speed, precision, and conciseness.

On top of all this, an AE can't skim. He has to know. A misquote, a miscalculation, even a single digit error is pounced on and seemingly never forgiven by either management supervisor or client.

An AE is sometimes recruited for the dirty work. AE's get the coffee. They rent cars and make reservations for the travelling team, including creative people. They have to go out drinking with the client.

AE's are even expected to schlepp the big black bag containing "the work." (This is where an AE—man or woman—should draw the line. Don't schlepp. It destroys your status as a serious professional and compromises your dignity. Seeing who schlepps tells me a lot about who's left holding the bag.)

An AE has to deal with peers on the client side, some of whom are out-and-out bullies who are insecure and being pushed from above. It is the AE who has to take the heat for agency lateness, sloppiness, and screw-ups. Which is why an AE's popularity ratings swing from "nobody likes me" to "everybody likes me" in the time it takes to say "the client's on the phone."

Some of My Best Friends

Life between account and creative people doesn't always have to be a test of character or will. Some of my best friends have been account executives.

Bill Thurber was the first. He was an AE on the Ford truck account at J.W.T. when I was a beginning writer. I remember the special spirit he had about his work and his writing, especially his call reports. (Call reports are written recaps of client copy meetings.) Bill's were dispatched from Detroit. They were expressions of energy, enthusiasm, and intelligence. What he wrote he felt; it came from him.

I was just a green kid making 100 bucks a week, so I didn't get to Detroit much. The call reports to me were more than inter office mail. They represented news from the front. And that's the way Bill wrote them, like a reporter. He never missed an opportunity to pat us on the back or to share meeting applause or to note a particular.

When Ford's district dealers raved about our commercials, he wrote about it. When the client was "ecstatic," it was mentioned in the memo. When Lee Iacocca, then Ford's ad manager, made it a point in an agency review to single out our efforts on Ford truck "as the outstanding element in Ford's TV advertising," there was a special memo saying so.

I gladly put work into Bill's hands. I trusted him to sell exactly what I gave him.

Steve Bretschneider is another example. When I last heard from Steve, he was the senior manager on the Coca-Cola business at McCann Erickson. I worked with Steve when he was an account executive on the Lehn-Fink business at S.S.C.B.

We were working on Lysol toilet bowl cleaner. We developed a thirty-second spot dramatizing a unique spout on the package that allowed the consumer to disinfect the "whole bowl" under the rim. This was an advantage we needed to demonstrate. But there was one hitch. Network policy would not permit a toilet bowl to be shown on TV.

We constructed a see-through plexiglass facsimile. Our plan was to present our story in an accurate yet tasteful, cosmetic way. All three networks refused the ad. Steve argued and then argued some more. But with no success.

Steve eventually went off the business, but in six months he came back on it as supervisor. The first question he asked was "What's happening to the toilet bowl spot?" Of course, the answer was nothing.

Steve went back to the networks and got them to approve the storyboard with the stipulation that final approval would rest on the tastefulness of the film.

We shot the commercial for $6,000. All three networks approved the film. It ran for years and was the first time any toilet bowl cleaner was shown in use. It gave Lysol an insurmountable lead in what had been a flat, unimaginative category. It would never have run without Steve's efforts.

Harris. Usually this is handled by the creative director, but for some reason he was unavailable and I had to do it.

I prepared well. I knew my stuff and came off in my usual "passionate, he really cares" style. Before I got back to my office, there was a note scribbled on my pad. It was from Artie saying how proud he was and that I had demonstrated to Harris that we really knew his business.

That was a turning point for me at B&B because it convinced me I could deal with the big boys in my own raw style. I still have that note from Artie. And I still miss his rah, rah approach.

Artie taught me the real meaning of partnership. He instilled that feeling in his group. We all believed we were "the chosen few." And believe it or not, it was actually fun.

If we didn't deliver, Artie was the first one to exclaim, "That's unacceptable." If he disagreed with a creative approach, he would never inflict his opinion or stop the work from being presented. You always learned what Artie's position was *before* a meeting, not during it. When we did a good job, he was always there letting everybody else in the agency know about it.

Artie knew something about creative people—how insecure we are and what big egos we have. He knew that a pat on the back would take care of both. As a result, most creative people would kill for Artie.

There is a fourth example—an AE by trade, a book-bum by heart. She helped me through this book. She kept me on track. She was my own best voice and she always gave me the feeling that I was better than I was. Her name is on the dedication page.

Chilling Expressions

I'm well aware that occasionally AE's are at the mercy of the creative team, spendthrift as we are with our giant egos, bad manners, and bad work. In many cases our egos are in disproportion to our supply of talent. We could also agree that just as many creative people are promoted over their heads as account people. Creative people can be lunks and even blivets.

Still, as an account executive, you have to coexist productively with the creative people. You must work hard at this relationship. Your power is patience. With enough patience, even the most talentless creatives can revise themselves into semiliteracy.

In this process, I urge you to avoid the two chilliest expressions in the advertising vernacular. The first is "the client won't buy it."

Don't use that. Ever. It restricts work to what the client expects versus what the client needs. And whereas a client should have some idea of what's coming, an agency should never present the expected. Your job as an AE is to be a seller of creative work, not a buyer. In fact, *never* begin a sentence with "the client."

I hate to admit it, but I've seen more than a few people go straight to the top with this act—continually selling out the creative product in pursuit of brownie points from a conservative management.

Yet, AEs are employed and paid by the agency, not the client. The work must first be good for the agency. If it isn't, how can it possibly benefit the client?

And I've never spoken directly to God. I never want to be burdened by an AE's idea of what God wants.

Second chilling expression: "I'm not comfortable with this." If *creative* is the most arrogant word in our special vocabulary, *comfort* is the most detestable.

Outside of your favorite clothes, if you can attach the word *comfortable* to any aspect of your life—job, kids, sex, marriage—you should re-evaluate it.

Comfort is old habits, formula, preconceptions, the ruts we can't get out of.

Comfort is the archenemy of what's biting, gripping, passionate, competitive.

Comfort is sleeping in the middle of bed. It never takes you to the edge where all the best ideas are.

Comfort is unchallenging, creates no waves, and gets old early. Comfortable is everything advertising shouldn't be.

Getting the Creative Team on Your Side

An AE's primary responsibility is to instill and nurture creativity in both client and creative. If you're an AE reading this, remember: Creative people don't have the organizational traits you have. Thus, your job is to encourage a spirit of entrepreneurship. There are obvious places for AE's to start: Be energetic, get excited about even a germ of an idea.

Creative people are suckers for enthusiasm. Encourage them to be audacious. You're not a boss or a judge, you're a leader. A successful campaign on your résumé is your big ticket to the next level or the next job. Think of yourself as a seller, not a buyer. (I know I just said that, but some things are worth repeating.)

Here are some specifics that can help in your relationship with the creative team.

1. Be relaxed with good humor and determination not to take the whole thing too seriously. You'd be surprised how this will affect your ability to read reality, which is at the heart of all sound advertising judgment.

5. Demonstrate early on that you can think. For example, when explaining a new assignment, write up a "starter kit" for your creative team. On Crest, I had an AE, Greg Walker, who would sit down and write every creative thought he had on one particular job, like "how to sell Crest to blacks." He sent me an entire study on blacks: habits, practices, beliefs. It was a springboard to ideas based on marketplace problems.

6. Have a sense of trends in the winds. Such as Hispanics as a major force in the 1980s, healthy eating as a goal for most families, chemical pollution of supermarket food, package graphics that keep pace with future stores.

7. Fight for more time for the creative process. Scoring brownie points with the client is not the measure of your success; quality work is. Scintillating campaigns do not happen in the same amount of time it takes to make travel arrangements.

8. Don't refer to copywriters as "my copywriter" or copy as "my copy." This goes against what is important for superior creative work—freedom.

9. Avoid a list of simultaneous creative assignments. It only results in a diffusion of effort on your part and splinters the focus for the creative people. Remember, creative people have a low tolerance for lists. They also get tired of things long before you do.

10. Set priorities early. Do it with brand group and creative in the same room. This eliminates bad feelings and bad meetings because you've taken the effort to get agreement up-front.

11. Go beyond a strategy. Write a clear, concise creative brief. Write it with the creative team. Include advertising elements such as language and what the film will look like. Don't let it be stilted. Write it with spirit.

12. Never agree to spend research money to break tied votes. It comes out of your profit sharing. Make certain each commercial has a difference you can test.

13. Trade up. Anytime you can talk with the group head instead of the copywriter, do so. Act like you're ready for the next level.

Finally, my own experience tells me that there is no job in an agency where one who is in earnest about learning to produce better work can make such enormous strides in so short a time as the AE.

How to Evaluate Copy

In your pursuit of career objectives, excellent copy judgment will take you to the top quicker than anything. Believe me when I tell you, when it comes to copy judgment, your own supervisor is probably suspect. If you put the following ideas into practice, you'll be a supervisor in six months or less.

What to Look For in a Storyboard

1. Is the execution surprising? Have you seen it before?
2. What will it look like on film? (Remember, this is the 1980s, and what people see is just as important as what people read or hear.)
3. Does the storyboard incorporate a visualization of the benefit? (A good example is the campaign for Sure antiperspirant: "Raise your hand if you're sure.")
4. Does the commercial have an idea stated as a benefit?
5. Does the commercial convey a product attribute or a consumer benefit? (An attribute is what the manufacturer puts into a product to make it work: Crest has fluoride. A benefit is what a consumer gets as a result: Crest gives your kids great checkups.)
6. Is there new information? (Information sells. It can be news about the product—an improvement, new package. It can also be news about the way consumers *feel* about your product.)
7. Does the idea translate to all media? (A great campaign should work on a matchbook cover.)
8. Can the idea be sustained over a period of time? Or is it just another temporary life-support system for the product?
9. Is the execution based on a believable premise? (Use your intuition on this one. Never forget that you're a consumer, too.)

Follow these guidelines and you'll be ahead of most creative people (including myself) who need to be reminded of things we long ago forgot.

Making Straight A's and Flunking Life

Getting an AE job these days without an MBA is not impossible, but it is unlikely. MBA's make up most of the account section of any middle to large agency. MBA's live and work by the numbers; they even dress by the numbers. They are rigid in that they have a preconception (and, therefore, the right answer) about everything.

This section is dedicated to this new breed—the kind who repeatedly test my limited intelligence and drive me well beyond type A behavior.

Their training makes them like this. They're the sort that prescribes a way of doing things. With a preconceived mindset that by definition rules out the magic that advertising requires and ignores the fundamental marketing princi-

that is being nitpicked to death. I will simply take it from the guppies before death can occur.)

Creative people are willing to go down with the ship. But AE's are occasionally willing to surrender to their training, which says that it's the numbers that make you successful and the unknown that makes you fail.

AE's dream at night. Creatives dream in the broad daylight.

An MBA might get you to the right answer, but it's usually missing the human stuff. The off-beat, the not-so-loving.

A pocket calculator will never lead you to a basic truth. Consumers are not statistics. They're people. They don't look at advertising with a copy of your ad strategy in hand.

The AE's definition of success is money, power, position, and career victories. Success for us is the reward of failing, of falling short, or correcting a fake position and never letting things alone. This is what advertising is about.

One more piece of advice, compliments of E.B. White, to be recited by AE's everywhere at the beginning of each work day: "There is no smooth ride as valuable as the rough ride."

Name Calling

By now, some of you are calling me names. For the record, I have completed a survey of the names that AE's and creative people call each other, usually after an internal copy meeting. Here are some winning names for bad creative people:

"He's a real cacamoid." Translation: A creative person who presents an assortment of caca. In common usage, a hack.

"A philodox." Translation: A creative genius who is in love with his own work—usually work he has done in the past that has nothing to do with the work at hand, which is dreck.

"A complete personhole." Proposed as a replacement for the more commonly used slur. This is a term whose time will definitely come.

Here are some winning names for bad account people:

"A bunch of gradgrids." Translation: People who measure everything. The closer to human nature they get, the more terrified they become.

"A total udney." Translation: One who loves but doesn't understand. Typical comments: "I love the ad, but I have a concern" or "I love the ad, but . . ."

"A puzzlepate." A universally accepted gibe to describe one who is continually bewildered by the simplest ideas. As in "I don't think I understand it." (A common retort: "I *do* think, and I understand why you don't understand it.")

Not to end this section on a negative note, let me offer some advice from the creative person's perspective to those of you who are AE's.

As an AE, you'll be expected to attend internal copy meetings and say smart things. This is where your training falls short. The AE's system of education usually favors what is measurable, predictable, and efficient. All this makes AE's less than spontaneous.

On the one hand, an AE is usually told by his supervisor to be quiet at meetings and listen. On the other hand, the quickest way to sneak up to the next level is to say something constructive in a copy meeting.

So, balance listening with articulating a respectable point of view. Assume intelligence. What you're thinking to yourself is usually the next thing your boss will say out loud.

To gain the respect of creative people, industriousness doesn't count. A helpful, guiding comment during a meeting will.

RESEARCH

In the words of F. L. Wright, "Truth is more important than facts."

Computer science has produced a discipline called artificial intelligence. It simulates human thinking and spins out what seems to be intelligent behavior.

The advertising version of this is quantitative research. It, too, passes for intelligent behavior.

The Artificial Audience

Quantitative research seizes on the horrifying tendency of clients to think that individual needs, dreams, and desires can be understood in terms of the multitude. However, a research multitude is no different from any other multitude. With a gentle push (*probe* in researchese), a multitude can be made to agree or disagree with anything, depending, of course, on the bias. And living by the numbers is the ultimate bias.

A research multitude is really a sampling of people from whom the

doorstop of a report. A detailed analysis audience—the masses. This method avoids the real audience, a single human being at the receiving end of the message.

In attempting to quantify everything, this type of research avoids the very thing that an audience desires most: escape from the condition that makes it a mass audience.

The Sin of Mass Appeal

It is understandable that clients gravitate toward the masses. There's a huge audience out there. Even a share of that market could mean huge sales.

But the error in treating your consumer as a mass can be seen in the cookie-cutter nature of the advertising itself. It is impossible to distinguish most products in most categories today. That's because, according to the people in research, "average is good." (Yes, I got that from an ARS man the other day. "Normal is good," his very words.)

The result is flatness and sameness in writing, visuals, personality.

Any commercial that requires imaginative input from the viewer will test badly. A commercial that lies there, frame by boring frame, and is open to only one interpretation will invariably score well. Respondents are able to "track it," to recall the main point of the commercial.

"We like to play Rosser Reeves and isolate the USP [unique selling proposition]," said the same ARS representative.

"Really," I chimed, "how'd you like to play Hal Riney or Tom McElligott instead?" He had no idea who these people were.

Clients who continue to use testing methods like ARS and Burke are buying a quack system that determines nothing in terms of persuasion, wearability, and attitude shift. We haven't demanded creativity from these worn-out research methods, so we settle for wobbly, one-shot answers.

I Can Be Very Friendly

Research is legitimate when it is properly used as a tool. Research was designed to *lead* to marketing solutions, not to judge creative work. It is the evolutionary aspects of research that can help the creative and marketing team.

I have research people telling me all the time: "We want to be friends with you guys, but you won't let us."

You want to be friends? I'll tell you how.

Start giving me feedback before I go to work. Stop second-guessing me after the work is done. I would never ignore research and the signals it gives at the planning stage.

Tell me about the product I'm considering. Is it ready? How does it compare with the competition? Is the name right? (For example, on Lysol, we were all set to call its new foam cleaner Lysol Bathroom Cleaner, a generic name. Research led us to Lysol Basin/Tub/Tile Cleaner—a much better name, because it's specific and tells the consumer what surfaces to use it on.)

Tell me about my flavor, my color, my formula, my crush-proof package, my flip-top dispenser, my new pump toothpaste, my lightweight, easy-to-hold box. Are they what the customers want? (We were testing packages recently for a new bleach. A lady with arthritis made the decision easy. She picked the package that was shaped so her hand could fit around it easier.)

Help me reposition my product. (Research did that with Fritos. Frito-Lay stopped its advertising for a whole year. The Frito Bandito wasn't hacking it. It took bare-boned concept research to isolate the winning position, called "meal accompaniment," which suggested to mothers that the healthiest side dish to give kids with soup and sandwiches was Fritos.)

Define my target audience for me. Don't give me big numbers; define my lead user. (Like you did for Schaefer when you isolated the heavy beer drinker— 20 percent of the beer drinkers in the United States drink 80 percent of the beer.)

Warn me when my product is less desirable than I think it is. (Like when you told us that black people thought of Crest as "the white man's toothpaste." You don't think this was a shock to P&G? It was to me. It was to Benton & Bowles, too. It led P&G to assign a black agency, Burrell in Chicago, to handle that segment of the market for Crest.)

When research starts dealing with the real; when there is a concern for human documentation rather than a devotion to optimizing the calculator; and when research addresses the unchanging man instead of bullshitting us about demographics and psychographics: that's when research is valuable.

Research proponents will undoubtedly find this section "flawed," laced with hyperbole and generalizations. That's okay.

I do little in my life to discourage hyperbole. And as for generalizations, that's the point, guys, I'll stop generalizing when you do.

The Hocus-Pocus Group

> Give me a darkened room with a one-way
> mirror in a suburban mall, a half dozen
> egg rolls, a comely moderator in a
> diaphanous gown, and I care not what the

on marketing productivity, they are the arteriosclerosis of the creative process.

A focus group is a quick test of creative material in its early stages of development. Campaigns, concepts, and execution are shown in rough form. This may include:

Storyboards.
Animatics (a storyboard on tape with a voice track and effects).
Livamatics (an animatic that moves).
Photomatics (a storyboard in polaroids).
Quick and rough film (a rank production of a rank idea).

Focus groups are conducted by quick-test research companies who operate out of suburban shopping malls. They employ energetic young researchers, resembling moonies, who intercept shoppers. Each shopper is given $15 or $20, cash, to participate in a group session. The maximum time for each session is about one and a half hours. There are 8 to 15 respondents in each group. If specific kinds of respondents are needed, such as users or nonusers of certain products, the recruiting is done by phone.

Respondents sit in front of a one-way mirror with soft drinks and cookies. Behind the mirror in a darkened room sit the client, the account team, the creative team, client research, agency research, friends, guests, and, in one recent case, a close relative. The observers feed on lox, brie, pate, caviar, whiting, dips, nuts, crudites, and on Long Island cold sesame noodles. The success of these lucrative and proliferating quick-test centers is dependent on the quality of the foodstuffs, not on the quality of the research.

There is a group moderator, usually a woman and often an ex-member of the agency research department. They are no dummies. They can sense a trend when they see it: the focus-group-as-a-crutch trend; the clogging-the-creative

59

trend; the help-my-shaky-judgment trend; the fixation-on-a-snug-fit trend.

They also know where the money is. They know that as career moderators they can double and sometimes triple their agency salary on the supplier side.

A focus group is commonly referred to by the client as "a learning experience." And learn we do. Clients don't cheat. We know who's going to make the copy decision for them. The focus group, bless their appetites, will.

They'll tell us what's relevant about the product, then we'll throw the same stuff back at them in the advertising, exactly the way they told us. Clients are notorious for this—if the idea ever does survive, the film is exactly what consumers expect to see and hear. This is the built-in comfort factor that dulls viewer capacity to react or regard the advertising with anything other than boredom. All of this takes forever. You can hurry copy, but never research.

Think of the Goodyear blimp—picture yourself inflating it with a basketball pump. That's research for you.

Groupthink Is No Think

Decisions made in focus groups are influenced by groupthink. We ignore our experiences and instincts. We forget that advertising isn't a science; it's a deceptively simple profession that practices the art of selling with imagination. I've seen the self-deceiving blinds in action. For Zest soap, we asked groups to look at some commercials. Although they liked the commercials, they questioned the basic premise that Zest gets rid of soap film. Time and again they said, "We never see soap film. Even if we had it, a towel would take it off." But soap film was the Zest strategy (it has been for years), and Lord knows you don't change the strategy even when it deals with a nonproblem that a consumer has never experienced. On the other side of the mirror, the brand manager was pounding the table, calling the woman stupid because she wasn't sympathetic to what he wanted to hear.

The client's curiosity was so manipulated that he became unaware that he could ask any additional questions. For example, "Well, you said you really liked the commercial. What did you like about it and why? Or, why do you like Zest?" (It is the number three or four best-selling bar. There must be some reason.) Or dozens of other product-related questions.

Contrary to the client's stated objectives, "learning" was the last thing on his mind. Three years later, the same client is still on the same "gets rid of soap film" strategy. Clients who overlook the tendency of groupthink to promote collective amnesia are the same clients who overlook other kinds of focus group bias.

The first of these is *group bias* in general. Many times groups are swayed and influenced by one dominant voice. This respondent usually hates the world, with advertising being number one on the hit list.

Second is *moderator bias*. If a moderator doesn't get the answer by probing, she'll push, bully, and browbeat to get it.

Third is the *comfort bias*. The control word with a lot of moderators is *comfort,* that is, the focus group is "comfortable with this or not very comfortable with that." As you already know, my criteria are quite the opposite: I write for edge, for bite, for outrageousness. Never for comfort. As a result, what most moderators get from me is conflict.

beating heart out of your message, you're foolish. You're running the real risk of turning a "film" brand into an "animatic" brand.

Burke: The Curse of Death

As befits its subject, this will be a brief account of a tyrannical idea—the Burke score.

At this writing, a Burke score is a one number predictor of a commercial's success or failure. It is the most widely used DAR (day after recall) system in the business. Telephone respondents are called 24 hours after a commercial is run. They are asked: "Did you see this commercial? If so, what do you remember?" The "score" represents the answer to that question.

Commercials live or die by that number. True, additional responses to a question are attached. They rate various aspects of the commercial's impact. But if you have ever read one of these surveys, you understand it for what it is: an assortment of grunts, pauses, drifts, dots, and dashes.

Burke tells you nothing about whether a viewer will be moved to buy the product or not—the factor called persuasion. Under no circumstances can any available type of research measure, project, or give a hint of what the persuasion factor will be. I routinely curse the research person who tells clients it can.

If I believe in anything, it is the residual value of advertising—the cumulative power of words and pictures to shift attitudes over a period of time and create a loyal customer. More clients are beginning to see this. So they don't rely on Burke as much as they once did. Although it's too late to be the first to dump Burke, it's never too late to get smart.

Sleazy Does It

Alas, an ambitious new Burke procedure called Selector claims to do the impossible—measure persuasion. Two days before a commercial runs, 450 respondents are sent a packet containing two questionnaires on the test program and entry slips for drawings of $50 worth of groceries. (Burke refers to this as a token of thanks for participating.)

The drawing is a way of testing whether the respondents were moved to switch brands after they viewed the commercial. The introduction of Selector has made the standard Burke obsolete. In fact, 70 percent of Burke subscribers now use Selector.

Author of all this is king of the crystal ball, Michael Von Gorten, senior VP of Burke's copy testing division. He says: "People place too much blind faith on us. My objective is to get people to use research more reasonably and less emotionally." Von Gorten "loves advertising." It's easy to see why. In 1984, Burke's total revenues were about $60 million, up 15 percent from 1982.

This man is dangerous. "Advertising isn't art, it's commerce," he says. "It's the difference between a novel and a well-written computer instruction book. A good copywriter is more like a guy who writes instruction booklets than he is like James Joyce." Such an inelegant and unthinking comment in a business where everything begins by thinking. Henry Miller could have had Von Gorten in mind when he wrote: "One has to be a low brow, a bit of a murderer . . . ready and willing to see people sacrificed for the sake of an idea—whether it's a good idea or bad." Which is why I want you to study the mug shots in Figure 4-18 carefully. If you ever pass this man on the street, you'll know what to do.

Research at Its Worst

Research is like the space program. It's obscenely expensive and everybody who works at it seems to be having fun. Research gives people jobs, it cheers them up, and it gives researchers the notion that they are part of advertising.

But the ones who perform in public aren't people—they are fire hydrants

Figure 4-18

who gush and gurgle. Meet Dr. Bob, a real director of research at a real agency. I met him in an article by Phil Dougherty of *The New York Times.* To Dr. Bob an ad agency is the equivalent of the human mind. The creative people are the id, artistic but not overly rational. The account folk are the superego. They know rules, what should be done. The two forces are at war. In between is the ego. "I

Dr. Bob (to creative team): "And what are our busy little ids up to today?"
Creatives: "Oh, off on another schizophrenic tear. And you, mein executive ego?"
Dr. Bob: "Field-testing some compromises, thank you."

Must I tell you that Dr. Bob got his first research job answering an ad looking for an analytical mind? And that he equates good advertising with nice guys? What must be said directly to Dr. Bob is this: If you really want to be part of advertising, stop the crap and start working as hard as the rest of us.

Intelligent Research Intelligently Interpreted

Research is not generally the road to the top in the agency field. Especially if you're a woman. Louise McNamee has overcome both hurdles.

She is acting president and CEO of Della Femina, Travisano & Partners, and one of the few research executives I ever heard who makes any sense.

Although I come down hard on the kind of research that tells you *how* to say it, the kind Louise produces tells you *what* to say. "Evolutionary research" she calls it. The kind that leads me to better ideas even as I'm developing others. I'm happy to test strategic stuff and never regret it. I'll gladly listen to the consumer until I'm sure I have something he wants.

I don't want to start out with a strategy dictated by a focus group. I want a street strategy. I want the right to go from there to my imagination to find the most intrusive way to say it.

McNamee explains the evolutionary process this way: "We want to provide creative people with the most insight and information possible—with as much access to as many people as possible at a time when they need it most—when they're trying to come up with a creative solution." This puts research into very friendly territory. McNamee's perspective bridges the gap between the familiar that tests well and the extraordinary that sells well.

His Master's Voice

Most of the material for this book and this chapter was gathered in the presence of Schroeder, my lovable lab. And since I read aloud most of what I write, he has become my most loyal, sensitive, and discriminating critic.

I find Schroeder to be much more reliable than most human beings. I can never fake him out. I can never whisper "snack" if there is none. If I want him to listen, much less respond, I have to tell him the truth.

Whereas many humans I know have trouble expressing any point of view, Schroeder chooses from a variety of signals: He lowers his ears, points (or drops) his tail, scratches, shakes. He even cringes by putting his paws over his ears.

My suggestion to clients is to buy a dog. As an audience of one, you can't beat a dog for integrity. Remember the old Victrola trademark with the dog listening to his master's voice? RCA was trying to tell us something.

With all of this in mind, try this: In your dog's presence, repeat out loud your next campaign. I guarantee he will never let you get away with a glib or easy solution. And the next time you have a recommendation to spend your company's profit-sharing or bonus poll money on report card research, read it aloud to your dog first. If she bites your head off, it serves you right.

ON WOMEN IN ADVERTISING

If you've come such a long way, why is Cosmo still calling you a girl?

My question is a reflection of the ironic state of women in most all areas of business. On the surface, many would agree with the Virginia Slims protagonist—women have come a long way. But looking beyond the smartly squared look and Ferragamo pumps, the facts take issue with that. Few executive women have what serious moneymen refer to as real wealth—investment capital—the kind that the new tycoons (all men) use to get *more* wealth.

Top women executives earn only 37 cents for every dollar earned by top male executives. In advertising, according to an *Adweek* survey, the average salary for women at the end of 1985 was $28,000; for men, $43,000. If you get out your calculator, you discover that agency men earned 54 percent more than agency women (more about this in Figure 4-19).

Not to worry, you say; more women are getting MBA's; young men and women are coming into the work force with equal credentials. From now on there'll be little difference in their paychecks.

Sorry. According to a recent Stanford University study, five years out of the university's business school, female graduates were earning $30,000 per year

Figure 4-19

Is this ad ... because it was written by a woman?

A lot of men must think so, because women in advertising with 5 years of experience earn 28% less than their male counterparts.[1] And that's _better_ than average for working women — who make about 60¢ for every dollar a man earns.[2]

That's not exactly liberty and justice for all.

Find out more about the status of Minnesota's working women and about their pay, power and poverty. Watch WCCO TV's five part "Cover Story." And if you are a woman, get your boss to watch.

Maybe you'll get a raise.

"Working Women" tonight through Thursday night on WCCO TV's 10 PM REPORT.

WCCO-TV

We're thinking news. We're thinking of you.

© 1984 WCCO TV

while their male classmates were earning $38,000. The Stanford women began earning 94 cents to the male dollar, but in five years slipped badly to 79 cents.

Even though there are large numbers of female MBA's in middle management, only a tiny percentage make it to the top. This hurts. Particularly when you consider these facts involve the wealthiest and most successful corporations, the ones that boast the most about their commitment to equality. If you want to verify this, get a copy of the best-selling business book of the 1980s, *In Search of Excellence,* which chronicles a dozen or so of America's most successful companies. Go to the index, which covers more than a dozen pages. Look for a woman's name.

I found one: J. Child. J for Julia. Who, I read on page 173, "loves Ray Kroc's french fries."

Why Advertising?

Dream if you will that in a man-dominated business there is something beyond vulnerability. What women want to hear today is about their certainties, not insecurities. And where is it written (except in *Vogue* magazine) that to be vulnerable is a female trait? I've always considered it a human one.

Business might be a man's invention and he still owns it. Yet, in business there is but one standard of success: bringing in a profit. It is the woman who dares to contribute a profit-making idea who gains instant equality.

Given this deceptively simple requirement—given this profit-alone standard, let us examine why today there is no better place for a woman to be than in advertising.

Women are the dominant influence in the marketplace. Women do most of the buying: 80 percent of all advertised products. Clients know this. They spend millions researching what women buy and why.

Women have a natural affinity for advertising because they use the products themselves. There's a much better chance that the advertising will be true to the product and avoid "dumb housewife" stereotypes. Advertising welcomes the fact that women listen better, pay closer attention to things. Women work harder. They have to. Men get the titles. Women get the work.

Catch-Up Time

"It's catch-up time," says Phyllis Robinson, first woman creative director at Doyle, Dane, Bernbach. "It's encouraging when you hear about women like Jane Newman, account planner at Chiat Day, and Louise McNamee at Della Femina achieving top managerial status."

"Are these just exceptional women?" I asked.

"Any woman," Robinson explained, "who's willing to believe in her own talent, who possesses an intelligent passion for things—the cut, the color, a feeling for the merchandise—who has a basic curiosity even about dull subjects, who understands the thrill of being associated with a great idea can succeed in advertising."

"Is that all a woman needs?" I asked.

"No," she added. "A woman must pick the proper environment. It's like parenting. Look for a balance of freedom and discipline, both at the service of selling something."

Jane Newman of Chiat Day echoes this advice. "Find a place where male bonding isn't important. Advertising is craft. Find a place with craft people. Getting it right at the end of a day, that's why I'm at Chiat Day—it's the solution that counts around here."

. . . only her hairdresser knows for sure," was once considered too suggestive and was turned down by *Life* magazine. When she presented it to the F.C.B. board (all men), they blanched. "The dirt's in your own mind, boys," she said.

Does she think that blondes have more fun?

"When you're a blonde," she says, "you don't have to be as pretty, the kind of aura that comes off your face—and, of course, being a blonde is *rarer* than being a middle brown."

"There's no real definition of what's pretty. I do think it's nice to know you're the best you can be" (another winning slogan)—"it's good for your ego."

According to Polykoff, "being a girl" has its advantages in advertising. "I took advantage of being a girl. The attractiveness and softness of a woman make it easier to function. I never gave up the advantages of being a girl. If you get to be more masculine, you're not as pleasant."

"Being a woman first," she added, "an advertising lady second, you manage to stay more a human being. You don't get sour."

Could a man have written these campaigns? Probably. But only a woman could have written them so well.

If there is a place where a woman doesn't have to defer her dreams, it's advertising. I believe that clients hunger for female brainpower. I believe that readiness to work is an advertising trademark and that the woman who is willing to work harder can't fail. I submit the growing number of present-day heroines as proof.

These are women with talent, stamina, and compelling personalities. They've offered the hope that if they could do it, others could too. These women didn't reach the top of their field by demanding office windows or shouting for raises. They arrived at an utterly simple conclusion instead: There has to be a profit. In a man-dominated business, that's the equalizer. And once you accept that principle, it's amazing how quickly all the other problems sort themselves out.

Three Portraits

MARY AYERS. I worked with Mary at SSCB. She was 20 years ahead of her time in every way. She was the first and only woman on the board. She was the first woman president of the Four A's. A gentle, intense lady, she helped establish the reputation of SSCB. Its first client was Noxzema, who underwrote the agency to get it started.

I had lost track of Mary over the years—but I never forgot her. I called Paul LeStayo at SSCB, a long-time colleague of hers. He assured me that Mary was "alive, healthy, and still beautiful."

"It's not very complicated," said LeStayo about what made Mary, Mary. "She never left anything alone. She was always stirring the pot." Before Cover Girl, all there was was Noxzema. A product with a single dominant idea—healthy skin. When Noxell's P.R. director came to Mary with the idea of Cover Girl cosmetics, Mary just applied the idea—"Beauty with medicine," Paul called it.

That was a unique position and still is. "Twenty-five years and still making millions," LeStayo said. Here's the Noxzema skin cream story as he tells it.

"Mary was still an assistant. A secretary who had bad skin kept coming to Mary for Noxzema, the big ten-ounce jar size. Up to this point, Noxzema was a product you used for sunburn and insect bites. Mary asked the woman how she used up so much Noxzema. Her reply: 'I wash my face with it.' The rest is marketing history, and so are the millions of jars of Noxzema that are 'used up' every year by women still washing their faces with Noxzema, not soap."

Mary herself makes it sound simple.

"I made money for the agency. We got the billing up to $40–50 million a year. And I had fun. I worked with awfully nice men. I got to pick my own people, and I had one advantage over the women I see today lugging these bulging attaches all over town. I could turn it off, and I did. I went home and forgot about it.

"As far as cosmetic advertising today, Cover Girl is still the only one with a real benefit built in," she said. "I see all this stuff today. I have to laugh. It's all so temporary, so generic."

Is there a connection between the legacy of a Mary Ayers and the fact that SSCB still has Noxzema, one of the longest-running marriages on Madison Avenue? I think there is.

LOUISE McNAMEE. I am not a friend of research. So, when I heard that the Della Femina agency, a creative stronghold, had named its top research partner as acting president, that was news. When I found out that person was 34 and a woman, I was flabbergasted. I called and arranged for a telephone interview with Louise McNamee, acting president and chief operating officer of Della Femina Travisano & Partners. Following are my notes from that interview.

Lyons: Tell me about women in advertising.

Women should have a nose for the environment of an agency before they go to work there. I was able to get over the hump by picking places with less corporate environments—medium-size agencies, for example.

Lyons: What helps along the way are men who are sensitive to this bias who don't just give lip service to notions of equality and who have enough self-confidence that they don't feel less manly when they see a woman get ahead.

McNamee: I've been lucky that way. When I was at Kelly Nason, Jerry Schoenfeld and Bob Palmer had all those qualities. "If you could handle it" was operating principle there—letting talented people do it, even crossing over into other areas beyond job description. I wrote copy, handled account assignments. That helped me expand my research background in strategy and positioning. That would never have happened in a big agency, and I would never be where I am today.

Lyons: You talk about research being evolutionary. You describe it as leading a creative person to a good idea and averting a war between research and creative. How do you get it to work?

McNamee: Again, it's different than at a big agency. Research here is not accountable to account management. Effective research is implemented by people who do the advertising. I have a direct line to the creators of the work. "What can be proved" is the wrong premise. I don't think of research as research. I approach it as a way to solve problems. The result is not a report card but ideas that literally end up in the advertising. At Kelly Nason, when Arm & Hammer suggested putting its baking soda in the refrigerator to freshen the air, that didn't come from numbers; it was making research work to help creative people look at products and their prospects in new ways.

Lyons: Is that the purpose of evolutionary research?

McNamee: The purpose is up to us in research to keep improving and finding better ways. One of those ways is to add new possibilities in the creative direction.

Lyons: Pet peeves? Do you have any?

McNamee: Not being open-minded. The world changes every day. Advertising is supposed to be a reflection of that world—if you're not open-minded to new ways, you're not current. You should get out.

Lois Korey. Lois Korey's airy, spacious, modernistic president's office declares in no uncertain terms: Woman at work. Or, better yet: Woman progressing at the speed of light.

I started the interview with a basic question.

Lyons: Does Korey Kay have a method? How does a smaller client compete for distinction?

Korey: A commercial has to be both loved and hated, loved by the people who love it, ignored by the people who hate it. I've always gone out of the way to make it a little outrageous, but with a smile . . . making fun out of the very people you're appealing to. But the judges of creative work are so fearful when they see a commercial like, for example, Federal Express. The people make them squirm—that's because they're so real. Fearful people are always looking for ways to kill work. They'll say something inane like, that's not our target audience. That stuff never works with me.

Take the Monk commercial for Xerox. Were we suggesting that our target audience consisted of monks 35 and over? Or that there was a real monk somewhere doing this? It was simply a drama of utter simplicity that showed an incredible copier overcoming an incredibly delicate job.

Take Charlie Chaplin. Is IBM suggesting that PCJr is for people under four feet four with funny mustaches who wobble when they walk?

Lyons: Do you believe in heroes, or maybe a mentor? Did you have a mentor?

Korey: Mary Wells. Mary floored me with her marketing insights. When we were at Tinker together, we had Braniff. First thing, Mary looked at the competition—and found the whole category colorless. From that came the idea of selling sex appeal for an airline. Nobody ever thought of that before. I remember when Mary said, "Let's paint the planes." Almost in unison, everybody in the room said, "If it were allowed, somebody would have done it long ago."

We checked with the Federal Aviation Commission and nobody ever had. Furthermore, they had no restrictions on the graphics or colors of the airplanes. The rest is history. Mary would never give in, she was always looking for a selling angle. That's what makes great creative work—curiosity and guts.

Lois Korey is very much a lady, but when certain words come out I hear a definite trace of New York.

Lyons: What's your pet peeve?
Korey: Creative people who back off when things get tough. Words like

Gender Bender

In a "Hers" piece in *The New York Times*, Katharine Pollitt asks: "Why are women psychotherapy's best customers?" To answer the question, she cites a study conducted in the late 1960s. The therapists sampled were asked to define "healthy male" and "healthy female." The healthy male was "active, independent, competitive, logical." The healthy female was "dependent, subjective, passive, illogical."

So according to those in charge of our psyches, women like Robinson, Korey, McNamee, and Polykoff, by definition, are sick. It's different for women in advertising.

Most of my friends in the business are women. And I am pleased to say they still are and have been willing to lend what I will call "graceful self-reliance" to these pages.

What they have to say about topics like money, sexism, careers, men in business, and being a lady not only serves to delight, but to demonstrate the earnest hopes inside.

On money: My mother always told me it wasn't ladylike to talk about money in public. And because I was so bad at math I should stay away from finance. "Find a good man, dear, and he'll take care of all of that for you." We're all victims of how we were taught to think. A lot of residue molding in our minds. I can't imagine where I'd be without advertising. Because of advertising, I'm a money-maker, not a budget manager. (Copy supervisor, mid-thirties)

On sexism: The work force in many agencies in town is close to 50 percent women. Sexism is an outrageous luxury that no profitable organization can afford. It means wasting one-half the agency's brainpower. (Personnel manager, forties)

On careers: I look back. I've never seen my decision to work in advertising as an office-versus-home decision or a woman-versus-bitch situation. Nor did I get into the business to take a man's job. It was a place where I could be my best. I was lucky. My agency was careful to have first-class work. That's why your choice of agency is very important. I look around. There are just too many other professions that allow you to be content with the second rate. Advertising isn't one of them. (Agency partner, 55)

On men in business: If a man can admire me for my toughness, I'll be very happy to honor him for his sensitivity. (Creative supervisor, forties)

Another view: Men will be men. In business they just can't be trusted or even counted on to deliver promises. Of course, women will always be women; we'll go on treating them gently even when they don't deserve it. (Account person, 28)

On being a lady: My mother could drive a tractor with assurance, but she always took advantage of being a woman. The attractiveness, the softness. I would advise you to never give up that advantage. I've seen women who have. It's just so sad. The more masculine they become, they just get very unpleasant. Another thing: If a man wants to pick up a check, let him. (Senior management, board of directors, fifties)

Another view: Women who get married to their jobs turn sour. Their only passion is for crisis. They become joyless. Being around them is no fun. I would say, don't just go for a career. Go for a whole life. You'll stay more human. Your friends and family will still recognize you. (Senior management, client side, retired)

Now I know why I prefer the conversation of women. It's somewhat like a breath of fresh air blown into an atmosphere of stuffy self-importance.

I believe it was George Meredith who said, "The marks of a mature civilization are its enjoyment of comedy and its appreciation of intelligent women."

I hope I have shown that whereas the rest of the business world might not be listening, advertising is.

Chapter Five

Day to Day

which is dull, corporate, vapid, and terribly friendly. It illustrates why I prefer the diaries of Samuel Pepys to most of the written communiqués that pass my overpapped and *overpapered* desk.

Mush to Malediction

Interoffice writing is filled with catch phrases and platitudes written by label experts who take pride in their command of marketing lingo at the expense of what is being said.

William Safire, in his book, *On Language,* says that English "is a stretch language. One size fits all." That doesn't mean, he explains, that anything goes. In most cases, "anything does not go."

Who am I to say? I break all the rules of precision. Sometimes on purpose, which gives me a certain malicious glee.

Arguing for Naturalness

Don't get the idea that I'm writing down rules here; these are only cautions taken from my own personal stylebook. They might not get you published, but they will get you an audience.

1. Make it like it's coming from you—your personal sound on paper.
2. Come right out and say it. The sharp word, the biting retort, the call to action, the flexing of personal muscle—all reduce our capacity for vapidness and agencyspeak. Read aloud the next letter or memo you write. Is there any rebel in your voice? Why not? Read the Declaration of Independence. You'll hear plenty of fight in our forefathers' words.
3. Don't meander. Know where you're going. Allow each line and each paragraph to advance the issue, point of view, or recommendation. Don't take me to paragraph three and then jerk me back to paragraph two.
4. Never use a ten-dollar word when a two-bit one will do: "And lo, the star

which they saw in the east went before them, till it came and stood over them where the little child was."

5. Get your idea down on paper. That will force you to get the rough edges out and give you time to process it, to hear how it sounds the next day.
6. Writing sparks other ideas. The more you write, the more the ideas keep coming.
7. Take risks. Try things. "Sometimes I play things I never heard myself" (Thelonius Monk). People remember the rough spots when everything else is smooth.

A good writer never gets lost in the ranks. Remember, a memo with real meat gets passed on and up.

Where do a writer's ideas come from? This is a question I'm always asked. When asked the same question, novelist Isaac Bashevis Singer responded with: "There are powers who take care of you, who send you patience and stories."

Take heart. There is a sending power in advertising, too. It comes in the form of a good and useful product.

Hemingway's Unflinchable Rules

In the early 1970s, *The New York Times* ran an article about a young news reporter for the *Kansas City Star* named Hemingway. His city editor gave Hemingway a style sheet with four rules of writing he never forgot:

1. Use short sentences.
2. Use short first paragraphs.
3. Use vigorous English.
4. Be positive. Not negative.

Reflecting on these rules, Ernest Hemingway said: "These are the best rules I've ever learned for the business of writing. I've never forgotten them. No man of any talent, who feels and writes truly about the thing he is trying to say can fail to write well, if he abides by them."

I have that article push pinned to my office wall. I've given out dozens to friends who've done the same. If you'd like a reprint, send a postcard to my publisher and we'll make sure you get one.

Memos: Wordplaque

A memo is the most widely used form of business writing. A memo can get you a promotion, get you a raise, get you in trouble. A memo can reveal a case of brain fog or a total lackwit. It can tell the reader that you have nothing of interest to say and, worse, don't know the difference.

A memo can get you instant respect, praise, response.

A memo is your personal calling card. It is asinine to write a memo that doesn't advance your cause or your case.

Most memos fall into three categories:

1. Stultifying—ego blurb for author. Lots of underlining and gray flannel

account executives, who write most agency memos, can take the blame for the glut of bad business writing.

Here are 13 steps that may help beginners find their way to a satisfactory memo writing style.

1. Before you begin, know what you want. Write down your objectives or main points. Starting with the words "The purpose of this memo is . . ." will keep you on track. This way you're not thinking of words, which fly by faster than your pen can go, but your main points, item by item.
2. Well begun is half done. From the start, the reader needs to be grabbed, held captive: "Call me Ishmael." "It was the best of times. It was the worst of times." "In the beginning was the word." If you're a reader, you know from first sentences like these that you're in for a great story. My own favorite first line is: "They threw me off the hay truck about noon" from James Cain's *The Postman Always Rings Twice*. The point: Make me feel I'm going to miss something great if I don't finish. This holds true for memos as well as novels.
3. Be upbeat, not routine. If you are bored, think of your readers. Not to bore is your first responsibility.
4. Write the way you sound. Not the way your supervisor thinks business writing sounds.
5. If your memo contains a gripe, that's okay, but first agree on one thing before you disagree on another.
6. Be specific. And (this is worth repeating) never use a big, heavy baggage word when a small, more active one will do.
7. Use nouns and verbs. When in doubt, leave the adjective out.
8. Remember accurately.
9. A memo is an ad for yourself. Layout is important. Make it easy to read.

Keep it short—one page. Use fresh ribbon in the typewriter and big ball type. Underline. Indent. Use big margins with lots of white space.

10. Edit. Be mean. Show no mercy. Assume it's overwritten.
11. Make a sale. What action do you want from the reader?
12. Don't try to impress me with your fancy signature. You're not signing the Declaration of Independence.
13. If you've written a clear, vigorous memo, you don't need to find ways to get off the stage professionally. "Sincerely yours" is sappy. You might as well write "laboriously yours." A "thank you" or "thanks for your help" will do.

I don't write many memos, but here's one that illustrates many of the previous points. Our agency had just lost the Nabisco account. It was a particularly tough loss because we had worked three long years developing trust with a client who had little when we started. The relationship on the brand level got so good they were about to give us some new business when top Nabisco management took both accounts out of B&B. Here's my memo (see Figure 5-1). A memo I felt I had to write.

I got an appreciative response from everyone, including our president (who wasn't cc'ed), plus a call from our CEO.

I didn't change a word—the first draft went out. Because I truly felt what I was writing, the vocabulary came from my heart. Most memos have no voice, or, more accurately, a false voice. For example, what if I came up to you harrumphing and said, "Hello, colleague, I want to hereby acknowledge receipt of your memo and beg to thank you for writing same."

You would consider me a fool or a distant relative of Mrs. Malaprop.

Jargon: Verbal Antics

The appeal of jargon lies in its deceptiveness. Jargon sounds like it means something, when all it does is lead the reader to ignore it because it's too damn much trouble to decipher.

A work request for a frozen fruit topping print ad went like this: "YAG we noted increased pie behavior in OND. Will send you the HUT numbers A.S.A.P."

Translation: YAG—year ago, OND—Oct. Nov. Dec., HUT—households using toppings.

What was I to think? Were consumers actually masquerading as pies? Or, was the author, like a character from Henry Miller, speaking lyric kink without knowing it?

Alas, all the poor account executive was trying to say was: "People eat more pies during the holidays. Can I have an ad soon?"

76

This is APPALLING—Acronym Production, Particularly At Lavish Level, Is No Good.

The next time you are tempted to play "jargonaut," read the ad in Figure 5-2 from United Technology's *Wall Street Journal* campaigns.

As a result of this ad, chairman Harry Gray has received half a million personal letters, plus phone calls, from people asking for annual reports, offering résumés for jobs, and interested in purchasing UTC stock.

The Invasion of Therapy Cliches

There is much talk of "touching" in advertising: Getting in touch, touching base, keeping in touch, and so on.

Figure 5-1

So we don't play golf very well. Are we going to whine about it? Or cry in our Rolling Rock about the way this business sometimes works?

Not this group.

No client ever had a more committed bunch—nor will this client ever have people who understood the very tricky margarine business better.

No group accomplished more to turn a narrow, suspicious, and oft-times mean-spirited client into a proud, boastful, and trusting client.

Their loss is Benton & Bowles' gain.

We all grew.

I saw Vance Smith become less timid, almost nasty.

I saw Courtney Stimpson roll over people to get a nagging project out of the way.

I had Wendy Greenfield come to my office to remind me that I shouldn't fold so easily on one of my own headlines.

I read countless business building memos from Richard S'Dao and saw him make many trips to East Hanover just to keep the client off our backs so we could do our work.

Me? I learned to bite my tongue a lot. For someone who has never considered patience a virtue, this was the personal equivalent of culture shock.

Can I tell you "it's been fun"?

That's out of character for me. I will tell you that I would gladly share a foxhole with any of you.

John

Figure 5-2

Keep It Simple

Strike three.
Get your hand off my knee.

eccentricities are the
promulgators of
triturable obfuscation.
What did you do last night?
Enter into a meaningful
romantic involvement
or
fall in love?
What did you have for
breakfast this morning?
The upper part of a hog's
hind leg with two oval
bodies encased in a shell
laid by a female bird
or
ham and eggs?
David Belasco, the great
American theatrical producer,
once said, "If you can't
write your idea on the
back of my calling
card,
you don't have a clear idea."

One waits in vain for these expressions from the human potential movement to grow dated, but they seem to have invaded our speech for keeps.

"Sharing" is another example. I am asked to "share my copy," "share my insights," "share my findings with the client." What we are talking about here is the exchange of information that any intelligent person would rather not hear. The only thing I've ever delighted in sharing was half a peanut butter sandwich with my first love in kindergarten. Her name was Donna. It was the first and only time the words "Thank you for sharing" ever made any sense to me.

The language we use in a communication business should by definition express instinct, thinking, or at least the truth. Dependence on "crosshatching" or borrowing from our gurus can only suggest a person who has been brainwashed to think, write, speak, and feel.

Word Packaging
Word packaging offers in the gaudiest of packages the emptiest of thoughts. I submit the following list of popular word packages with the warning that you proceed at your own risk.

Enhanced scope of cooperation.
The need to generate agency capabilities.
Intensive-related product orientation.
Impact on the issues.
An interface session with the client.
Potential bicoastal issue.
A major crisis problem.
Strategic foundation stones.
Fairly narrow copy parameters.
A major thrust in the history of client/agency amity.

These are language antics, and any school of business that condones them should have its license revoked. Not to be confused with the history of amity, I offer the following minor thrusts as retorts.

An account supervisor wants "to eyeball the copy." *My reply:* "Only if you send out 'Come to the eyeballin' invitations."

A memo reminds me "that we are in the twilight zone between a go and no-go situation." *My reply:* "In either case, visibility is zero."

A hard-nosed, hardball-playing account manager informs me that the agency is "between a rock and a hard place." *My reply:* "Is that any more painful than sitting on the horns of a dilemma?"

A new business manager asks for "a deepening dialogue on bedrock issues."

My reply: "I've been there before. I end up digging a hole out of which I can never escape."

A research document concludes: "Performancewise, the new campaign proved a failure." *My reply:* "Nowise."

A bifocaled account supervisor says: "I see it as a problem of no specific size." *My reply:* "It is because it is of no specific size that tackling it is so difficult."

In a debate over copy direction, an account woman wants to discuss "the parameters of our collective vision." *My reply:* "Forget it, my parametric pressure is high enough."

William Burroughs claims that "language is a virus." If so—jargon and fake erudition are as annoying and catching as the common cold.

My objection is not on linguistic grounds. It has more to do with formulas for living, which I abhor. If you respond with a formula, you've denied me of a thoughtful and considerate response. If I confide in you, if I seek your honest advice, if I ask for your support or simply enlist your help to get something done, I can think of no greater letdown in confidence than to be met with a "thank you for sharing this or that with me." I also know something else about you: You say what you've been trained to say, not what you feel or think.

MEETINGS: GIVE ME LIBRIUM OR GIVE ME METH

Meetings are the antithesis of action. They are forums for big talk and big egos but hardly ever big decisions. You can gather all the charts, blow-ups, and people you want to fill the room, but in the end someone has to act. "I'll get back to you on today's meeting." How many times have you heard that beauty? Meetings are defensive, conservative, speculative, never aggressive.

The proof of this is the fact that meetings seem to take on a life of their own. Most meetings are extensions of prior meetings. This week's meeting demolishes or tosses aside all the facts inherited from last week's meeting. There are several reasons for this. The one person with the power to say yes or no is never at the same meeting twice. Those who do attend do so "wearing several hats." Add to this attendees in swivel chairs practicing 180's or 360's, and you have a recipe for a slow, painful death.

Most meetings are games. Their main purpose is to provide a medium in which the subject survives—a pet project, a delaying or holding action, a smokescreen, or make-work where the client perceives agency activity, but where, in fact, nothing is happening.

Whereas baseball is a game of cumulative tension, a meeting is a game of cumulative grunts, pauses, shifting eyes, and piss calls. Time is never a factor. Theoretically, a meeting could last forever.

I recall Jerry Della Femina on this subject in *Madison Avenue*—"They pull the trigger and we can see the bullet coming. Then they call a meeting. Then another. They invite more people and they muddle around 'looking at it.'

"There's no getting out of the bullet's way once it's fired; you just have to wait longer for it to hit."

What counts in most meetings is who wins, who makes allies, who holds whose hand. Never bring up the truth in a meeting unless you want to be thought of as a madman.

A Competitive Forum

A meeting can also serve as a competitive forum where upper management gets the morning line on the troops. This is especially pertinent if you're in the middle ranks.

Advertising has hundreds of managers in their late thirties who have just gotten their last promotion. They have 15 to 20 years left, but nine out of ten are about to hit the career-ending wall.

A meeting sorts them out because a meeting takes full advantage of the pack mentality. Most of these middle men have a strong aura of ambition. And their bosses are highly aggressive themselves and feed off their subordinates who are still struggling to get ahead.

I can't tell you how many times I've seen a middle manager go nuts in a meeting thinking it was "his meeting." He'd do the set-up and background preamble, but when the meeting got to the meat, bang. In stepped his boss, who literally took over. The most humiliating and personally deflating career event is to have *your* meeting taken over. The ones who allow it are quickly sorted out. The ones who are crafty enough to get back into the meeting (all the time

you handle people. If there's one positive aspect of a meeting, it's this. A meeting is a great way to seed and grow ideas through interaction. In that spirit, I offer the following tips.

1. *Know who's going to be there.* Knowing this is more important than what will be said. The account director from the agency would never dream of attending a meeting that his counterpart, the marketing director, wasn't going to. A meeting is a game of level versus kind. "Level" is hierarchy, mutual impressions, brownie points, keeping score. "Kind" is kind of thought, kind of person, kind of quality.

2. *Become a student of the chop-chop school.* Chop-chop means to cut through. This requires a strong ego and a person who knows his own strength. At a recent copy meeting, we were going on and on about a commercial that we all loved, everybody except the advertising manager. Obviously, he didn't like it and was trying to be a gentleman about it. Finally, I turned to the advertising manager and said, "I won't take it personally; why don't you just say 'I hate this shit' "? He looked up, shook his head up and down, and said "I hate this shit." The next minute, the meeting was over and we were on our way to the airport. At least we all knew we weren't going back to whip a dead storyboard.

3. *Learn to lay pipe.* This is the best way to perform like a virtuoso. Get on the phone before the meeting with your counterpart or even the next level up. Get his overview, his concerns, find out where he's at. You'll already have a good idea of how the meeting is going to go and you'll be able to anticipate events so well that your agency cronies will think that you've got ESP.

4. *Read gestures and grunts.* Facial expressions, personal eccentricities, nervous tics speak volumes. Learn to read them. I once had a client who doodled in meetings. If he began to retrace his doodles, digging his pen deeper into the same lines, I knew I was in trouble.

5. *Avoid the I should'a feeling.* Coming out of a meeting, the most sickening sensation is the "I should'a *kept* my mouth shut" feeling. One of the best ways to avoid this is to listen. Really listen, so that the other person gets the sense that

you *are* listening. So often I've seen fake listeners who can't wait for the speaker to stop so they can get their two cents worth in. The reflective nod acknowledges the sincere listener.

6. *Avoid vagueness and nonsense.* People get away with all kinds of this stuff. "Let's keep our options open" is a classic example. What exactly does that mean? It means that the speaker has a self-promoting fear of making up his own mind. I prefer Ed McCabe's dictum: "When it comes to advertising, I want to keep all my options closed."

The next time you hear bullshit, stop the meeting, turn to the person, and say something like, "That's interesting. Could you send us all a little note on that idea?" This accomplishes one of two things: He'll shut up, or it will force him to rethink what was probably a bad idea to start with.

7. *Know when to throw a tantrum.* I once dealt with a product group head who was master of indecision. At a promo meeting for Crest toothpaste, I had an idea for a Rose Bowl Parade float for Crest gel, featuring the Crest Team and the Cavity Creeps, who were the cartoon characters we used on our Saturday morning TV commercials for kids. I thought it was a terrific idea then, and I still do. Well, the brand group went on and on about cost and time implications and logistics. Finally, I jumped up and said, "You people are a disaster. It's the best kids/moms promo we've ever had. All you guys can ever think of are T-shirts. I'm leaving." And I did. The next day I got a call from the client. "Let's talk about that Rose Bowl idea." He saw firmness. When everybody else is weak, don't ever worry about strong-arming.

8. *Never duck a question.* If you don't know—if you aren't 100 percent sure— say so. Never guess at an answer, particularly a number; they'll hold you to it. If there's a foul up, admit to it. "It's my fault" can get you more respect than you'll ever imagine. It also says you have the confidence to fix it.

9. *Don't be a one-man band.* There's strength in numbers. Learn to back off and let someone else in. Always give collective credit.

10. *Don't play musical chairs.* Never, never attend a meeting that can't begin until more chairs are brought in.

11. *Have the last word.* Assuming people respect your opinion—wait. Let others thrash it out. Sooner or later, they'll ask you what you think. Give a short, impassioned point of view and stop. This happened just last week at the end of a two-hour C and R (comprehension and recall) research meeting. "It's your commercial, John, what do you think?" On cue, I took out a quote from this book on research and read it out loud, pretending I'd just thought it up. Everybody thought it was a wonderful summation and went away happy. Moral: Never underestimate the importance of having the last word.

12. *Learn terrorist tactics.* Sometimes you can scare people into action. One trick I use is to put myself in the competitor's shoes and think up methods to destroy my own client's business. Start with the sentence: If I were the competi-

tion, I'd. . . . Since most decisions are based on fear anyway, why not milk it? This tactic also plays to a marketplace fact: Patience is less and less a marketing virtue.

How to End a Meeting
The next time you're at a conference table, look around at the crowd. Can

Here are a few choice tales from some of the more memorable meetings I've attended.

I once knew a very fox-faced management supervisor who always came to meetings wearing the first 50 pages of the L.L. Bean catalogue. Unfortunately, he had no more control over his syntax than his clothing. In a particularly excruciating copy review, he said, "Gentlemen, this product is on a deathward down-spiral. I have no panaceas, nor do I propose any silver bullets of truth, but we have to face reality. Guys, it's the copy."

"Hey, it's not my fault," I said, as I turned my chair north. "I always thought reality was north, in the direction of P. J. Clarke's."

Then one of my art directors piped up: "I always thought false profits were north, reality was east, empty words west, and the Jersey shore south."

In one brutal screening (that's when agency and client meet to view a commercial for the first time), the client, not being very articulate about why he hated the commercial, finally mumbled, "It's the wallpaper." The producer looked at him and queried, "What do you mean, the wallpaper?" "The wallpaper," he repeated, "it's too Jewish."

One of the best one-liners I ever heard occurred after a meeting at Boyle-Midway, the most bullysome clients I ever worked with. The agency's management supervisor, who began the meeting with us, ended up standing behind the division president bad-mouthing the copy he loved an hour ago. After the meeting, a writer in my group went right up to the guy and said, "There's two things I can't stand about you, Kenmore. Your face."

Practice Chutzpah
As can be seen, a meeting is an all-enveloping presence. You just can't escape them, unless you are ingenious enough to come up with a legitimate excuse: "Tomorrow's a Jewish holiday" and "I've got jury duty" can be useful.

"It's the wallpaper.—It's too Jewish!!"

The next time you're tempted to call or attend a meeting, remember: You can never make money for your client holding a meeting. Conditions change too fast. Today we're all at the mercy of the marketplace, and committees just can't keep pace. What's more, you can't reduce every problem to a case history. Given any sensitivity in the room, you have to have the chutzpah to squelch unrealistic priorities, to put your finger on the pressure points, and suggest immediate action in areas that can affect your client's business *now*. Act like it's the day before retirement and you're not afraid to dare.

Your persuasiveness, your passion, and sense of caring can be infectious. The most important thing about any meeting is the feeling you have leaving one.

Do you come out recharged and full of ideas, or do you come out confused, depressed, and very tired?

ON PRESENTATIONS

Spontaneity, surprise, glee, and a promise of excitement to come. This is the

needed to sell your idea, your agency, or even yourself to a client you want to have and hold.

Value Added

A presentation is the magic moment in an agency's advertising life. It represents the essence of our craft, that is, asking for and getting the order. Against the inertia of tradition is the presentation that puts your agency up in lights; the "spots" are on you, there is drama, and you're up there trying to win over that tough critic in the first row. It is the unfolding of tone and personality, of talents and resources, of nonintellectual biodata—people to be exact—who will make it easier for the client to distinguish between levels of *measurement* and levels of *thought.* When a client leaves the room exclaiming, "What a show!" he really means what a performance, what timing, what orchestration, what insight! It means that your presentation netted applause, not yawns.

The Force Is You

It isn't every day that you get to speak for your agency, and yes, it can be scary. But what better way to stand out, to prove that you know your stuff, and to gain simultaneous respect from upper management on both sides?

There are four kinds of presentations:

1. New business.
2. Copy.
3. Internal.
4. Seminars or speeches.

Following are some of the small points I use to help me maintain my own equilibrium when called on to perform.

New Business Presentations

In this case, you are presenting to an audience of strangers. It helps to know their identity. Have they been quoted? What is their background? What kind of agency do they employ now and why are they here? You can't guess about the answer. Tailor your pitch to the prospect. So many agencies parade advertising they've done for other clients that the entire presentation becomes a "shill" for the agency versus a feeling of "Hey, these guys understand my problem" or, even better, "they really *defined* my problem." Content, therefore, is everything. If the content is good, the chemistry is good. By all means, make it short, crisp, with a unified agency point of view.

Strangers make up their minds fast. So, set the mood early. Be lighthearted. The spirit of play is a telltale measure of your self-confidence. Don't hide behind lecterns, podiums, or conference tables. I always present on my feet. Clients see enough paper shufflers and "readers" who wet their lips turning pages from prepared notes.

If you are presenting storyboards, pencil in beforehand one-word "keys" on each frame. They can act as triggers to help you present point by point, not word by word. Describe what *you* see in the finished film, the potential of the idea on film, the feeling of the film itself. Give no client the benefit of a projectable imagination. I've had clients, even the ones I know, say "I can read boards." I can't. Leave nothing to the imagination. I am not suggesting that clients have no imagination. All I'm saying is that you don't need an independent set of images on top of the images you already have.

Emphasize how different or how new the agency solution is to the competition and why. Size up the crowd. Move in close to the person who counts the most. Play to him and to the ones on either side of him. If it's a toss-up at decision time, one of them is going to sway it one way or another.

Most of us are possessed of a markedly imperfect instrument—our voice. In my own case, the softer I can talk, the less "pitchy" I am. Getting up close is important. That way, I'm not so much presenting as I am having a one-to-one conversation about a subject near and dear to the client's heart—his business.

Always give examples of how by sheer digging and tenacity your agency was able to come up with an unusual solution. When I spoke to Phil Dusenberry, BBDO had just won the Apple Computer competition. "We educated ourselves about their business," says Dusenberry. "We sent our people to computer school. We actually did a crash course on Apple." The lesson here: Sweat the details, shoot for the moon on the first shot. Clients are always more interested in hearing about the investigative capability of an agency than the predictable screening of the agency reel. Get to it. Give the client the sense that nothing matters, except his product. Cut down on boring mug shots of agency personnel. As a client, I want to know two things—who is going to solve the right problem, and who's working on that problem seven days a week.

Always sum up. A strong climax swings the hung jury. Go see the movie *Inherit the Wind*. Watch Spencer Tracy as Clarence Darrow destroy Frederick March as William Jennings Bryan. See how digging deeper helped David slay Goliath.

Finally, I never rehearse in front of the agency. I attend the rehearsal, I

welcome as a roaring kitchen hearth. An ex-radio announcer, Kent delivered every line with the quiet persuasion of an experienced con man. He would approach a storyboard, glance at the first frame, and grin to himself. The client couldn't wait to hear what Alan thought was so funny. Just before he finished the board, he would pause, walk the length of the conference table, turn, and deliver the copy twist or selling line. It was the most tantalizing bit of theatrical moxie you could ever imagine. Clients fell for it all the time; they'd produce a spot just to hear Alan read the copy again.

By and large, however, creative people are lousy presenters. Sometimes we think all they have to do is show up with pushpins to tack up our brilliant work. If we think about it, we know that brilliant work is the toughest sale there is.

Phyllis Robinson claims she puts as much energy into presentation as the work. As an example she talked about DDB's first presentation to Clairol. The product was Nice 'n Easy. She related the story this way:

> The strategy was the same, naturalness, but we changed everything else—we went away from the stiff cliche of the bouncing bouffant to a visual of natural hair with natural women saying natural things. It was the first advertising that recognized the "me" generation. That was our line: It lets me be me. The Clairol people were extremely upset. We broke all their sacred rules. It was advertising that would make little old ladies sweat. But we did over our own research to sell it. We showed the client what was really going on out there. We went into presentation with incontrovertible arguments. It was a flow from strategy, to work to presentation.

Helping the client to understand the thought process that led to your solution always makes you and the agency look smarter.

Why did you choose one particular execution over another?
What human reality does the idea tap in on?

If the solution comes from something the client said, say so; it makes him feel like he's part of the solution.

Make sure the client *sees* the work the same way you do. Describe the details that add up to your vision of the finished film. Think of it as a kind of illumination to the big picture. It can be the difference between "Yeah, yeah, yeah" and "I see."

Remember that all clients have rules for evaluating copy. Make the client play by *your* rules. I always give the assembly four or five things to look for in the work. These are *my* objectives. Clients will always write them down. They forget their own bias. This helps clients make intelligent comments. Put yourself in his place. He's seeing unfamiliar work. Maybe there are three or four boards to go over; you're asking for an immediate reaction and evaluation.

Say, one management level has already seen the work and now it's the big boy's turn. Make the big boy sit next to you. Present directly to him. Take the work down off the wall. (Don't worry about the others; they've seen it.) This serves to command attention and a one-to-one conversation. It also promotes silence from the rest of the room. The effect is much like when John McEnroe is serving at Flushing Meadow. You can always hear a pin drop because no one has the guts to break the silence.

By this time you've been on long enough. Thank him for his attention and let the account person sum it up. One last word. Don't ever resort to arm twisting like "You're going to love the work." You might as well say "If you don't like this, you're an idiot."

Part of your strength as a presenter is rooted in your respect for the client's opinion. It's an awful mistake to give the impression that you're distrustful of his intelligence. Learn to fall on your sword for the right things, such as the style and content of your main idea.

If, on the other hand, you detect certain agency folk jumping on the fence or if the client begins to resemble a horse trader—"You give me my three frames and I'll buy the board"—pick up the work and exit. If pressed for an explanation, either of the following will do:

1. Ideas have feelings; you're hurting mine.
2. A good ad carries one idea—we'll go back and have another.

Some clients you see more than others. Like the ones in town that you don't have to take a plane to see. Close-quartered clients tend to have schizoid mood swings. This is destructive to good work and good relationships. I had one such client. She resented the fact that she even had to be there. A copy meeting interrupted travel plans for another whirlwind swing through warm weather sales districts. She would come in and say "I have 15 minutes." I would say, "I only have 10; maybe we should do this later." That seemed to clear the air, and we would have our copy meeting.

In longer term relationships, never let a client get a "book" on you. Presentation is preparation. It's mental. There's a lot of up-front thinking.

like this is much like open heart surgery, only it's your creative values up there on the table. Even if those values constitute a devotion to high standards, they are open to never-ending transplanting.

When management is dominated by creative people, gutter wisdom prevails: street-talk headlines, verbal color, risky unforgettable stuff. The work gets out the door because *management* creates it, and generally it soars. Getting a still-breathing idea out the door through a menacing noncreative management composed of thoroughgoing twits should be considered if not a performing art, at least an unnatural one.

If account people would stick to their knitting and be sellers of advertising, not buyers, we could downgrade internal copy presentation and get on with the show.

An internal copy meeting can be both practical and analytical. It can be the perfect time and place to test the "mettle" of your current employer. Are you and management able to co-exist in a common cause, or are you a party of one? The answer will constitute rewards or fester animosity. It is a career imperative to determine as quickly as you can why some agencies orchestrate music and others run off program notes stuffed into spiral binders.

Seminars or Speeches

Audiences aren't so much interested in content as they are in contact. The listener wants to feel like he really exists in the speaker's mind. An effective speech gives the audience what they long for—an identity. Author Kurt Vonnegut says, "They (the audience) simply want to learn from your tone, gestures, and expressions whether or not you are an honest man."

Putting yourself at the center of your subject helps. Last year I was invited by the American Cancer Volunteers to introduce a new campaign to 1,500 volunteers who were meeting in New Orleans as part of their Synergy '85 program. The morning of the speech I got up at 5:30 to write it. I can remember the sound of the barge horns on the Mississippi. The idea for the speech seemed to erupt from a warning blast, a kind of signal for a surprise you didn't plan for—like being volunteered for a job you really didn't want. "I was volunteered to do a campaign for the volunteers," I said. "What began as a pain-in-the-ass job ended up a joy because it forced me to relearn a lot of basics I'd forgotten. I relearned that the best of what we do comes from information and the energy of people outside myself. I relearned that people are humanists and that made me less cynical. I relearned that there are no homogeneous people any more than there are homogeneous volunteers. I relearned that people hunger for information; they want to learn as much as possible about your product or service or company. I also relearned that as advertising experts, we should make sure to be as gifted as the products we speak for. In the process I became like all of you—a believer, a willing volunteer."

The speech was only four minutes long and led to a rousing theme—"The Gift of Life" written by Nina Murphy, a writer at McCann Erickson, and composed by George Grant of GNU music. The whole audience went wild, they held hands, they clapped, and I got a curtain call. After the whole thing was over, many people came up to me with tears in their eyes. I was baffled and even embarrassed until one lady said, "I've been a volunteer for 25 years, but this was the first time I ever felt my presence acknowledged." I managed to put her in the center of things. I gave her an identity. It was truly a humbling experience. When Alan Erickson, vice president of American Cancer Volunteers and himself a 25-year-veteran, wrote his thank-you letter to Benton & Bowles, he said it was the high point of his associaton with the American Cancer Society and that our campaign for the volunteers would, *in fact,* save countless cancer fatalities. It's hard for me to believe that anything we do in advertising could do that. It sure puts dryer sheets in perspective.

Method Acting

As with anything else, the enemy is self-doubt. Part of your success as a presenter is realizing what you do well. If it's a maverick, if it's grit, if it's dazzle, even if it's the little kid in you, it'll play.

This is an ego business—that makes it difficult and sometimes detestable—but there's a healthy ego, too. We all have our *methods,* our own school of acting, the style of approaching things. The best and most satisfying way is for you to be true to that.

Don't let "The Suits" take that out of you. Presentation is an event. Be a showman. Do what it takes to make your audience see and feel the same things you do. Even if it means stealing the show. If there is madness to your method, so be it. No audience hangs around for less.

ON TIMETABLES

I understand how critical the management of time is. If I ever forget, I have the account executives, advertising's answer to the egg timer, to remind me. Issuing timetables ("Let's keep on top of the creatives") is a major part of their job. Most timetables are followed by a "When can we share the work?" phone call. "Work"

revisions. Nobody thought it was funny when she opened the package at home the client, but it cured her. She never again promised the client a meeting I wasn't prepared to have.

The Big It

The most frequent comment I receive as a group head is "The work is terrific, but it takes forever." The *it* in that statement is nonnegotiable—the *it* (a scintillating creative solution) is represented by the last increment in Figure 5-3. The graph suggests the disdain that the process has for *it*. It's like someone asking me for a "two-week idea"—in advertising you can always get more money, but never more time. This squashing of creative time is not an aberration. It is a repeated felony. I have, on occasion, drawn my "warped" timetable for clients who look, laugh, and nod. Still, advertising life goes on. And the quivering finger points to the creative department, where great is always late.

A Reverse Solution

Section three in Ecclesiastes begins, "To everything there is a season and a time to every purpose under heaven. A time to be born, a time to plant, to pluck up, to kill, to break down," and so on.

So wonderful are those rhythms that they inspired the pop classic "Turn, Turn, Turn." Here are some additions I'd like the future rewriters of the Bible to include for believers in good creativity.

> There is a time to call the client and say, "Do you want it now or do you want it great?
> There is a time to stop pampering research, who get ten times the time the rest of us get to do anything.
> There comes a time to honor the fact that the biggest roadblock to *solid, right-headed* work is not enough time.

Figure 5-3

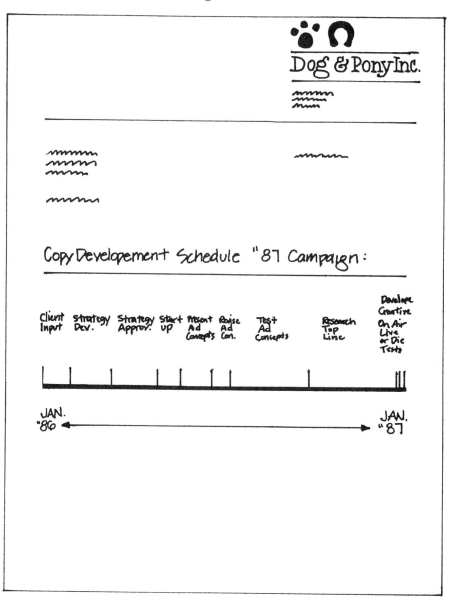

There is a time to make the account person sweat, not because the work is so late, but because we took the time to make the work so different.

There is a time for creative to realize: When it's great, nobody remembers that it was three weeks late.

blew it all out of the water. The same thing occurred after the second 20 minutes, and again after the third. We spent a simulated six weeks killing one bad idea after another. When it came time to present our solution to the other groups, we had zero.

There was clear-cut learning from that simple exercise. Here is a summary:

Be patient with the creative process.
Have the courage to throw out bad ideas.
Too much evaluation stops the building process.
Don't stop an idea from coming, even if it's dumb.
From dumb comes smart.
Work in small groups; committees can't create good copy.
It's easier to fall in love with your own idea than someone else's.
Good executions take, if not forever, a long time.
Keep pushing; there's always something better.
Call an idea BS if it is.

The conclusion written by the Procter group said: "This was a terrific experience, providing firsthand insight into the trials and tribulations of the creative process."

National Trash Day

I would like to propose that we establish a National Trash Day to honor the wastebasket. When we talk about advertising as a service business, we should think of the wastebasket. Nothing gives us more service or is more worthwhile. When you make a list of the ten greatest tools in the creative process, always leave room for the round file and leave room in there for timetables that remind you that *it* "was needed yesterday."

I understand how pressure can be a great catalyst. That's why I intend to open up a Martinizing store when I retire. Instead of dry cleaning in one hour, I'll deliver copy. I intend to clean up.

On Managing

Care about your subject, be energetic, and keep it emotional. These are the commandments I follow as a writer. After seven drafts, I found it impossible to apply them to the subject of management.

In separate cover stories, three news weeklies proclaimed management as "the dominant theme of the 1980s." While it is always reassuring to get my news in triplicate, the subject seemed too big for me to handle.

Then, the new breed of managers I kept reading about was too awesome to contemplate: "Elite, value-driven, hands-on, they were peak performers, pragmatic dreamers and egalitarians who were capable of reinventing corporations with theories that were on the leading edge of things."

For someone operating with little more than his hunches, this was intimidating news.

These men, soaring aloft in the upper air—I knew nothing about their brand of managing. I'd never even been to a power breakfast; how could I have anything of value to say to the serious student of management?

I had one option. I could always, as Casey Stengel advised, "look it up."

I did.

From my local library director, I learned that, next to self-help, managing as a topic was the largest growing nonfiction section in the library.

I was welcome to browse, she said. And browse I did.

I began with a best-seller. Its antibusiness-establishment tone borrowed heavily from Robert Townsend's amusing and very readable *Up the Organization*. This book, however, was written by a former lawyer and present sport-celebrity manager who, without the benefit of an MBA degree or much originality, sets out some of the lessons he's learned.

To make a sale, I am told to learn everything I can about the customer. To build a business, I am instructed to begin with a quality product. I learned the value of a power breakfast (always order your muffin before you talk turkey). Above all, I should be "honest, moral, and aware of the joys of silence."

If only the author had followed his own advice, he could have spared me this book.

Quickly, I moved on through the managerial stacks. I learned how to manage up, how to manage down. I learned how to be a "super" manager, "beyond even mega."

I learned how to fight FUD (fear, uncertainty, doubt).

I learned tricks of the management trade from none other than George S. Patton: "Grab 'em by the nose and kick 'em in the pants."

I learned how to take charge like Teddy Roosevelt, how to shoot the "executive rapids," and how to perfect the "art of foreplay" when combining business with golf.

I eventually found more than 900 books in print whose titles contained the

a book.

After three days of serious browsing, I was at 43 titles and counting when the library director threatened to have me arrested for loitering.

The experience left me suddenly confident of the value of my own observations. And with the realization that sometimes writing about a subject as sweeping as management requires more than savvy and education. Sometimes it's nothing more than sheer luck—like crossing a New York street.

I would try my hand at the subject.

Unbosslike Qualities

The idea of being a boss has always run contrary to my image. On the surface, I keep people at arm's length. I glare. I intimidate. I terrify. I have a short fuse. I am exacting on myself and expect the same from others. The combination of these elements usually results in internal combustion and at least a two-alarm fire.

Yet here I am, a creative director. Some people saw something in me and came to the conclusion that I could lead people. When I look back, I'm astonished at how objective they were about my skills. My outside defenses had nothing to do with the reality of developing into a leader.

The habits of a lifetime did not disappear overnight. But managing people put me in touch with the other part of me—the more likable, more competent half. And the more controlled half.

My energy shifted to other people—their feelings and welfare, and making sure my people got full credit *and* compensation for their contributions.

I became less adversarial, less hostile. I no longer felt a need to waste energy fighting for control. By definition, I *was* in control.

In advertising, managing means it's your business—you run it. I don't manage an office or a space or other managers; I manage a product. In this case, the creative product.

Changing the Atmosphere

To accomplish this, talented people aren't enough. You've got to create an atmosphere. I don't mean a physical atmosphere; I mean an atmosphere of concern.

Ralph Ammirati put it this way: "People here know that we're here for them 100 percent of the time. Marty [Puris] and I aren't going to be here forever. We want to pass our way of doing things on. It's so much better than hiring people from the outside who bring in all their bad habits."

To establish this kind of atmosphere, you gotta get everybody believing in the same thing: that great creative work is possible.

I started by putting myself on the line for the work to top management and the client. By example, I was saying to the world that creative excellence is both a means and an end. It's not just a question of better business; it's the *only* business. Speeches and theories are one thing, collective responsibility is something else. Creativity is not something you have an occasional interest in.

By being an advocate for my people's work, I established a record of guts. As a manager, it's the number one way to get and keep respect. As a boss, my role was more submerged than visible. If they needed me, my people knew I was there. They had my support.

The hope always is that this spirit will permeate the whole agency. It's not enough that my group wants it or I want it—management above me must want it. The most obscene joke in the world is a square agency hiring a hot-shot creative. It's like taking a rose and planting it in the desert. The whole thing is a question of climate.

Partnership

All of this spills over into the account section and over to the client. This is where creative and business consideration come together. Advertising is a collaborative business. The key is matching people. There are just too many mismatches in this business, too little respect from both sides. The same care that a creative department takes for matching talent needs to be directed on the account side. The account executive should have the same concern for quality as the copywriter.

"When we hire account people at Needham," says Keith Reinhard, "we don't care about what degrees they have. We want to see their reels. It tells us what value they place on creativity in their careers."

From partnership comes immediacy and quicker sales for the work. For example, I'm not afraid of going to the client with roughs, thumbnails, or scribbles. I involve a client early in the process. Sometimes they have real good reasons why I shouldn't keep going—they know more about the product than I ever will.

If a client wants to tell me *what* to say, that's okay. *How* to say it is my call. This makes the client feel like he's part of the whole thing. It's a sure-fire way to avoid bad meetings (the single biggest drain on an agency's productivity) and the

that trust, you'll never get anything worthwhile done.

"Gangbangs"

I never want outside help on my business, and I'm sure most other creative directors don't want it on theirs. That's why I keep my group busy on our own work and avoid letting them get drafted to help out with other accounts. Then there's no excuse for the common complaint among the doers: underutilization.

I hate "gangbangs." I'll tell you why.

When working on someone else's account, you never get all the information; you're solving a problem on the periphery.

It's not your business. It's not that you don't care, but if you don't come up with a solution, you're not going to cry in your beer. "Gangbangs" destroy accountability. And accountability, the belief that this piece of business *is* yours, is everything. With accountability comes morality: not honesty or taste, but the sheer rightness or wrongness of your solution.

You never get full credit. And that's how you get paid in this business—by getting full credit.

You lose control. Or worse, your idea gets bastardized. Or even stolen. I've seen names on storyboards magically change overnight.

I feel I'm accountable to my people. I want each of them to collect on their brains and ideas—"accounts payable" I call it. Creative "gangbangs" don't pay off—for anybody. They solve a problem, but not for long. All they do is buy time and help to get a client off the agency's back.

Bypass

Most of what I know is big agency life. It's overstructured and runs on hierarchy. Sometimes I get a phone call or a memo that's addressed only to me (because I'm on the level of the sender). I never withhold this information. I make certain to re-Xerox the memo with *all* of my group's names on it.

As a result, my group knows there is no such thing as classified information. And I avoid giving them the very natural feeling of being left out. It puts people's noses out of joint—and sometimes it's impossible to rectify.

If I hire people to solve problems, why shouldn't they know as much as, or more than, I do?

What I'm talking about is a style of management that gets me loyalty. If I have loyalty, I don't need a master's degree in situational relationships; healthy attitudes and good work tell me that I'm doing things right.

Smaller Is Better

Six months at Ketchum in New York have more than sufficed to crack my big-agency tendencies. It's a lot like pitching in Fenway Park: You learn the value of a good pitch and you pay the price for a bad one. Managing a small creative unit builds an immediate sense of independence. You know the job is in *your* hands.

A small to medium-size agency has another powerful advantage. It leans toward a nonblaming structure. Everyone is expected to be a significant contributor. "It's more than a charming ability to talk advertising," says Ralph Ammirati. "We force one another to interact."

"The smaller you are, the closer you are to the client's problems," says President Don Just of the Martin Agency in Richmond. "You can't insulate yourself. Performance gets high visibility."

Conclusion: Anything that increases distance between key agency people and the client is not advantageous to the partnership.

Managing by Not Managing

I do a lot of managing by not managing. My group knows that. Do they ever take advantage?

Never. Let me give you an example.

I come in early in the morning—7:30, 8:00. Does that mean everyone should be in at the crack of dawn?

Hell, sometimes half of my group gets in at 10:00. They'll be the first ones to admit they're not on fast time in the A.M. But nine times out of ten, the same people were together the night before at a working dinner. And whatever the problem was, it's already solved. Never judge your people by the hours they keep. I know people who come to the office on Sunday. It looks good to the supervisor, but it has nothing to do with work. All they're really doing is making long-distance phone calls to all their out-of-town friends.

On the other side of the coin, I have an art director who does her best work asleep. "I wake up in the middle of the night with the damndest ideas," she says.

Because of this, she keeps a night pad on her night table to jot them down. The key thing is to leave a good person the hell alone.

Said another way, I don't care who makes me look good.

A good creative director is a "director of thinking," says Mal MacDougall, "but a great creative director is the one who is respected for his own work."

3. Editorial gift.
4. Evaluative gift.

With Women in the Group

My group is predominantly women. Are there any special concerns? Let me answer this way:

Managing is understanding. Understanding needs. Understanding talent. Understanding individual differences.

I have never changed my style or conceded a managing principle because anyone was a woman. My brain wouldn't let me, and the women I work with would be furious if I did.

Recently I went to three of the women in my group privately and asked them, "Outside of being equally obscene, why are we still together?"

Answer one: "You're the only man who says exactly what he thinks and gets away with it."

Answer two: "I trust you. You have my best interests at stake."

Answer three: "I'm continuously learning."

Number three has been promoted to my level. Am I happy? Of course not. I'll never be able to replace her.

Office Politics

Politics leads most creative directors to heebee-jeebeeville. Avoid the natural habitat of the politician: meetings, lunches, cloakroom stuff. Don't ever assume you have an *unspoken* agreement with a presumed ally. You might as well take a python to bed.

The trick is to take advantage of a system that demands that you exercise tenacity with your ideas and rewards you well for seeing an offbeat or unpopular one through.

Here's a choice bit of advice from Ayer president Jerry Siano. "The first thing to teach a talented person is to be political." His definition of political? "How to sell an idea." Now there's a man with his politics in order.

When I asked Siano for specifics, he said: "First you challenge yourself, then you challenge me. Learn to participate in the decision, mix it up with the client. You gotta mix it up."

Mistakes

Sometimes big mistakes can be fixed more easily than little ones. As a manager, I have to be an observer, a sensitive observer. I find that most mistakes aren't mistakes at all; they are little "tics" that reduce presence, authority, confidence, and listenability.

In client meetings, an account person I worked with began every sentence with "In all honesty." He came off as puffed-up and insincere.

A management supervisor ended most points with "okay?" He was begging for approval.

An older writer in my group would always say, "I'm showing my age." He was.

An account woman was always saying "Sorry" or "Excuse me" when there was no apparent reason. She didn't think of herself as a force. She was apologizing for her presence. Other people agreed.

A producer was always walking the halls biting her nails. It didn't paint a reassuring picture. If there's one thing I need from a producer, it's reassurance.

Often you can turn mistakes into an advantage. I'm not advising this as a practice, but on occasion at meetings with clients I'll take the rap. I'll pipe up and say with a smile, "Blame it on me" when it really wasn't my mistake at all. It has the reverse effect: It gives people the mistaken idea that I'm a gracious soul. It also gives the impression that I have: 1) the humility to make a mistake in public, and 2) the confidence to fix it real quick.

One Priority at a Time

Advertising is filled with independent cusses. Especially creative people. I like to keep them happy—so I try to run an autonomous group. First, it cuts down on levels of approval, which bog down the creative process. Second, it keeps upper management out of your hair. From what I've seen, the quickest way to get into trouble is to set too many priorities. Simultaneous crises, I call them.

So, I never set, or allow other people to set, a *list* of priorities.

I set *a* priority. "Tell me one big problem that needs to be solved *now*," is the first thing I say when tackling any new piece of business.

The second thing I say is, "I'm a lousy juggler. I only do one thing well at a time."

This may sound like a luxury in other businesses, but not in advertising, when you're constantly working with people whose main job is manufacturing crises.

The one priority is set by agreement with the account group, the brand group, and the creative group. The biggest task is to get the client to agree. Most

problem gets solved *for good*. It can turn a multilayered behemoth into a sleek operation and turn desperation (crisis) into accomplishment (peace of mind).

Being a Manager

Being a manager is not something I aspired to be as a kid.

But being a manager is a wonderful ploy to get my creative way.

Being a manager is a way to demonstrate that I'm not just a trained seal who performs at copy meetings.

Being a manager is a way to demonstrate that I can think. I can talk. I can market. I can be strategic with the very best of them.

Being a manager gives me an outlet for my combustibility: I can let my enemies know I'm still smouldering underneath.

I can let my clients know that I care, that I have a passion for my work and they will get me "from the dirt up."

I can let an uneasy management know that any attempt to round out these edges will get them nowhere fast.

Being a manager helps me to put my advertising life in my own hands.

Being a manager lets me work on my own inadequacies in public. It also beats poverty.

The more I read about managing, the less sensational the subject becomes.

In researching this section, most of what I read seemed inflated with equal pressure—hot-air hype geared to propel people of consuming ambition to the top of the corporate heap. They all sound strangely alike, this army of closet guppies. I just think it's different in advertising. We are propelled more by impulse; in some cases, it's all we have.

My own impulse came to me in the form of a wee small voice inside. If I listen to that voice, it tells me all I need to know about managing. "Behave well, remember that our little craft isn't the Second Coming." Add to that this tiny

103

prayer that Red Smith, my favorite sportswriter, used to utter: "Lord, give me sense."

My job (and I am listening to my wee small voice now) is to simplify a very simple business.

Advertising is really pretty basic. Problem. Product. Consumer. My job is repeating basics like "you can't make decisions without making mistakes." Failure is not a bugaboo.

My job is also remembering the essential difference in advertising as a profession. While other businesses are referred to as "people businesses," advertising is a sheer energy business. My job is to turn on the energy—that's where the edge is.

If I can feel the difference in the hallways, then I know I'm going to see a difference in the work.

Chapter Six

On Clients

3. Client has patience, long-run purposes and objectives.
4. Client knows his customers better than his competition.
5. Client anticipates trends.
6. Client takes risks and exceeds his wildest dreams.

I can be very friendly with this kind of client. I can quickly set up an environment where my agency can be a legitimate partner, not an adversary.

THE SPIRIT OF PARTNERSHIP

All talk concerning the "good client" falls under the catchword *partnership*. Talk to a hundred agencies and every one will cite commitment to the partnership principle. Out of these hundred, only a handful have the passion and balance (smart people/hot creative) to deliver. These agencies are mostly midsize, where continuity and accountability reign.

Partnership demands that everyone be accessible to the client, including the creative team. This forces them away from the sometimes limited view of their typewriter or drawing board. It leads more quickly to the whys and the hows and helps avoid the bear traps along the way—client blind spots and preconceptions, a client who has been insulated by habit, or a client who makes easy submissions to dullness.

Partnership helps the agency base its creative approach on reality, not naivete. What good, for example, is a brilliant campaign if the premise is abstract or doesn't tap in on what's happening in the marketplace? What good is a brilliant campaign if it never stands a chance of running, much less building your client's business?

As a working partner, we must develop a persistent curiosity about the client's products and be vigilant about his competition. Look at the historical reel, know what's worked and why. Dig for product magic. Learn to aim your client's money. Don't be too hasty in recommending TV. Maybe something closer to the consumer at decision time, such as promotion, is better. Learn to talk with the client P.R.D. (Product Research and Development). Every day you'll be learning more about the client's product. All this makes you faster on your feet. There's no better confidence-builder than holding your own with a tough client, especially when the subject matter is *his* product.

All this changes client perception. Agency people are no longer outsiders. They are perceived as assets, as committed as any of the client's own people.

"IT TAKES FOREVER"

"If advertising people were dentists, it would take 25 people to pull a tooth." This is from Mal MacDougall, president of Hill, Holliday, Connors, Cosmopulos in New York. This comment emphasizes the number one complaint of clients about advertising: "It takes forever."

When I interview clients, some changing their current agency, other complaints I hear include:

> They bring too many people to meetings.
> They're reactive. They do what we tell them to do—they don't lead us with great ideas.
> They don't think strategically—they think *process*.

There are steps we can take to minimize these complaints.

The single best step is simple: Pick up the phone. In 15 minutes you'll have it straight from the client's mouth. This way you avoid overreacting to every client mood swing or knee jerk as reported by a nervous third party.

Utilizing a direct line to your client counterpart eliminates countless internal meetings, eliminates relying on other people's maps that presume to set the proper course, eliminates useless junk like call reports written two weeks after the meeting, and eliminates fighting the wrong battles.

Until I applied some of these principles, I assumed that every client was two people: one excellent, one dreadful. I assumed they were dogmatic and doctrinaire when they were only being decisive. When this kind of client said something, the odds were that he really had said it. In a business where 99 percent of the time the very opposite is true, you'll appreciate how valuable a straight line to the client is.

Pick your client's brain. But remember that *perception is proper selection.* Learn to sort out the meaningful from the trivial. Don't let a client dilute your priorities. Everything can't be important. If you pay attention to everything, nothing gets solved for good. What you usually end up with is chaotic direction from the account group resulting in a demoralized creative group.

Finally, my experience tells me that you can never know more about your client's product than he does, *so listen.*

A superb example of listening is the work for Perdue chickens via Scali, McCabe, Sloves.

Chicken maven of the Western world is Frank Perdue—clucky, hawklike

you so in the advertising. This dedication to a cleaner, more edible bird has helped Frank Perdue earn a 60 percent market share on the Eastern corridor, a per-pound margin that's several hundred points over the industry, and sales of $800 million.

Perdue supplies the facts. Ed McCabe, creative honcho on the account, supplies the charm and personality.

Here's McCabe on a seemingly effortless collaboration that's lasted for over ten years:

"There's only so much value in listening to a client. Sometimes what the client thinks is important goes beyond what the consumer thinks is important. As for our relationship, I understand the consumer from a commercial point of view as well as Frank Perdue does from a product point of view—we've established a general truth. We've both come together on this over a period of time."

In a footnote to the Perdue approach to selling, which has been labeled by some as feisty, McCabe added: "Frank is contemptuous of his competition rather than combative" (see Figure 6-1).

CLIENT TYPES

If you have a naive faith in the benevolence and good nature of ordinary people, you will be disappointed by many of the clients you meet. The more you analyze them, the more bewildering their inconsistencies become.

I don't wish to dwell on these; I just want to get them out in the open and out of the way.

Here are thumbnail descriptions of clients who should be approached with caution. These are the types who never have ulcers. They're just carriers.

Figure 6-1

The Bully

A world-class hater. Seizes on negatives rather than analyzing reasons for agency recommendations. Then beats on agency. Agency role is reduced to taking dictation: "Put the name of the product in the headline, make the package bigger, let me tell you about this commercial my wife came up with," and so on.

creative work point by strategic point. Resulting advertising is exact as a yardstick and just about as dull.

This was Pepsi in the 1970s, a submissive second to Coca-Cola. But look what happened the minute they took on Coke with the Pepsi Challenge. Positions reversed. Number one now responds to number two, and share period by share period, the choice of a new generation becomes a reality.

No Abiding Relief

This client resents the need for advertising. Considers it fluff. Would rather spend $35 million on deals at supermarket level than spend one cent on the consumer. Sustains product life by buying share and shelf space. Answer to any competitive threat is to drop a coupon into a blizzard-turned-avalanche of coupons (180 million were dropped in 1987).

Mediocre middle management. Kill themselves so fat cats at top can take home all the gravy. Result is a great deal of contempt for corporation. This spills over to contempt for consumer. Client thinks he's doing consumers a big favor by letting them buy the product.

This client should develop a list of consumer promises—desired features— and test them with the lead user. This would bring middle managers closer to what the consumer wants rather than what the boss wants.

The Incrementalists

Would be better served to be in brain surgery. Hires incrementalists. If bottom line goes from 90.99990 to 90.99992, they are immediately promoted. Mavericks not encouraged. Operating philosophy is "safety in numbers." Corporate version of the "Stepford wives": This client hires nice, gray, amorphous agencies whose favorite expression is "let's not make waves."

This client gladly settles for number two or three position across many categories. Strategies are bland, aimed at the masses, never a targeted group. No consideration for consumer or psychographics or emotional terms.

Decision making is decentralized; no shared values from the top. I worked on Fleischmann's margarine, a Nabisco product. It had no cholesterol, no salt. Yet, Nabisco also sold peanuts and snacks loaded with salt. Company got very touchy when we presented a strong antisalt campaign.

What Can I Get Away With?

Working philosophy is: If copy isn't being challenged by competitor or investigated by FDA, there's something wrong with it. Claims sound like legal briefs. Riddled with ominous weasels. Demonstrations in commercials show no marked differences—yet superiority is asserted in voice track. Products are extensions of managers—bugs, roaches, and assorted hemorrhoidal tissue. Spends zilch on research and technology. Uses available chemicals to spawn product spin-offs. (I've worked with only one client like this.)

By the Numbers

To this client, marketing process is a ritual. Works from diagrams and easels depicting success-failure arrows; would be better suited to directing SAC pilots from underground silos in Colorado. Strategies are overburdened with too many ideas. Spends hours, days on semantic minutiae. Gets off on massaging the numbers. Decisions are based on complexity, never quick intelligence that springs from native intuition. Can be 90 percent sure of recommended actions, but mentality suggests a 6-to-12-month wait to be 100 percent sure.

Is slavish to research. Recent reformulation of Coca-Cola to New Coke is a good example. Research told Coke management that younger people preferred a sweeter, more Pepsilike taste. Like all broad-based research, it failed to account for consumer's loyalty and emotional allegiance to the product.

Against the Grain

If you were to put the clients described in this section together to work on their own advertising book, the title would write itself: *Advertising Made Difficult.* Yet, for every client who begins with bias, blind spots, preconceptions, fear, trembling, or disdain for consumers, there is always one that begins with a strategy that incorporates a marketing solution. Bold advertising is just one of the many by-products. This client we will call the "against the grain" type.

This type of client frowns on annual objectives or annual anything. This client is distinguished for: dedication to making an honest product, entrepreneurial smarts to tell the right people, and an iconoclastic marketing plan.

Case in point: Timberland.

Against the flood of expensive imported shoes that fall apart in a hard rain came the handmade quality brands—Bass, Reebok, and Timberland. For years, the Timberland boot was sold through army-navy stores and L.L. Bean. It took

Leonard Kanzer, president of Marvin & Leonard, a Boston-based agency, to slot Timberland right.

Marketing solution evolved from marketing niche. At Kanzer's suggestion, Timberland began selling the boot as a fashion item for outdoor yuppies and backpackers. The agency bought space in *The New Yorker,* sold to Bloomingdale's,

breaking-the-rules thinking (see Figure 6-2).

THE CHALLENGE

Complaining about who won't take risks is easy. I think it's a cop-out. One, it's not your money, and two, complaining is never a big challenge—persuading your client to take the smart risks is tougher.

When Bounce, the fabric softener from P&G, took its advertising out of subterranean laundry basements and concentrated on the way people feel about clothes softened with Bounce, that was a risk. But in the end a smart one.

People are attracted to fabric softeners because of softness, scent, static control, and convenience. The new Bounce promise of "clothes you can't wait to jump into" imbued the product with these attributes. The feeling and energy of the advertising sold the product. Gone were the dull ladies, dull laundry, and dull lives. Risk in this case was made positive because it took advantage of the clothes revolution and the consumer's desire to feel comfortable and feel good.

When I think of impressive clients, I usually think of one person, maybe two, who symbolize the values of that company. By values I mean strong beliefs. The belief that advertising should tell the facts in a disarming way without tricks or hogwash. The belief that advertising should reflect imagination, daring, independence, and energy. The belief that this image will eventually rub off positively on the consumer.

The following client case histories illustrate in very different ways some of these beliefs.

Iacocca

In my advertising lifetime, there hasn't been a harder consumer charger than Lee Iacocca. The Iacocca I see today is astonishingly close to the Iacocca I observed in 1965. I was a junior writer at JWT on the Ford truck account.

111

Figure 6-2

WHY THE BEST BOOTS AND HANDSEWNS MONEY CAN BUY ARE THE BEST BOOTS AND HANDSEWNS YOU CAN SELL.

Over the past few years, we, at Timberland, have developed a reputation for making quality footwear.

It's a reputation that we feel is well deserved.

Because while some manufacturers may combine a few of the features we put into our boots and handsewns, no other manufacturer combines all of the features.

Obviously, this commitment to craftsmanship benefits people who buy Timberland products.

But it also benefits people who sell them.

OUR BOOTS COME WITH RUGGED SOLES, LEATHER UPPERS, AND HIGHER-PROFIT MARGINS

At Timberland, we've always put higher quality craftsmanship into our boots, so our dealers can get a better price for them.

And they do.

Today, Timberland boots are the fastest-selling premium quality boots in the United States. And they sell at a premium price.

Our boots also come with something else other boots don't come with: built-in consumer demand.

Which means that you can sell a pair of Timberlands in less time than it takes to sell a pair of ordinary boots. And make more money.

THE FIRST LINE OF HANDSEWNS WITH THE QUALITY OF TIMBERLAND

For us, making a line of quality handsewns was a tough pair of shoes to fill.

Because, as the makers of the world's finest boots, we couldn't come out with anything less in a handsewn.

Timberland handsewns, including our boat shoes, are made from the same quality materials as our boots.

They are made with the same quality craftsmanship. And, most important, they come with the same high-profit margins and built-in consumer demand.

WE'VE SAVED THE BEST FOR LAST

Unlike other manufacturers, we've never thought our job ends when shipping begins.

Every year, we invest more money in consumer boot advertising than any of our competitors.

And this year, we'll be putting more money than ever before behind our handsewns, as well as a new boat shoe.

We also have the most complete dealer support program, including p.o.p., in-store promotions, and dealer co-op.

The result of these investments?

Well, just in the last few years alone, Timberland's growth has been unmatched by any of our competitors. And our dealers' profits have grown just as quickly.

See, we told you we were saving the best for last.

Timberland

Iacocca, at the time Ford's general manager and advertising manager, was my first client. In those days, most copy meetings were held in Detroit. If my group head, Bill Muyskins, didn't handle the meeting, our creative director, Harry Trealeven, did.

I never made the traveling squad. I depended a great deal on call reports

To illustrate this point, Iacocca alluded to the campaign that the Dodge agency was running. It was increasing Dodge sales, not by drips and drabs, but by as much as 70 percent. The advertising was centered around one theme, The Dodge Rebellion. Twenty years later, Iacocca borrowed from these thoughts with The American Revolution, Born In America, The Pride Is Back campaign. "You have to have an overall slogan," he repeated, "a ribbon to tie the package, a framework that we can slip anything into."

Some say that virtually everything American automotive management does seems to be a day late and a dollar short. This is especially true when you compare Detroit with the Japanese, whose mystical management rituals consistently beat American manufacturers to the punch and to the sale. Iacocca might not have the resolution of a samurai, but has something (for his market) better—an abiding faith in the American way. Here he is in a monthly copy meeting:

> How much will it cost us to clobber 30 markets for 60 days? How much? Two million? Three million? Five million? You tell me. Don't sweat the budget, open it up. Get something good and we'll come up with the money. This is a ten-million-car market, let's go get it. GM is weak. We'll never have a better opportunity than right now. It will take added advertising . . . and a lot of other things . . . but with a rising penetration in a rising market. . . . now is the time to get more money.

I don't know of an agency that wouldn't kill for a challenge like that.

In a quick and not altogether shallow time, where, according to Andy Warhol, everybody will be a celebrity for 15 minutes, clues to Iacocca's durability and steady performance over the past quarter-century are worth noting. Very early on, Iacocca found something he loved—cars, the making of cars, the thinking, the look, the smell, the feel of cars. He has stuck with it. Please note these lessons I gleaned from Iacocca:

113

His concentration on a single-minded strategy: Giving the paying customer his dollar's worth. I don't know how many tailors, carpenters, electricians, plumbers, and bankers can say the same.

His decisiveness: There's a strong sense of "let's do it" running through the man that attracts talented people like a magnet.

His innate salesmanship: To the consumer, there's just enough humility in his voice to make him totally believable. To his people, there's enough fire to let you think that if you really did come up with a better idea, he'd follow you through a mine field to sell it.

His ability to put his finger on the market segment that isn't being satisfied and build cars for them: Mustang for all the Walter Mitty's in the world; Fiesta, the car that saved Henry Ford in Europe; and the K-cars for the value-driven American drivers.

His assertiveness: "Be opportunistic." "Grab the market while it's there." "Talk directly to the competition and hit on its weakness." "Have a theme, a string, through the advertising." "Consistency throughout all media."

Iacocca's belief in advertising, his emphasis on simple values, his personal involvement in monthly advertising reviews, and his abiding belief in his own people were the catalysts that helped his managers down the line implement familiar Iacocca strategies.

Consider what Iacocca has accomplished for Chrysler by applying these same principles. In the mid 70s Chrysler's ROA was a -8. During 1984–85 it was a $+20$. Twelve percent would have most stockholders jumping for joy.

I was a 100-dollar-a-week rookie writer in the 1960s, but it all got filtered down even to me—the energy, the sheer joy at your occupation, the lesson of giving the consumer his dollar's worth. It made the swinging worthwhile. Facing a client like this one on my first trip to the plate was like being served a fat pitch every time up.

One surefire way to get an instant argument is to ask the question—is advertising an art or a business?

The story of Iacocca and his Ford team gives us a hint to the answer. With dedicated labor at their craft, they were able to develop it into—what, an art form?

Maybe. If it wasn't art, it was a skill that gave huge pleasure to an awful lot of people on both sides of the fence.

Procter & Gamble

Procter & Gamble has been called many things in its time: the Calvinists at Sixth and Sycamore (a reference to P&G's address); the wounded lion (a position they find themselves in due to fierce competition); Hack's Heaven (referring to the company as a haven for mediocre creative work); the Colossus (referring to revenues in excess of $13 billion); and a long-slumbering giant (one who wakes up and discovers the world has passed him by).

Each look at Procter seems to reinforce the fact that there are some icons about whom there is no final truth. Only stories and assessments, various portraits by various writers. Following are my own personal stories.

single building in the Procter kingdom and the plant for Charmin, Luvs, Pampers, Bounty, and White Cloud. There I would learn everything I could about Charmin.

Visiting Mehopony offered substantial clues into the mind, motivation, and pursuit of quality that established P&G as a respected client and a formidable marketer: Imagine 75 acres under one roof. Imagine a building that housed a 50-car freight train. Imagine 150 18-wheel tractor trailers emptying raw goods and picking up finished products in one day, 65 railroad cars doing the same, and shipments in excess of two million cases per month. Imagine owning your own forest to provide raw materials. Imagine 20–30 percent of the energy and steam technology required to run this plant coming from recycled "bark strips."

These indicators dramatized for me the strong need that Procter has for meaning, the strong notion they have about themselves and their way of doing things that has become a sort of culture. To get an appreciation, I asked my friend Mark Ketchum, who managed 2,500 employees at Mehopony, to comment on what seemed to be a Procter hallmark: getting ordinary people to do an extraordinary job.

"Everything we do is based on merit and contribution," he said. "The best jobs are rotated. Teamwork. Team concept is the cornerstone of how things are accomplished. The cost results and work systems here are rated within the company as the best."

To understand Procter and the real key to its sustained financial performance is this final insight from Ketchum. "The price of making this system work doesn't count; quality that comes from workers who are treated fairly doing the work they do does count."

Of course, none of this helped me kill Whipple. (He wins every "Burke-off.") He remains, along with Morris the Cat, Charlie the Tuna, and the Maytag repairman, as one of our most durable of personalities.

115

I did realize this: Few American-made products today have been improved compared to the number whose quality has been diminished by slipshod work or second-class materials. The crisis we face in this country is not the lack of big ideas—it's lack of quality work. What sets Procter apart from the rest?

Hear this from a most unexpected source: "One thing about Procter—it's not their marketing that makes them number one, it's what's in the box." Speaker: Helmut Krone.

The test market. I say that commitment to quality is more the reason for Procter's success than marketing smarts. The exception to the rule are Procter's individual brand managers, who are willing to trust their own ideas, outwit the Procter system, and ultimately get the idea out to the customers.

The story of how they applied Procter's existing paper technology to make the world's first disposable diapers is an excellent example of the difference between just having an idea and implementing one.

Pampers was first test-marketed in Dallas—in the summer. They bombed. Although Pampers kept the baby dry, they were too bulky and too hot, with no ventilation. Lots of babies got heat rash, eczema. The brand group went back to P.R.D. (Product Research and Development). Together they came up with a lighter, more breathable version featuring an inner lining that let liquid in but not back out onto baby's tender skin.

Again the product was tested, and failed. It wasn't because Procter didn't have a superior product—the cost to the consumer was too high. The product was there. The need was there. What was Procter's answer? They simply built another factory to manufacture more Pampers. Consumer demand took care of the rest. At double the dollar volume, they could sell it to the consumer for less. Today the disposable diaper market is in the $2.8 billion category.

Marketing smarts is one thing—keeping at it is something else.

The fatal blind spot. Examples of Procter's commitment to "winner" products with meaningful differences form an impressive list. Crest, the first fluoride toothpaste and the first to win the American Dental Association seal of approval. Bounce, the first fabric softener that could be used conveniently in the dryer. Charmin, the first two-ply toilet tissue. Dawn, the first dishwashing detergent designed to work specifically on grease. Today, most of Procter's competition has caught up with its ingredient technology. Everybody has fluoride, all fabric softeners make clothes soft, fresh, and static-free. And so on. Many of Procter's products are technically superior (measurable in the lab), but the differences are not consumer noticeable. As a result, Procter's advertising tries too hard to dramatize minuscule differences. The copy is factual, appealing to logic, but hardly ever to the emotions.

Not long ago I was talking to a Procter brand manager assigned to a new bleach product. I pointed to a demonstration of two shirts with no noticeable difference, but claiming that one was whiter and brighter. "As long as you assert

116

superiority, that's enough," he said. Not exactly a shining example of respect for consumer intelligence, I thought.

Because P&G is so committed to quality, it rarely introduces a new product or a product improvement unless the product has superiority.

This devotion to quality has led to what I consider a serious Procter blind

Lever's Aim was the first gel that touted taste. Beecham's Aqua-Fresh was a three-color entry resembling the American flag. The white fought cavities, the blue had great taste, and the red freshened breath.

Number two Colgate went head to head against Crest with MFP, Maximum Fluoride Protection. Crest held to its 25-year-old strategy as the unsurpassed leader in cavity protection.

If your life's work happened to be incremental share readings, you could see that Aim and Aqua-Fresh were chipping away while Crest and Colgate shares remained flat. You didn't need a competitive analysis to get the message: Fluoride was becoming the price of entry; taste was the name of the game.

In focus groups, gel users told us over and over "all toothpastes have fluoride, they all do a good job."

Just as clear was another fact affecting the toothpaste category: Kids just weren't getting as many cavities as they used to. Cavity prevention wasn't nearly as urgent. "Getting my kids to brush is the problem," mothers would say. "Give me a toothpaste that makes brushing fun," or "I need to make brushing a habit." Clearly, the consumer was messing up Crest's 25-year-old "head set." As one lady said, "Kids can't fight cavities until they get something on the brush."

Even with the high degree of loyalty that Crest had built over the years, one beleaguered Crest mother said, "I use Crest, but my kids insist on a gel. We're a two-toothpaste family."

If you don't listen to a *lead* user, to whom *do* you listen? Crest would need a flavor gel. And quick. In this kind of competitive environment, six months is forever. That's how long it took P&G's upper management even to give the brand group the go-ahead to develop a gel.

While Crest was leisurely test-marketing its gel in Burlington, Vermont (another six months), Colgate beat it to the punch by introducing wintergreen-flavored gel nationally. What's more, Colgate "sampled" its gel. Procter, against B&B's pleading, didn't. With share dwindling, we finally introduced new Crest gel. Slowly we began to build share back up. Six months later, after a major internal debate, P&G went back to a cavity-protection story.

To this day, Colgate still features its wintergreen flavor in all its advertising. Crest hardly mentions it. I'm convinced some consumers still don't know that Crest has a gel.

It seems almost benign to talk about the importance of staying on top of the consumer. Despite all the lip service about the customer being right, it's the Procter tendency to do what it's predisposed to do.

The gel that Procter had eventually developed was excellent. We encouraged the company to do a taste test with kids to see if we could get a preference. Crest could stick to its long-standing strategy, but frame it around marketplace relevance: "Crest, your favorite cavity-fighter, is now your kid's favorite taste." At the time, Aim's copy was very close with a line that had a mother say, "My kids love the taste, so they may be brushing longer." (Note the legal weasel *may*, which destroys, for me anyhow, the reality of the thought.) A smart client would have challenged the agency to pursue that direction, something like "My kids love the taste; brushing's getting to be a habit around our house." At least it states a reality, a human entry point that might allow the mother to nod yes.

But we could never convince Procter that taste was a factor in purchase decision. "Crest isn't a flavor, it's a pre-eminent cavity-fighter," a brand man once said. In this case, client preconception was more important than reality.

As of spring 1985, projected share figures show: Crest 32 percent and losing; Colgate 29 percent and gaining.

If it sounds like the story's over, you don't know Procter. With the summer of 1985 came a $37-million introduction of Crest's "tartar control formula." Industry sources say that already Crest has picked up three to five share points on Colgate.

A subsequent vignette is the arrival of its new pump dispenser. Whereas Procter is last of the national brands to have a pump, it differentiates its entry by offering two pump sizes, a four and a six ounce, the *two most* popular sizes. Additionally, the Crest pump provides flavor stability, while in some of the pumps a flavor change is perceived over time.

The pump—which is still another way to make the act of brushing easier and more of a habit—now holds 12 percent of the $1 billion category. Household product analysts call it a defensive move, but the latest Gallagher report shows something else: P&G is doing the shaving. Crest's midsummer 1986 market share is 38.2 from 29.5, proving again that underestimating Procter can be dangerous.

Procter will always be blue-sky, big-idea people who would much rather reinvent the wheel and start from scratch than refine or improve what they have.

The company is monomaniacal about quality. To Procter, quality is the best investment possible, which is why it never passes off novelty for invention. Given the fact that the drastic shortage American businesses face is not new or improved ideas, but pride in our work, there can be no higher striving than quality. If Procter could only learn to be big and act small at the same time,

Q: What bugs you most about the agencies you work with?
A: They fall into the administrative trap and their creative product falls with it.
B: Too compliant, too obedient. [When probed,] "They're dull."

Lysol
Follow the shopping cart. Chart the critical five seconds, the instant of purchase decision. The product that gets the ride home is the one with the strongest brand image. Although the average supermarket contains 4,000 brand names, only a fraction of them have a brand "image." Six factors distinguish the products that do:

1. A significant point of difference leads to the highest purchase intent.
2. The point of difference is something the consumer needs.
3. The need is enhanced by a high degree of efficacy and quality.
4. Efficacy is linked to satisfaction, which is linked to loyalty, which is linked to willingness to pay a premium price.
5. The advertising builds the brand as opposed to simply the product.
6. The package is so faithful to that image that it sells off the shelf.

If you push your own shopping cart, you know the long-term winners in the "brand image sweepstakes": Listerine, Green Giant, Pepperidge Farm, Oscar Mayer, Coke, Campbell's, Kellogg's, Budweiser, Marlboro, and Lysol.

It was on the Lysol account that I got my basic training in package goods. Two client names stand out: Hal Danenberg, division president, and Jack Hughes, group products manager.

119

"You start with having to win and you work back." I don't remember who, but I remember one of them saying that.

A recent phone interview with Jack Hughes, now president of Mennen U.S.A., suggests that the key to product success is a strong brand image that builds an emotional attachment to that brand.

"Our objective," says Hughes, "in everything we did, was to reinforce what Lysol was to the user: the efficacy elements—a conscious effort to link brand name with the benefits. So many products within the same category have interchangeable advertising. Never Lysol. We guarded against diluting its power. We never went with quick-impact ideas and proliferation."

As an example, Hughes cited the "I Love My Carpet" product. "Associating the name Lysol with that kind of product is something we would never do."

"The big boys like P&G," continued Hughes, "can bring out a product, position it to the broadest market, and spend a ton delivering the message. We were small change by comparison. We did niche marketing long before the term came into fashion.

"To our Lysol customer, there's magic in that can. When you get behind that mirror [referring to focus group sessions], you've got to pay attention to *two* things: what women say and what they actually do. Take Top Job and Mr. Clean. They're good cleaning products. But the Lysol user wants more than just looking clean, she wants it smelling clean. We dimensionalized clean for her.

"That's why every competitor who came after Lysol has failed. They tried to be Lysol. They tried to compete on a parity basis. They never learned from their mistakes. They didn't understand the Lysol mystique—the faith and belief our user had. Competitors who compared themselves to us only infuriated our customer. The Lysol name is stronger than an image. Attacking Lysol was like attacking mother."

I asked Hughes how he judges his agency.

"By the boxes I move," he flatly said.

What do you look for in the agency's creative leaders?

"A person who thrives on response and takes up the challenge. A person who is always looking forward. A person who recognizes his contribution on the basis of what's happening to my business."

How did he learn to think?

"The same way you learn to write," he said, "by revising your failures. You learn by your failures. You have to remember your failures and not repeat them."

And what does Jack Hughes think of today's new managers?

"Let's put it this way, John. They don't teach risk-taking at business school; they teach risk aversion. They analyze things to death. They're more concerned about their own careers. They lack guerrilla instincts."

Warm and Friendly

Keeping pace with the future store is the future company, Campbell's, whose sales have gone from 2.8 billion in 1981 to over 4 billion in 1986. By 2001, this once-stodgy client will own its own supermarket. Here are six reasons why:

and Vlasic pickles, an upstart that literally took over the market from well-entrenched Heinz and now commands a 62 percent share.

4. *Consumer relevance.* "We're obsessed with the consumer," says Herb Baum, Campbell's president. Advertising reflects the corporate credo—"Focus on the consumer"—and plays to major trends, such as the healthiness of food (as illustrated by the slogan "Soup is good food" and Figure 6-3), working women, speed, and convenience.

5. *Faith in advertising.* "We put our money where our mouth is," says Baum, who came to Campbell's Soup from Needham in 1978. Baum credits president Gordon McGovern. "When Gordon came, we became marketers, not just manufacturers."

6. *Initiative to try new things.* "Prego and Le Menu are two examples of what happens when you encourage research and development people," says Baum.

When I asked Baum to personify Campbell's soup, he simply said: "Warm and friendly." Based on that interview, I went out and bought the only stock I own: Campbell's soup.

QUESTIONS FOR CLIENTS

As discussed up-front, "why does it take so long?" is a client's number one frustration. Not to cop a plea, it "takes so long" because creativity is a by-product of digging, sorting, listening, and plain hard work.

There's enough advertising out there that addresses the trendy and explains the far-out and obscure. I'm satisfied when I can get to the obvious.

Figure 6-3

HEALTH INSURANCE

One of the best ways to insure good health, is to eat a well-balanced diet that includes nutritious foods like Campbell's Soup.

That's not just our opinion. The fact is university researchers found that soup plays a significant part in a nutritionally healthy diet.

That Campbell's Tomato Soup up there, for instance, is an important source of vitamin C. While Campbell's Vegetable Beef contains more than 1/3 of the day's allowance of vitamin A in just a single serving.

And not only are most Campbell's Soups a rich source of nutrition, they're also light on your stomach, and easy to digest.

So when you're picking out a good health insurance policy, remember to pick up a few cans of your favorite Campbell's Soups.

If you have any questions, talk to one of the best insurance agents around. Mom.

CAMPBELL'S SOUP IS GOOD FOOD

Creative people today have plenty of ideas like that. What we need are clients who will let us do something with them.

There are plenty of answers to the question "why so long?" But why string them together on a page when I strung them out in a book?

So, I'm turning the question around to you. As a client, if you answer these questions honestly, you'll have an inkling as to why you can't get better copy, faster.

> Do your copy evaluations pass for a brand of geometry, where you sit and judge copy by degrees rather than the whole?

Are "word-smithing" and "nit-picking" your favorite avocations?

Do you rely on benefit or support strategies for creative direction, as opposed to a written creative brief that reflects what your lead user feels?

Do you inhibit emotional, image-driven work because you can't measure it effectively?

Does your company's reel look like home movies?

Does there exist in your company a mercenary refusal to treat production values as a great lever to an ultimate sale?

If yes popped up a lot, I can tell you who you're not: You're not a client who would approve a Max Headroom, a Joe Isuzu, or an Ed Jaymes. You're not Visa, Tide, Levi's, Bayer, or Calvin Klein. You're the other guy who is spending ten times what these guys are spending just to get noticed.

If

If nothing is working.

If every attempt to establish a meaningful relationship with your client has resulted in a series of meaningless disasters.

If you avoid the dull grind of yet another client meeting like the plague.

If, instead of merely crumbling a client communiqué into a small ball, you tear it into eighths or sixteenths—it's definitely time to take the client to lunch.

In New York, I suggest Exterminator Chili, a diner-type eatery at the corner of Church and Walker. Chili there comes in three grades: *residential* for likable, gentle-type clients; *commercial* for the lukewarm; and for the client you never want to see or hear from ever, the *industrial*, which is served with a fire extinguisher. Note: This establishment has no beer license. Make sure not to bring any.

Chapter Seven

On Strategy

Strategy is the starting point in the advertising process, a premise that the consumer has to live with for the rest of your product's life. The sheer rightness or wrongness of that premise determines success or failure.

HAVE TEETH, WILL BITE

All kinds of people discuss strategy, argue about it, spend countless days on specific language, fly-specking, semantic differences: "Is the word *charismatic* an apt description for a dryer sheet user?" "Is there a difference between *yuppie* and *consumptive?*" and so on.

Everyone has his or her own definition of strategy. I think it would be convenient for our purpose here, if we all worked with the same definition. . . . mine.

A strategy is a carefully designed plot to murder the competition.

Any idea that makes your competition hate you, cry foul, fire its agency, or quietly invoke Chapter 11 qualifies. You might disagree with that narrow definition, but that's the one we're going to be working with in this section. It gives rise to these corollaries:

Any premise that lacks a killer instinct is not a strategy.

Any premise that doesn't reflect or include a consumer's crying need is not a strategy.

Any premise that can't make up its mind or that is overburdened with more than one objective or idea is not a strategy.

Any premise that represents compromise or group-think is not a strategy.

Any premise that is embalmed in stiff, predictable language—phrases like unique formula, the best possible, on the cutting edge, state of the art—is not a strategy.

Any premise that addresses the whole world—women 3–93—is not a strategy.

Any premise that is interchangeable with that of another product in the category is not a strategy.

Take a look at your own advertising. The odds are that you could change the category without losing sense because the message is so generic that it could apply to products in any number of categories. Millions are wasted every year on strategic positions already occupied by a competitor.

Amazing indeed how few strategies make any attempt to link brand name and product position in a pre-emptive way. By contrast, do you have any trouble,

problem—throw it away. It doesn't have any redeeming sales value.

I have to wince occasionally when agencies form *creative* review boards. Even if the creative is right, how could it survive 18 layers of approval? The successful agencies have *strategy* review boards that have the toughness to agree on one tightly defined objective up-front.

Often I have heard creative people decrying the lack of freedom. But, honestly, there is nothing a creative team appreciates less than direction from a creative director or account manager who says, "Do anything you want, but do it great." There's plenty of freedom in that speech and you can go off and be as vague as you want. I'd rather have the kind of freedom that starts from the precision of an interesting, informative, honestly written, long-term strategy.

"Give me the freedom of an extremely tightly defined strategy." That's Norman Berry speaking, Ogilvy & Mather international creative head. "We try to tie brand names to the consumer emotionally. We never stop until we have a long-range solution. There's no such thing as a 'for the time being' strategy," he adds. Berry doesn't have much trouble luring top creative talent into his fold. Executional freedom is much more important than strategic freedom.

SOME SPECIAL PLEAS

Let's assume that you're a client and most strategies across your own brand lineup are inadequate. Although they might express your product's benefit and reason why, they lack direction in terms of target audience and character and have no long-term purpose.

Let's assume that your core group with its team of equals, brand manager, account manager, and creative team are starting from ground zero. The objective is killer copy based on a killer strategy. Drawing on my own experiences, following are a few special pleas for clients, account, and creative folk alike.

To creative: Never begin copy without a good picture of your user, your strong markets, and your competition. Make sure that picture is qualitative. Get involved at the start; those who commit to a strategy must be the same people who solve the problem. Remember, it's more fun to solve a creative problem that *you* agree with versus a dictated solution from somebody else.

"Creative people should be trained to solve the *relevant* problem, the problem that *they* had a hand in defining. Be willing to be accountable for all phases of your work," urges Bob Levenson of Saatchi & Saatchi Compton. "That includes strategy that isn't just a fancy marketing exercise."

To account people: Never let your client agree to a strategy on judgment alone. The irony of this business is that a client invariably will approve a strategy on judgment, but ask him to do the same with copy, and he'll ship you to Terre Haute on a store check. Make sure your strategy is consumer-approved and -tested. Make sure acceptance is based on genuine need. It can be practical, physical, emotional, or psychological, but it must be genuine.

At Chiat/Day it's the solution that counts and strategy shapes that solution," says account planner Jane Newman. "Getting it right is never done in isolation without the consumer." Adds Jay Chiat, "Strategic planning is the key to selling important ideas to a client. It just makes it easier."

"At Campbell's," says Herb Baum, "we're obsessed with getting the consumer into our strategy. Most companies test advertising; we never do. We test 'promises,' a list of benefit/attributes that consumers rank in order. V-8 juice is a good example. Consumers told us that V-8 was good-tasting and good for them, but they never considered V-8 in their choice, which led us to 'Wow, I could've had a V-8!' It has worked very well for us over the years."

Most strategies suffer from regularity. Don't be afraid of a colorfully written one. And never lump strategic timetables with creative timetables.

To clients: Strategy is only half a word. Strategic position is your goal. Is that strategic position occupied or is it truly preempted? Don't exclude emotions as a trigger. Remember "You deserve a break today?" Those five words revolutionized perceptions of fast food joints. McDonald's isn't the Four Seasons, but the strategy offered an acceptable eat-out alternative. To a harried mother, "acceptable" is sometimes a luxury.

Make sure to get your strategy approved from the top. "Top" here means whatever level constitutes company go-ahead. It is in the strategic area where a top executive can set standards up and down the line. By doing so, he exposes his thinking process to the people who will be running the place in a few years. It's a proven method for establishing a corporate culture.

Once you are convinced that you have the right strategy, give the agency the time to create and *produce* it well.

No Place for Pipsqueaks

Phil Dougherty, not-so-mild-mannered ad reporter for *The New York Times*, calls adland the place where make-believe and reality walk hand in hand. Unwittingly, Dougherty has pinpointed the exact location of many existing strategies.

Volvo

The basis of many American-made products is the proposition that says: Let's give the consumer what's acceptable as opposed to what's best. Buttons fall off your once-laundered shirt, a shoe strap breaks at the sight of your ankle, zippers go off their track. That new put-together toy or gadget is missing parts, and the parts you have don't fit. Your new car over-heats on the way home from the showroom. Funny, you never hear about that happening to a new Trident submarine. So, it can't be because Americans lack know-how; it's because all too often labor doesn't care.

I could easily launch into a "pride in your work" speech, but this years-old strategy for Volvo, the Swedish import, makes the point. Volvo's Built To Last strategy, supported by the fact that nine out of ten Volvos registered in the United States since the mid-1970s are still on the road, is just one of the reasons why close to 40 percent of all cars sold in this country are made somewhere else. This explains why in 1986, for the first time in U.S. history, more workers were employed in service industries than in production. In Sweden, it's the architects and designers who get rich, not the junkyard operators and mechanics.

Until Detroit gets the message and stops showing contempt for the car buyer, the pulling power of this strategy will have eternal appeal. See one of the original ads in that series in Figure 7-1.

This attack on cars that destroy themselves by the mere act of carrying themselves around surprised a lot of industry moguls, but not the American consumers. Establishing a quality and luxury priced position took Volvo time. It also demonstrated a willingness to build a brand as opposed to simply the product.

Figure 7-1

Here's the same strategy continued. This advertising explicitly addresses the disparity between what's best and what's accepted:

[Sound effects: Fife and drum marching music throughout]
Announcer: In nineteen hundred fifty-six, Volvo had padded dashboards. Twelve years later, all cars had them. Encouraged by an act of Congress.
In nineteen hundred fifty-nine, Volvo became the first mass-produced car in the world with safety belts as standard equipment. Nine years later, all cars had them. Inspired by an act of Congress.

128

All told, Volvo had six important safety features before Congress made them law.

[Sound effects: Drum roll. Music continues]

Announcer: At Volvo, we don't wait for an act of Congress to make our cars safe.

product that appealed more to its handlers than to its eaters. First, Pringles came in easy-to-handle tube containers. Second, each tongue-and-groove uniform chip came stacked tightly against every other, eliminating breakage. Third, Pringles was easy to stock, providing more facings per foot. Last, Pringles had longer shelf life.

Time magazine described "new-fangled Pringles" as "dehydrated mashed, cooked potatoes stacked in tennis ball-like cans." Today, when I see a can of Pringles, Wise potato chips come to mind, for two reasons: (1) there's a wise old owl on the bag, reminding me of what a smart buy I'm making; and (2) a commercial I saw in the mid-1970s attacking head-on the concept of a high-tech chip.

This commercial is the work of my friend and former partner, Dick Levy, who now runs his own place, Levy, Flaxman. When I told him I'd be referring to him as "Killer Levy" in this chapter, he couldn't wait to start shooting. "We took Procter head-on. We were natural, they were fake. I wasn't even on the account, but Needham [Harper & Steers] was about to lose the business. So, when I heard about the idea of Pringles, this strategy kind of wrote itself.

"When Borden's saw the commercial, it didn't take much convincing to run it. The upshot was tremendous. It forced P&G to take Pringles off the shelves and reformulate it to a more natural chip. It helped the smaller regional chip makers fight back. Our commercial made Pringles easy to attack. This made it tougher for Procter. They weren't able to bulldoze the store manager into more shelf space and corner positions.

"Even today, with an improved product, the true potato chip lover won't ever forget the original product. New-fangled Pringles and old-fangled Wise really stuck in their minds. Pringles is half a successful product at best and a good example of how disastrous it is not to know your customer. If there's one thing potato chip eaters like, it's not uniformity. They like different sizes and shapes. They don't mind a broken chip or two. Procter never bothered to ask them."

Figure 7-2 shows the print translation of the campaign.

Who says creative people aren't strategic?

THE PEPSI CHALLENGE

Comparative strategies can be deadly. They can backfire and the product attacked actually gains sales. That is what happened when Datril waged its shoddy attack on Tylenol.

At its deadliest is the comparative campaign in which number one can expect not only a reverse in sales but also a diminishing of its image. For this kind of advertising to work, it must strike the right nerve. The Pepsi challenge did. The nerve it hit was Coke's religious attitude about taste. Coke's dignity was being attacked, and it wasn't prepared. It got too offended. Worse, Coke's always defensive response over the years, culminating in the reformulation fiasco.

In his new book, *The Other Guy Blinked*, Roger Enrico, president of Pepsi-Cola, U.S.A., refers to Michael Jackson as a kind of Pepsi icon. When I talked to ex-P&Ger John Costello, then at Pepsi, now at Wells, Rich Greene, he said, "Pepsi wasn't an upstart. We really had a taste advantage. The Pepsi challenge leveled the playing field. Jackson put us over the top."

Moral of this strategy: When the attacked overreacts, push it.

AT THE RISK OF BEING A NUDNICK

I began this chapter with my own narrow definition of strategy. It comes from my compulsion to see results increasing at the same rate my own blood courses.

The question arises, is there not an alternative guideline for the ladies and gentlemen in the audience? Put another way—why can't I just be smart? Aren't brand groups who follow the polite but bright approach sometimes just as successful? Yes. The crop is incredible. And I'd like to mention a few:

Prego is the spaghetti sauce that comes with real beef, spices, and seasoning already in the jar. Advertising claims, "It's in there." Proof to the Aunt Millies and Ragus of the world that just when you think you're hot, someone may come along with a story that says you're not (see Figure 7-3).

A.1. steak sauce's "turns hamburgers into steakburgers" position is brilliant. It takes a specialty item and gets it on the table right next to the mustard, mayo, and ketchup.

"The soup that eats like a meal" gives Campbell's Chunky instant credibility as more than just a stomach filler. It plays off a negative consumer perception of thinner soups as a not-too-nourishing dish. "Food business products are differentiated less and less," says Campbell's Herb Baum. "Chunky is a superior

Figure 7-2

Figure 7-3

product and it is seen that way." If Campbell's seems consumer-driven today, it's "because management changed and marketing became emphasized."

If Levi's is a legend, it's because the company doesn't play it safe. Witness its loose and casual $38 million campaign touting its shrink-to-fit brand 501 jeans (see Figure 7-4). Never before has such an investment been made on a single

$500 million in 1987. Pepsi now claims that Slice, a strong second to 7-UP, is ahead of Sprite in areas where it's sold.

Compare the current Michelin tire strategy—"Because so much is riding on your tires"—with any other in the category. Compare the Michelin babies romping in a playground of tires with ads for the competition. Tiresome, never-

Figure 7-4

ending running shots of tires plowing through puddles. The outtakes alone must equal the entire footage from *Heaven's Gate*.

In the most redundant category in the business, Michelin stands out (see Figure 7-5).

At the other end of a quick-strike strategy is the one with the patience of Job. Appropriately, the peanut butter called Jif is a Procter brand. "Tastes more like real peanuts" the strategy says. That's why choosy mothers choose it. It took Jif 25 years to make it, but it is now America's number one choice—a fact that chairman John Smale proudly pointed to at a recent stockholders' meeting.

Think of your strategy as a set of directions—a human hypothesis leading to a creative solution. This can't happen in isolation with old rules and formats. Solutions come from the street, not the boardroom. You have to include, know, and reward your customer.

Don't be afraid of strategies that rely on common sense and human nature. While human nature is universal, it works. "Fly the friendly skies of United"— somebody believed in that advertising, so today they own it.

Don't be greedy. Define the genuine needs of your lead user. Avoid the quick fix; think long term. Make certain to tap in on some part of human nature, which never changes. The right strategy comes from reality, which is never a

Figure 7-5

collection of hunches of a committee. Inevitably, a great strategy will lead to a great execution.

How to Introduce a New Product

, ...g ....g.

Rather than simply bemoaning the whole problem of loser products and the speed with which the newer ones disappear from the shelves, let's list the questions we should ask the next client who suggests one.

Is There a Crying Need?

In the early 1960s, Pampers answered a mother's need with a product that made her baby more comfortable and gave her the feeling that she was taking better care of the child. Today the disposable diaper business is worth $2.7 billion.

Can You Demonstrate Product Superiority?

Is your product, by its very name and nature, superior to existing products, and can you clearly demonstrate the advantage? Gillette's Trac II razor is a long-running example. Trac-Two sounds like a terrific idea, but there was potential for consumer confusion. The need was to demonstrate how one blade just nips a whisker and how the second finishes it off. Which is why you'll see an animated depiction of this in every Trac II commercial.

Is the Product Adaptable?

We resist the words *new, improved,* and *introducing* as trite. But these words not only add years to a product's life, they help establish it and keep its leadership position. The minute you come out with a new product, improvements should be hatching back at the lab.

P&G's Bounce was the first dryer-added fabric softener. In just ten years, it introduced (1) two scent improvements, (2) an unscented version, which now accounts of 17 percent of Bounce users, and (3) a breakthrough stainguard ingredient that prevents future stains from setting in your next wash.

Can the Existing Product Be Improved?

An improved package can be as valuable as a product improvement. Scope's new plastic bottle helped gain more than a stride in the share race with Listerine. I remember the commercial we created to introduce it. In slow motion, we dropped both Scope's new plastic bottle and Listerine's glass bottle onto a hard-tile bathroom floor and froze at the hit point, as a pair of bare tootsies stood surrounded by flying glass from the Listerine bottle. The commercial ran one week before Procter & Gamble got a letter from Warner-Lambert claiming everything from dirty pool to disparagement. It was so pathetic that it almost made *me* cry. The Procter people, of course, being the courteous types they are, discontinued the spot, but the damage was done.

Is the Product Extendable?

No Nonsense pantyhose is now No Nonsense fashion. The pantyhose comes in wide band, knee-highs, comfort tops, comfort stride, ultrasheer, sheer to waist, and queen size. Their display rack dominates drugstores and supermarkets, and so does its long-time promise: "No Nonsense pantyhose at a no nonsense price."

Keeping Pace with Campbell's

Since the early 1980s, the Campbell's Soup Company has been the undisputed leader in the new products race with 334. (My source is Dancer, Fitzgerald Sample's New Product News.) Campbell's is also leading in *successful* introductions—Le Menu and Prego spaghetti sauce are just two.

As early as 1990, Campbell's expects to kick its tin-can image by developing a plastic container suitable for its flagship condensed soup line, that, according to president Herb Baum, could be microwaveable. If you don't think he's on to something, consider that 50 percent of America's kitchens already have microwaves (80–90 percent by the year 2000) and that lessons in microwave cooking are included in most adult education programs.

This adventurous corporate approach is not without costs—a huge marketing investment, doubling advertising expenditures, and encouraging people to try new things.

Baum explains Campbell's new products philosophy this way. "The consumer is into a grab-and-run style. We want it quick, convenient, with no cleanup, they're saying. Campbell's strategy is to offer the consumer every kind of soup in every kind of container they could have."

This reflects the philosophy that you have more than one pocket for your money. "We don't mind competing with ourselves," Baum adds. "We'd rather come out with new products than have somebody else beat us to it."

Campbell's stands to save millions in packaging and shipping by switching to the lighter, cheaper plastics. Here again, Herb Baum: "The tin can isn't as easy to open. The can is not user-friendly" (a term Baum likes to use). "We're in the soup business, not the canned soup business; we have met consumers' needs and desires as they happen."

When I asked him about the risk of tampering with a national symbol like the Campbell's can, Baum said, "the real risk is marketing myopia."

million strong. While the subject matter gets lighter and lighter, the magazine gets fatter and fatter—and more successful.

There are new product entries that don't belong to any established market. Black & Decker's Dustbuster comes to mind. It's a small cordless vacuum cleaner whose recharging unit hangs on a wall. While GE was diverting its efforts in big ticket items, B&D single-mindedly pursued innovation. Introduced in 1979, Dustbuster cleaned up to the tune of ten million units.

The package is important. When Hershey came up with its New Trail Granola Bar, they thought they had a winner. But the package wasn't tempting, the product shots were boring, and the copy was too low keyed. The package lacked design personality. Hershey decided to put healthy, all-American looking athletes on the package, and develop a single brand color, brown—which was closer to Hershey tradition. The new package was tested and had immediate impact. The lesson here is that people don't initially buy a product, they buy what's wrapped around it.

If you think you have a winner, sampling is the quickest way to find out. The sooner you can get the product into the consumer's hands, the sooner you can measure *repeat* purchase. Always time your trial with peak advertising. The equation: Peak sampling effort, peak advertising frequency. And include cents-off coupons in the free sample. Why? Because consumers today prowl the aisles for discounts. They opt for saving rather than their favorite product. It's a price-off mentality. Get used to it. If you've got a good product and offer a free sample and a cents-off coupon, you've given the consumer three good reasons to like you. I can't think of a better way to start a relationship.

Are You Willing to Spend?
Quick-hit budget plans never work, especially when you're up against the big boys. The Fleischmann's margarine people at Nabisco wanted to get into the

oil business. Their no-cholesterol, health-related heritage seemed a logical fit for cooking oil. They set as their objective a four-point share, but were willing to spend only around $4 million, when the category was averaging $12 to 15 million. Additionally, Fleischmann's oil was undifferentiated. The product had the same reason-for-being as the three leaders. Nabisco brand management seriously believed that Crisco, Wesson, and Mazola would let them waltz in and grab a quick four points without a battle. It wasn't exactly a six-day war, but it was close. Another example of a client whose appetite for success outgrew the size of its commitment to advertise.

Upping the Ante
In the mid-1970s, it cost $10 million to get a new product off the ground. In 1986, it was $80 million. By 1988, the average cost will have broken $100 million. One reason is the urge to merge and acquire companies in the package goods area. To me, this is an admission of failure: "If I can't create success, I'll buy it."

Name-Dropping at the A&P
While package goods are hot, unpackaged areas—produce, flowers, deli, breadstuffs, gourmet—are even hotter. Check out the produce and salad sections—Chiquita bananas, Sunkist lemons and oranges, Signature salads, California grapes and raisins, Orval Kent's Salad Singles, and even Andy Boy broccoli. People never bought broccoli by a name before. In 20 years, there won't be such a thing as a nonbranded commodity. Identity and quality are too important today.

As new products proliferate, shelf space gets tighter; as the fight for space intensifies, the failures multiply. In this "demarketing zone," some experts feel that trench warfare (price-off and deals), not brand loyalty, determines purchase. I don't agree. Strong brand image today is better than money in the bank. It's a chance for the big to get huge. There is an old saying that "the worth of a thing is the price it brings." Perceived value commensurate with quality and consistency will always win.

Flankers
Given that kind of atmosphere, the smart companies continue to drive sales with flankers—spin-offs of brand name products—*provided the brand name is strong*. The highly visible success of Diet Coke and Cherry Coke are examples. Another is Ivory soap. It would be much easier for P&G to sell one Ivory brand, but they wouldn't sell as much. Net market share is the bottom line. When Ivory soap went down, its flanker Ivory Liquid took up the slack. Sales of both together netted Procter a gain of over two points.

The Right Name

The right name can drive a new product for years. Clinique for face and skin; Obsession for the possessed; Meow Mix, the cat food cats ask for by name. Dopey, corny names work for functional products: Elmer's glue, Murphy's oil, and Zud are my favorites.

Although it is true that new products require a combination of strategy, perseverance, and luck, finding a good name is 50 percent of the battle.

Throwaways

I figured we had reached the end with disposable film, but, alas, a disposable watch for under $35.00. Swatch. One of the top five new product entries in the 1980s.

New product winners are generally hatched by a person who is obsessed with his own idea. Success has more to do with creativity, invention, and discovery than with prescriptions and formulas. Outside of the fact that a new product has to be makeable, marketable, and competitive, the only rule is to break the rules or destroy the myths.

Myths

All new products are new ideas. Not really. Take the cumbersome old headphone and a noisy transistor. Put them together and what have you got? A Walkman. It's light, it's comfortable, and the sound is great. Walkman is a staple item for those who make spending a habit.

Gimmicks don't sell. Wrong again. Glad's Glad-Lock was devised to cut into Ziploc's recloseable bag market. The Glad-Lock brand features one blue track and one clear track. The colors tell consumers when the bag is actually closed. This is based on the fact that every family has somebody who doesn't close the bag. People found it fun and easy to use. And the seal was sure. It has surpassed all sales projections. "The color change seemed like a trivial idea," said president Ernest Potischman. "Then somebody came up with an idea from the first grade that appealed to the kid in all of us."

Pull, not push. You can't push technology on people, but sometimes there's a readiness to take advantage of hot trends. Heavyhands is a fancy, hi-tech dumbbell. The manufacturer, AMF, calls them aerobic weights. Smartly designed in high-visibility red and blue colors and displayed in a strategically designed see-through package, the product is the focal point. This combination of unique product visibility and packaging with the high-ticket price that would justify a Bloomie's or Hammacher Schlemmer retailer resulted in first-year sales exceeding 10 million bucks. Easily the best selling new fitness item in many years.

You can't improve on a paper clip. 3M's simple but infinitely helpful brand of self-sticking notepads, Post-it notes, played a major part in the editing of this book. My assistant, Holly Ricci, used them constantly to edit or make suggestions. They were almost ubiquitous.

She didn't have to remove parts of the manuscript. Comments were "posted" exactly where they were appropriate. No paper clips or staplers were ever needed. Post-it notes are adaptable—Holly used the small ones to me, I used the large ones to my editor.

Ideas come from above. McNuggets. Conceived by a franchiser, the idea resulted in making McDonald's the second largest chicken retailer in the United States.

THE GOOD OLD DAYS

The more I talk about new products, the fonder I get of the old ones. Like the ones my mother saved—my tin soldiers; my cast-iron fire engine; my agate shooter; my all-wood, 33″ Nellie Fox Louisville slugger. If I never have to work on a "state-of-the-art" gadget, I won't mind. My advice is to take care of what you have and remember what Andy Rooney said: "Very few things you buy will be the answer to the problem you bought them to solve."

Chapter Eight

On Copy

to be scared again. So I'm going to spend some time looking for a limb to climb out on."

Who can confidently say what ignites a certain combination of words in a writer's head, causing an explosion in the mind of a consumer? Inspired copy is a high mystery. And books, even the worthwhile ones, attempting to explain it are mystery stories in thin disguise.

Everybody has his own rules. In a chapter devoted to copy, David Ogilvy, in *Ogilvy on Advertising,* begins by quoting "God is in the details." Then, in prose phrased as direct orders, he covers them all in just 32 pages.

Defining sound copy principles is no different from defining sound business principles. A recitation of these lessons appears in the glut of current management best-sellers. However, for cleanliness, accuracy, and brevity, the winning definition is this by Leo Burnett: "The greatest thing to be achieved in copy is to be believed, and nothing is more believable than the product itself."

In truth, there are no infallible guides to writing effective copy. No guarantees that a person who follows every rule will be able to write clearly.

Understand. The view here is from the trenches, not the chateau. My observations are drawn from a copywriter's experience of writing. My purpose is not to soften Ogilvy's commands. Although I know that dogs and kids attract more viewers and that copy should break for easy reading, I also know that rules and formulas for copy have never been so futile and ineffective as they are today.

STYLE SPEAKS LOUDER THAN WORDS

An ad written with style is communication through revelation. What you believe is exposed in your work. If the person who writes the ad is crass, dull, or tricky, it shows. If the person is sincere, friendly, and informative, it shows. As a consumer you get the immediate sense that "that person knows me, he knows my problem."

Copywriters with style do not remain incognito for long. Nor do the products they speak for. When I speak of Ed McCabe's style, I don't mean his command of the prepositional phrase. I mean his passion for breasts.

Announcer: Ladies and Gentlemen, the president of Perdue Farms, Mr. Frank Perdue . . .

Frank Perdue: I've got a problem here that you can help me with. My breasts aren't moving as fast as my legs. For some reason, people are buying a lot more of my Perdue chicken legs than Perdue chicken breasts. Of course, I really appreciate the support you're giving my legs. But we've got to get this breast problem straightened out or there'll be no end of grief. You see, a chicken only has two legs. And no matter how you slice it, you can't get more than two breasts out of one chicken. Now I'm not one to complain about having a few extra breasts on my hands. But I'm on the brink of a major leg shortage. You're just going to have to start buying more Perdue chicken breasts, or I'm going to have to start coming up with three-legged chickens.

Announcer: When it comes to chicken breasts, Frank Perdue is even tougher than you are. He has to be. Every one of them comes with his money-back quality guarantee.

It takes a tough man to make tender chicken breasts.

Perdue.

McCabe's dedication to Frank Perdue's breasts makes this copy inevitable as well as enjoyable. I have the same regard for Ed McCabe as I have for any writer who seriously approaches his craft with kidlike enthusiasm for something great.

Style allows me to believe over and over that advertising was invented yesterday. As I write, I am looking at a full-page ad ripped from yesterday's copy of *The New York Times*. This case history ad (for a New York agency) was so shockingly original and unexpected (see Figure 8-1) that I had to write to one of its creative directors to applaud it.

The agency (McCaffrey-McCall) had just been fired by its client, J.C. Penney. The copywriter (Ted Shaw), who had poured 14 years of heart, guts, and soul into Penney's business, wrote the ad the same day the agency was fired. He showed it to agency president David McCall and within 24 hours it ran. When I called Ted Shaw to ask him what prompted the ad, he said "I just wanted to show everybody we had a little class over here."

I only wish that I had written it myself. Nor am I alone in my admiration of its style. At this very moment there is a client who is thinking to himself, I wish my agency had style like that.

Figure 8-1

Tinkerers Be Damned

If any young writer doubts that the style is your best revenge, let him try rewriting a familiar campaign theme and see what happens. This from the ink-stained Leo Burnett:

Come to where the flavor is. Come to Marlboro country.

Here we have ten short, easy words forming a simple declarative sentence. Yet this arrangement has demonstrated a certain durability; the campaign is now well into its third decade. See what happens when we tinker:

Flavorwise, Marlboro country is where it's at.
If you like flavor, you'll love coming to Marlboro country.
Looking for flavor? You'll find it in Marlboro country.
There's only one place to come for flavor . . . that's Marlboro country.

It seems unlikely that Burnett could have made the line stick (unchanged for 25 years) with any of these variations. Try some other lines. See what happens when we alter the words to these classics:

Let your fingers do the walking. Alteration: Don't waste gas and time, shop in the Yellow Pages.
The one beer to have when you're having more than one. Alteration: Drink a lot of beer? Schaefer is the beer to drink.
Reach out, Reach out and touch someone. Alteration: Long distance brings you closer together.
I am stuck on Band-Aids, 'cause Band-Aid's stuck on me. Alteration: My Band-Aid's stuck on me, that's why I'm sticking with Band-Aid.

The writer's meaning in the altered lines is still intact, but the music is gone.

When writing headlines, if you haven't gone too far, you haven't gone far enough. When you're convinced that it's great, go for ten percent more. "Polish, polish, polish," says Phil Dusenberry. Headlines are fragile and particularly vulnerable to the tinkerer's sweaty hand.

Note the headline (Figure 8-2) that I did when I was a troubleshooter at SSCB.

What I was up to was relatively simple. Advertising hasn't been attracting the best and brightest talent from the college crop for ten years or so. The all-type ad is an attempt to get this group's attention, break down misconceptions, and present my case. When I presented the ad to our president, he said, "Great, but let's change the headline."

"To what?" I asked.

Figure 8-2

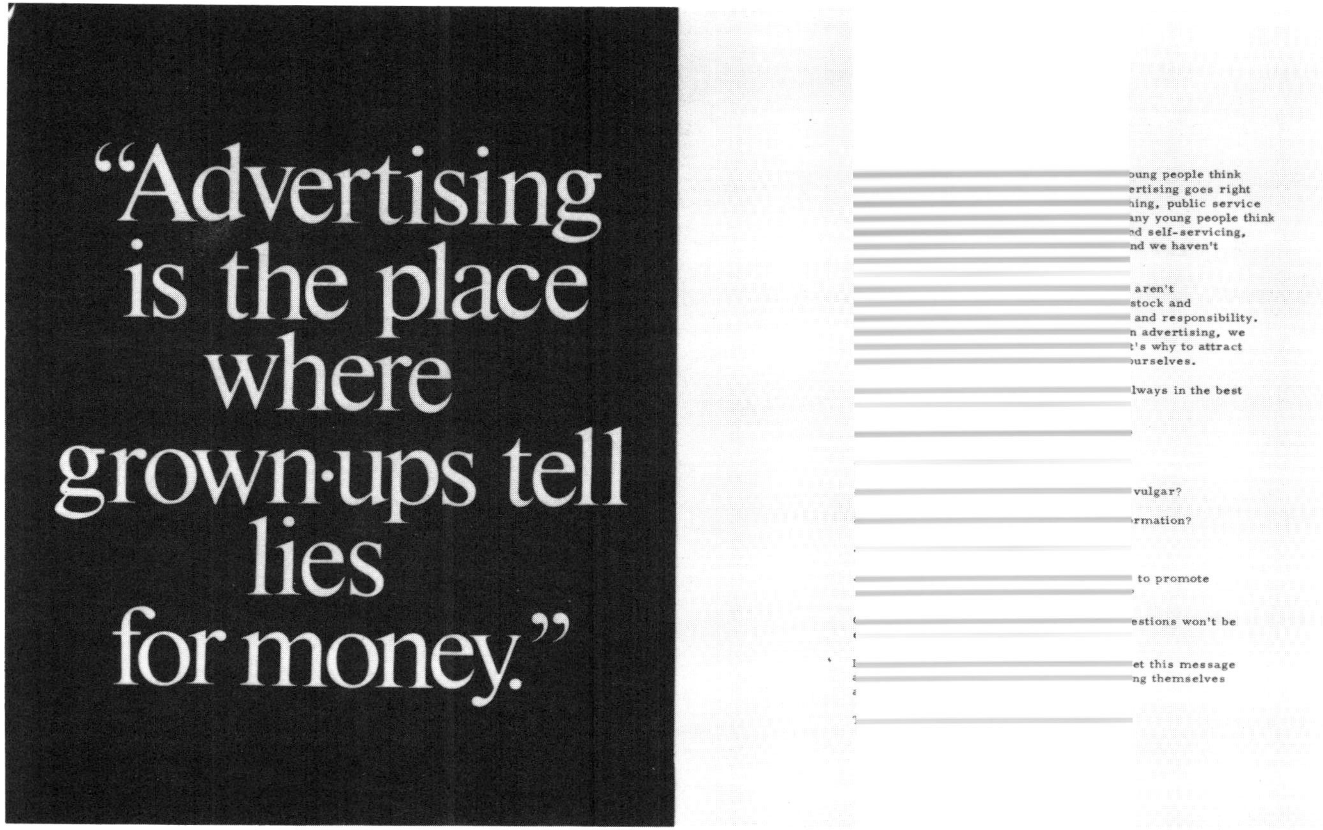

"Advertising is the place where grown·ups tell lies for money."

oung people think
ertising goes right
hing, public service
ny young people think
d self-servicing,
nd we haven't

aren't
stock and
and responsibility.
n advertising, we
t's why to attract
ourselves.

lways in the best

vulgar?

rmation?

to promote

stions won't be

at this message
ng themselves

"Something positive like "Advertising is a great place to work," he replied.

There's only one explanation for irrevocable differences like this: Advertising executives have careers. Copywriters don't.

Style: An Increment to Sales

Copy style not only reveals the spirit of the writer, it reveals the spirit of the product. Style is an increment to sales. The product is given its distinction by the very style that the writer lends. Following are the works of seven writers. Their magics are various. They offer considerable instruction on the merits of emotion, hunch, warmth, candor, and what Leo Burnett calls "intelligent daring."

Compassion revealed: AYDS campaign (Figure 8-3).

Here is a writer with a real sense of mission. The typewriter was not her first stop. She took the trouble to try to understand the suffering and anxiety of being fat.

She sat down with overweight people to find out how the product changed their lives.

Figure 8-3

She writes as a close friend would write to another with sincerity and compassion. The writer: Ruth McCarthy.

A knowing humor revealed: Ziploc storage bags (Figure 8-4).

This writer possesses a rare talent indeed. He knows how to be funny and sell the product at the same time. He doesn't decorate with humor—the humor

...ᵐᵉ ᵐʸ ʲᵒᵇ ᵃˢ ᵃ ʷʳⁱᵗᵉʳ ᵉᵃˢⁱᵉʳ.

A killer revealed: Volvo campaign (Figure 8-5).

No ambiguity here. The writer is a killer. His style is quick, stilettolike. His headlines ring with bareboned logic. His target: Detroit and sloppy automotive design that ultimately leads to premature death. When the American car owner was demanding value, this copy delivered it in the form of a European import—Volvo.

The writer: Killer McCabe, who has this to say on style: "It's not fair to inflict your own style on a strategy. If this was a killer ad, it was only because Volvo found itself in a killer marketing environment."

A rebel revealed: Levy's campaign (Figure 8-6).

"It broke all the rules. That's why it's my favorite ad," says veteran Judy Protas about this Levy's classic. "It said what people didn't say out loud. The old man [Bernbach] encouraged it. And the client was thrilled," added Protas.

The little girl revealed: Clairol's "Does she or doesn't she?" campaign (Figure 8-7).

This writer knows how to take advantage of being a girl. As she says, "The attractiveness and softness of a woman make it easier to function—that's why I've always said, 'Don't give up the advantage of being a girl.' "

Does this writer really believe that blondes have more fun? "The thing about being a blonde is that you don't have to be pretty. There is a kind of aura of light that comes off your face when you're a blonde, which is much rarer than being a middle brown."

This campaign made hair coloring appealing, not something to be ashamed of. It was the forerunner of new wave campaigns that broke away from the old U.S.P. school, which made up a problem and then offered a manufactured solution.

The writer: Shirley Polykoff.

A little kid revealed: Lipton soup (Figure 8-8).

Figure 8-4

517

(vo): Since 1975, lettuce is up 61%.

MAN: That's a lot of cabbage.

(vo): Mushrooms 46%.

WOMAN: Indeed!

(vo): Grapes? 82%!

MAN: It's fruitless.

(vo): In today's economy, you need Ziploc Storage Bags.
With their unique seal, Ziploc Bags are a zip to lock,
and they stay locked...so foods stay fresher, longer.

BUGS BUNNY: What's up Doc?

(vo): Carrots! 138%

BUGS: Oh, no!

148

Figure 8-5

Point of fact. Three little kids—a photographer, an art director, and a writer.

The objective was to catch the magic of the line "It tastes like Mother just made it" for Lipton soup.

First, the photographer shot dozens of rolls of film. The picture had to work hard. It had to communicate fun, warmth, and satisfaction.

Enter the art director and writer, who tells the story this way: "From the mass of photos, our "W's" picture leapt out at us. Then occurred the mysterious

149

Figure 8-6

process called creativity. To the right picture we added the right headline. When they came together, the rightness was irrefutable."

When that happens you feel a lot like a little kid yourself.

The photographer: Howard Zieff.

The art director: Tom Melahan.

The writer: Eli Kramer.

Style is not a trick of grammar or a slavish devotion to copy principles. Style emerges from an attitude of the mind. It is something you demand from yourself. The winning approach is by way of simplicity, order, and sincerity, thus drawing the consumer's attention to the sense and substance of the product.

150

Figure 8-7

If the copy idea is the result of first-class thinking, the mood and temper of the writer will come through, but never at the expense of the product.

REMINDERS FOR WRITER AND CLIENT

The following section contains a number of my own observations. I don't mean them to be rules, although they are presented in that form. If you're a writer, consider them reminders of things you already know but sometimes forget. If you're a client, think of them as guideposts in judging your advertising.

Figure 8-8

"The W's tickle when they go down"

And the O's roll. And the K's go bump, bump. And the L's wobble. It's a happy inspiration, this new Alphabet Vegetable soup from Lipton. It has alphabets shaped from enriched egg noodles . . . a gardenful of crisp, fresh vegetables, a sea of brawny beef stock. It's exactly what you'd expect from Lipton: another delicious soup that tastes like Mother just cooked it.

Does It Have an Idea?

You've got what it takes . . .
Share the spirit . . .
Share the refreshment . . .
Share the joy . . .
You never had it this fresh . . .
Tasty, tangy, tempting . . .
Go as wild as you want . . .

This is not a parody. These are headlines from that crowning achievement in graphic confusion, *People* magazine. None of them is an ad because none of them contains a clean, emphatic selling idea. Now, into the gray sameness drop a real idea:

A benefit line presents a compelling idea in a memorable set of words. Most ads do not bother to include a benefit. They are merely small deluges of adjectives. Another magazine, please.

> The civilized way to surrender . . .
> The most glamorous women use . . .
> A gift of good taste . . .
> Sturdy, trim, capable . . .
> Winning, worldly, and well-bred . . .
> The joy of good living . . .
> His nose is twitching and there's a smile on his face, chances are he's
>   dreaming about brand "X" dog food . . ." (Chances are he's a sick puppy.)

Now, in the midst of this, drop a benefit line:

> The oil that saves you gas.
> So advanced, it's simple.
> Everywhere you want it to be.
> The bread spread (Figure 8-9).

If these sentences seem almost childlike, recall such lines as "To be or not to be" or "All men are created equal." Ed McCabe was right: "Show me something great, and I'll show you a bunch of monosyllables."

Is It Visual?

Juicy copy. Juicy visuals. That's Hot 'n Juicy, my all-time favorite fast food campaign. Straight product sell sells product, not writer.

To Dick Rich, copy is not so much style, but a way of thinking. "Wendy's believed it had a better hamburger. They had this line: 'Quality is our recipe.' All

Figure 8-9

There's one more sandwich in there somewhere.

A sandwich just isn't a sandwich without the tangy zip of
Miracle Whip salad dressing from Kraft. "THE BREAD SPREAD"

I did was add visual enjoyment to that thought. It sounds so simple. Anyone could have done it. But they didn't. I did.

"It's a combination of marketing intuition, defining the right problem, and applying your creative skills. I've always felt what a person does is already within that person. My stuff *feels* like my stuff."

Like all great copy, the words create their own visuals—Wendy's customers go to great lengths not to have juice drip on their clothing. My favorite: Two

154

nuns protecting their habits. While McDonald's and Burger King do a good job, they also have a ton of money. (What do you think they bill a year? Whatever you guessed was off by $50 million, on the low side.) For something that goes in someone's mouth, nothing put it together like Hot 'n Juicy.

Figure 8-10

It's like opening a present.

companies get so wrapped up with technique they forget that they have to sell things to people. We sold love."

Take Risks

Earlier in this chapter, I said that there were no rules for writing successful copy. What I can give you is the number one rule for failure: Write to make everyone happy. Don't do it. If you're willing to try for something great and it fails honestly, it's better than running an ad in gray-safe land. If you're a writer, insist on the freedom to fail. If you're a creative director, the most important thing you ever do is to leave a talented person alone.

By playing it safe, you run the biggest risk of all.

The writer of these ads knows where the real pleasure of the business is. This ad (Figure 8-11), sponsored by the Episcopal Church, takes on religion's upper crust—TV ministers, and charismatics who would rather be born again than just saved like the rest of us. The only regret I have is that it wasn't my church that ran it. I'm sure it caused hostility in the church community and cost the Episcopalians dearly at collection time.

On risks, the creators, Tom McElligott and Nancy Rice, had this to say: "A strong campaign that wasn't bitten to death by the usual array of committee guppies." Taking risks with words always involves a battle. Most people are afraid of words because they are afraid of making mistakes in the open. Clients and even agency personnel will contend that the "average reader" won't understand such copy. Remind them that no such mythical person exists.

Use Nouns and Verbs

Nouns and verbs give copy its succinctness, toughness, and directives for action. Use plain declarative sentences. The following posters and postertype pages are explicit examples (see Figures 8-12, 8-13, and 8-14).

Use Words and Pictures

If the picture is worth a thousand words, the right picture with the right words is worth a thousand more.

In this Torn Ocean ad for El Al Airlines (Figure 8-15), the words by themselves supply all the information. But with the visual the power of the ad is magnified a thousandfold. The lesson here is that words and pictures together persuade consumers better than copy or pictures alone.

Don't Push the Belief Factor

Nothing is more wearing to a writer than the endless urge to magnify minuscule differences in parity products. This happens when a client believes that he has to persuade consumers that his product is superior to others in the category. Take a commodity like soap. One client for ten years has been on a

(Text continues on page 160.)

Figure 8-11

Figure 8-12

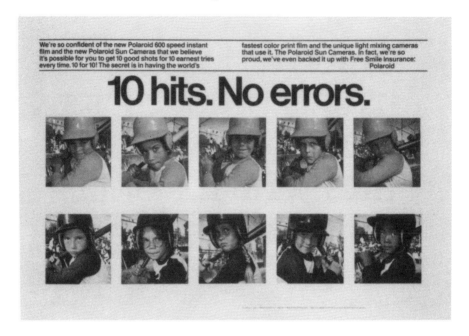

Figure 8-13

Figure 8-14

See Jane burn 30% more calories.

Tests prove that running with Heavyhands not only increases aerobic capacity, but also burns between 30% and 100% more calories than running without Heavyhands.

At the same time, Heavyhands help tone and strengthen major muscle groups *throughout* the body, while decreasing the danger of injury.

Find out why more and more serious runners everywhere are using Heavyhands at your local running store. **Heavyhands™ from AMF.**

Figure 8-15

strategy that claims that his soap doesn't leave soap film; therefore, you'll feel cleaner with his product. The fact is, you can't see or feel soap film. Soap film is beyond the consumer's experience. "Even if there was soap film on me, my towel would get it off." We heard this over and over again in focus groups.

I have actually seen this client in his own frustration say, "What's wrong with them? Don't they understand they've got soap film?" Yet, this soap is an excellent product. It would be better served to dump a strategy that supports an element of disbelief and start with a more believable premise. Like Dial's deodorant position—"Aren't you glad you use Dial? Don't you wish everybody did?" Or

160

Safeguard's unique "the smallest soap in the house" positioning. Or Dove's "one-quarter cleansing cream" story.

Generics

Most products are identical. This is especially true in the highly competitive

All mouthwashes fight bad breath, but only one "Fights bad breath . . . doesn't give medicine breath."

All hand lotions relieve dryness, but only one gives you "intensive care."

All detergents clean clothes, but only one is strong enough to get at the "ring around the collar."

All express services offer overnight delivery, but "if you absolutely, positively have to have it," you'd know where to go.

All fabric softeners offer softness; only one gives you "clothes you can't wait to jump into."

There are many performance luxury cars available; one is "the ultimate driving machine" (see Figure 8-16).

Does It Bury the Idea?

In a recent ad for Aim toothpaste, there is a strong copy idea, but it is buried.

The copy in the ad focuses on something else—cavities. Although important, cavity prevention is fast becoming a generic benefit. All fluoride toothpastes are generally accepted as effective in fighting cavities. What's more, the category leader, Crest, has for 25 years singlemindedly employed superior cavity prevention as its reason for being. In a commodity category, Crest users are extremely loyal. Yet, this ad goes head-on against established competition. Lever knows the score, yet they forge ahead and try to be Crest when they can't.

Aim should try something else.

Aim was the first gel. It quickly netted Lever Brothers a 6–7 percent share of market (one share point equals $7 million) with a copy line that told the world to "Take Aim against cavities." Now, in a category where taste and price are the name of the game, all of Aim's competitors have gels.

So, where's Aim's leverage?

Figure 8-16

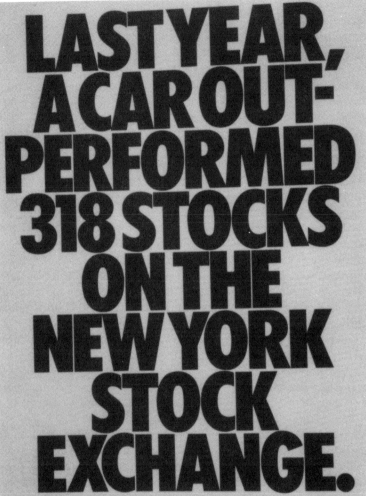

The leverage is in what we hear again and again in focus groups. "Getting my kids to brush regularly is a hassle. I wish there was a toothpaste that would make brushing fun."

Therein lies the buried treasure. A single line that has appeared in Aim's copy since its introduction, but it is never leveraged. It suggests the perfect

Clever is the writer who is not content with ordinary questions, but must invent kinky ones. A headline in *Glamour* magazine asks: "What kind of woman dingos?" It all depends on what kind of dingo-bat she is.

Clever is the writer full of three-dot leaders whose best ideas occur on the 3:45 out to the Hamptons. This in *Vogue:* "Here . . . for the summer . . . the perfect soap . . . your lovely face, your skin . . . de-filmed . . . de-flaked . . . de-turged." We will "de-turge" them on the air, at sea, and on the beaches.

Clever is the writer who believes that the first thing he puts down on paper will be of gripping interest to everyone. For a New York City bank, a headline introduces us to a "Major milestone in personal banking." Will Major Milestone please report to the copy general's office?

Clever is the writer who speaks a language all his own. An ad seeking funds for an organization committed to Christian brotherhood refers to a recent get-together as an "Interrace interface." He's not heavy; he's my interface.

"Clever" is not an endearment. To have one's copy referred to as clever is the kiss of death. Clever copy for the most part is an ego-blurb that will repel any intelligent reader. It says that you're a show-off, take short-cuts, and have nothing to say. It tells everyone that you haven't done your homework.

Young writers should understand: Copywriting is more than word-slinging. As defined by Len Sugarmann, "Great copy is usually a balancing act between relevancy and the unexpected."

DOES IT CONTAIN WEASELS?

Weasels are small deceptions. (Note the weasel in the preceding sentence!) They are the leeches that suck believability out of copy.

In the travel section of *The New York Times*, a resort hotel offers an English-type grille menu. Unhappy the tourist who arrives to find a hotel-type hotel menu.

A product for hemorrhoid sufferers offers "temporary relief in many cases." "Temporary" is fleeting, and in "many" cases there is no relief at all. "Many" is a sinister "double weasel." The word not only qualifies the number of actual cases (does it mean thousands of cases? a thousand? several hundred? several?), but qualifies what this copy desperately wants to say: "all cases."

Beware the natural margarine and the all-expense free trip to Honolulu. Exercise extreme caution with the birth control device promising 97 percent effectiveness (when used according to instructions). If your glass is only "virtually spotless," chug-a-lug your beer straight from the bottle. Avoid "fresh carton tomatoes." They give salads the distinct taste of cardboard. Steer clear of the boutique that sells "tailored shirtings." It's a good way to lose your shirt.

If your kids eat a lot of cereals, watch out for: "Time for some complete breakfast with Count Chocula." This ranks up there as one of the more repellent constructions of our time. There are more than just a few parents in the cereal business who should be ashamed of the junk they try to sell to their own kids.

Resist weasels. Even at the client's request. Remind him that his audience does not consist of visiting Martians. If that doesn't work, remind him of the guy you know at the F.T.C. The point is, if you've got an honest concept, you'll sit down and find an honest way to express it.

SOURCES

The secret to winning copy is curiosity about every aspect of your business. It's what a writer does on his feet that counts.

Be forever a student. Learn all you can about the category. Look at competitive reels. Make sure the account group writes up regular analysis of the competitor's copy. Try to figure out where the enemy is vulnerable. Copy capitalizing on a competitor's weakness can hurt and even put him out of business.

Go to client meetings. Listen—you might think you know a lot, but nobody knows more about his product than the client. What a smart client says can and often does lead to solutions that you would never think of yourself.

Spend time in the supermarket. It's an opportunity to get one-on-one with the consumer. Learn how other people shop. Why they pick one package of hot dogs over 20 others. It may be for price: a ten-pack of private label hot dogs could sell for up to $1 less than, say, Hebrew National. Some hot dogs cost as much per pound as steak. But mothers are fearful about the contents of hot dogs. If they have the confidence that it's "real meat," they'll pay the premium price. So sell quality.

At my local Grand Union, I meet a lot of friends. I always ask them why they pick brand X. The answer I get back most often is "I have a coupon." In today's price-driven economy, it only demonstrates just how persuasive your copy has to be to maintain brand loyalty.

That's not all you can learn in a supermarket. You can learn cleanliness,

commercials. It means millions of additional "squirts" to Lysol business.

On Crest, letters told us that loyalty to the product was well over the norm in a fickle category. Advertising for Crest always makes sure that the loyal user gets a reassuring pat on the back.

Finding extended uses for your product can lead to a total restaging of an old product. Look at Arm & Hammer's baking soda. It meant millions of new sales when the copy suggested putting an open box in the refrigerator to absorb food odors.

The time you're willing to spend away from the typewriter gives you one huge advantage—you know more. Curiosity, more than any other intangible, provides the highest measure of a person's talent.

Finally, God knows how many hours I've spent asking myself if I was really put on this earth to write about bad breath and cavities. I'm not Updike. But I'd like to approach the next ad I write with optimism. I'd like to think that the next thing I do is going to be famous. That's important to me.

I'm as free to tell the truth, to strive for excellence as the next writer. I'm content at the typewriter and grateful that I'm still at it. In this respect I have never had the urge to apologize because I get paid for doing what I love to do. When the thought of writing another line hangs over me like an ugly cloud, I often console myself with this prayer: Lord, provide me with a useful product, short copy, and an inescapable benefit.

BORN OR MANUFACTURED?

Can copywriting/talent be taught? Mal MacDougall, of Hill, Holliday, Connors, Cosmopulos/NY, says no. "Copy is a second part of the word. A writer isn't something you become. It's something you are."

Gene Federico of Lord, Geller, Federico, Einstein is emphatic: "No. You can uncover talent. You can instill a kind of energy that drives talent to kick themselves and never be satisfied. But taught? Never."

Bill Backer, who at the age of six wrote his first song, says, "99 percent no—it's something you're born with, a desire very early in life to write or draw."

Ed McCabe says no. He quit school when he was 15 to work in an advertising agency. For some, education is a liability.

Although there are good schools, courses, and instructors, nothing substitutes for a real job at a real agency writing on a real assignment. In an agency, you learn firsthand:

The constraints of the business.
How to write under pressure.
The importance of relevance and clear communication.

Talent is in the genes. You can't teach it. You can nurture it, fire it, fuel it with a desire to accomplish something constructive. You can encourage an attitude that settles for nothing less than excellence. You can supply certain guidelines and tools. You can provide chemistry and an environment where people are free to fail and have fun. You can create a sane asylum for talent, and that's it. The only possible thing to be taught is the value of hard work.

Finally, my own experience tells me that experience counts heavily. I remember a "60 Minutes" segment featuring Garson Kanin. He tells the story of a Connecticut town that suffered a total power outage. No one could fix it. Finally, they found the man who installed the system. A very old electrical engineer living in a retirement home. He went to the power station with a mallet and started tap-tap-tapping until he tapped one switch and all the lights came on. He sent a bill to the power company for $1,000.02. He itemized the bill. Tapping: 2 cents. Knowing where to tap: $1,000. That's what experience does for a copywriter. It tells you what to tap. And who.

CORPORATE ADVERTISING

The business of business is very much on the scene. The galvanized faces of CEO's grace magazine covers. Their stories bulge the business stacks in libraries and book shops.

As late as 1984, *Forbes* averaged 34 pages of corporate ads per issue. Witness the Ginzazation of Times Square, where Sony, Panasonic, Toshiba, and Hitachi billboard their American presence.

Scanning corporate advertising in the *Wall Street Journal, Business Week, The New York Times, Time,* and *Fortune,* I was hit with an idea for a new game—Just Buzz. Wanna play? Look at these three columns:

systems	confidence	excellence
commitment	tomorrow	trust
spirit	achievement	technology
research	science	future
soaring	understanding	quality

Or, if you want people to invest in your computers, "Systems winning your trust" says it very nicely.

Touting its new Zip Code Plus Four delivery service, the postal department "Is addressing tomorrow, today." As a frequent addressee, I depend on the postal service for fleetness (getting money to my impoverished son at college). To me, a word is a word and "zip" ain't it. "Turtle code" or "What the hell's your hurry?" code would be more accurate.

So at first glance, corporate advertising appears to be cliche-ridden, boring, lofty, and self-serving. Setting its own booby trap, it brags, it spews copy points, it refuses to talk to people like people. It's all the things we dislike about big business: phoney, calculated, and unfriendly.

Yet, there is an irresistible need for corporate America to stand up and stand for something today. There must be numerous examples on the up side.

I called a person who should know: Fred Poppe, chairman and CEO of Poppe Tyson (an agency that specializes in business-to-business advertising) and author of *The 100 Greatest Corporate and Industrial Ads.*

I said, "Fred, I want this book to be positive. What can I say about the state of corporate advertising and why it's so awful?"

Poppe conceded that he, too, is tired of "esoteric corporate ads that address themselves to the energy crisis, pompous self-serving corporate-conscience ads on environmental posturing." And he added, "I'm fed up with legal mumbo-jumbo from lawyers who stop us from writing old-fashioned hard-hitting ads."

Poppe claims that corporate ads can still "sizzle and sell something. I'll send you some material that'll change your mind."

As promised, a package arrived the next morning with several articles penned by Poppe plus a copy of his book. This was good stuff. In one article, Poppe asked: How do you create a good corporate ad? The same way you create a good campaign for any product.

167

Define your target—who do you want to reach and how do they now perceive you?

Analyze your situation. What's good? What's bad?

Develop a strategy—what do you recommend doing?

Deal with *the* top honcho. Poppe attaches considerable importance to this. He says, "nine out of ten times the CEO or president is the corporate conscience. He's the one you must have at all the input meetings. He's the one who approves the plan, the budget, the work, if he's smart," adds Poppe.

Leafing through Poppe's selection of "the greatest," I realized these were not as much corporate messages as they were simply great ads.

I recalled a quote in the Poppe material by Phil Dougherty of *The New York Times:* "Corporate advertising is like dropping coffee on a dark blue suit; makes you feel nice and warm, but nobody notices it."

The difference here is that I *did* take notice. The ads in Poppe's book span 60 years. Without exception, every ad was driven by a strong concept. The "Keep America beautiful" series by Marsteller, Inc., for example, which featured Iron Eyes Cody, a native American with a tear rolling down his face.

Most books on advertising include this "man-in-the-chair" ad for McGraw-Hill written by Henry Slesar in 1958 (see Figure 8-17). The publisher prints 15,000 copies a year to handle requests. The ad has run in Russian, German, Italian, French, and Chinese.

This is one of my all-time favorite campaigns (Figure 8-18). It's spacy. No drapery. Doesn't look corporate. The concept is ballsy and provoking. The copy instructs the reader on the value of this prestigious business medium. The picture, sullen and stubborn, captures, as Poppe observes, "their insight into the Oriental mind."

Typical early Doyle Dane (Figure 8-19). Stock photo picked by Bill Taubin. Great copy by Chuck Kollewe. Again, Poppe: "The last sentence is worth quoting because it says in very few but beautifully written words what kind of image Olin wanted to convey."

That's why, in the jungles of Vietnam, or throughout the world, the war against disease will go on long after man has made peace with man.

"For years Sears Roebuck had the image of a chain of schlock stores that sold a lot of cheap merchandise," says Poppe. I picked this ad (Figure 8-20) because it was easy to understand how the customer could think differently about a corporation that was willing to talk differently about itself.

The Sears ad recognizes the consumer as primary. The subject matter is humble and human. Created by Ogilvy & Mather in 1963, it is yet another

Figure 8-17

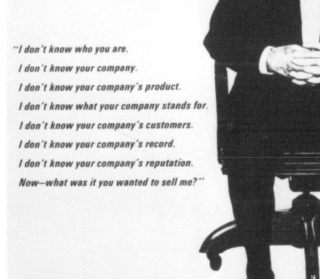

"*I don't know who you are.*

I don't know your company.

I don't know your company's product.

I don't know what your company stands for.

I don't know your company's customers.

I don't know your company's record.

I don't know your company's reputation.

Now—what was it you wanted to sell me?"

MORAL: Sales start **before** your salesman calls—with business publication advertising

McGRAW-HILL MAGAZINES
BUSINESS•PROFESSIONAL•TECHNICAL

Figure 8-18

Not for all the tea in China

Unlike the Russians (and their Pepski generation), the Peking regime in China isn't about to encourage the sale of Coca Cola—or any other American soft drinks. At least not now.

Will things go better with Coke in China if and when formal recognition from the U.S. comes? Maybe so. But one thing is certain. With one-fifth of the world's population, and an economy 50% larger than Britain's, China has the long-range interest of many an American marketer who is export-oriented.

In a recent article "Lightbulbs for the Lamps of China?", Forbes takes an illuminating—and highly scrutable look at Mainland China's import/export picture now, and in the not-too-optimistic future.

It's the kind of important, timely editorial coverage that continually attracts the readership of America's key executives. Those at the very top. And those determinedly on their way there.

In fact, Forbes rates first in the measured reading preferences of America's top management. The research firm of Erdos & Morgan made a reconfirming study of this among the corporate officers in 1300 of America's largest companies. The results of this study showed Forbes to be read by more of these top management executives than any other major business or news magazine.

No wonder Forbes was the *only* magazine in its field in 1976 to register a second record-breaking year in a row for advertising page gains. And is the clear winner as the fastest-growing business or news magazine of the past decade, with an advertising page gain of 72%. Compare that, for example, with Business Week—down 28% in that 1966 to 1976 period. Or Fortune—down 26%.

We look forward to new Forbes records in 1977, created by advertisers who select their media on the basis of advertising performance—ours and theirs.

Darn clever, those capitalists, to know that we're just their cup of tea.

FORBES: CAPITALIST TOOL

example of how an existing photo can spark a concept. According to Poppe, "When copy supervisor Bob Pasch saw the photo in a photographer's sample case, he decided he just had to build a Sears campaign around it."

Corporate Logos
Figure 8-91 is dedicated to the work of the great Saul Bass and to the client

rather succinctly: "It's market development 1990."

In the teeth of five major competitors, I.P. is staking its corporate edge on the positive feelings that younger audiences (high school, college students) will have about the firm in future years.

This campaign illustrates the *kind* of person young people want to hear from. Kurt Vonnegut tells how to write with style. John Irving on how to punctuate. Tony Randall on how to increase vocabulary. Malcolm Forbes on how to write a business letter.

The campaign underlines one of this book's dominant lessons: The most powerful kind of communication is the kind that generates positive word of mouth. Did you read this book? Did you see that movie? Have you tried this product?

I find it amazing how many times I've used the ads in this series to help make life a little better, easier, or richer for myself or those around me:

> At my request, our local library displays a stack of Michener's "How to Use the Library" near the reference section for high school and college kids.
> I never fail to pass out Vonnegut's "style" essay to new members of my copy group.
> Account people are forever grateful when I refer them to Edward Thompson's *How To Write Clearly.*
> My oldest son, "the English major," was turned in that direction thanks to essays by Steve Allen and James Dickey on the classics and poetry, respectively.

About the evolution of this campaign Fuess said, "It's a lot of work." Each ad takes four to five weeks to research and over a month to write and rewrite (young copywriters take note).

(Text continues on page 176.)

171

Figure 8-19

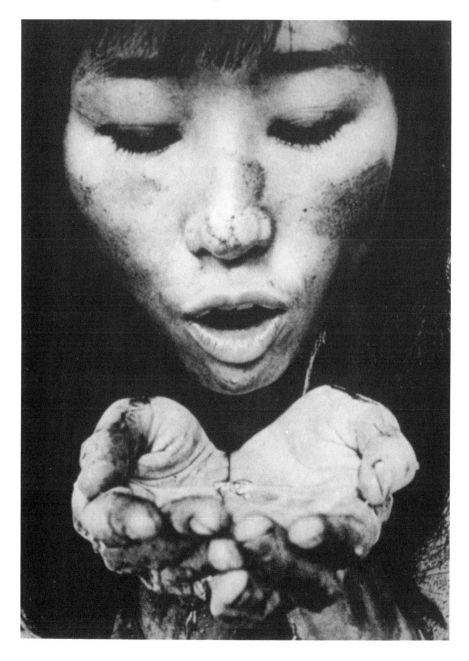

Figure 8-20

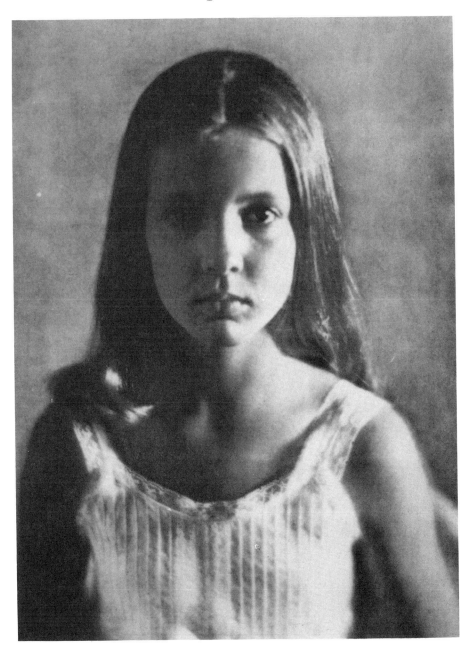

Bring your daughter to Sears, Roebuck and Co. for her first bra and girdle. Sears figure experts are trained to select the correct garment for every woman. But they take *special* pride in starting a youngster out right.

REMEMBER the day you bought your first bra? Was it an exciting, grown-up kind of day? Or awkward and embarrassing?

Sears takes great care to make sure its young customers remember this day with pleasure. Sears bra and girdle people know how to make your daughter feel at ease. Many of them are *graduate fitters*. This means they have completed Sears highly comprehensive figure-fitting training course – and passed a stiff written and oral examination.

Nobody asks, "What size?"

Your daughter's first step for her first bra at Sears, is into the fitting room. The Sears graduate fitter will keep her measurements on file at the store – and bring them up to date as she grows, and as her measurements change. This written record lists her size, figure type, style of bra and the fitter's comments.

But this is by no means a service for young girls only. When you go to Sears to buy a bra or girdle, the Sears fitter can measure you as carefully, too. And when you choose a Charmode bra or girdle at Sears, you can be sure of its quality and workmanship. For example, the elastic in the Charmode Cordtex® bra wears *longer* than any other elastic tested in the Sears laboratory.

Free alteration—on the spot

If a garment doesn't fit you *exactly*, it must be altered. Often the Sears fitter goes right to her sewing machine and makes darts and tucks on the spot. Free.

Other alterations are free, too. Taking in the hips of an "all-in-one" for a woman with a full bust and small hips. Placing flannel strips inside a girdle for extra comfort. Changing the position of garters. Special fitting of surgical and maternity garments.

Sears fitters know every woman can have a better figure – with a bra or girdle that *fits*.

The Sears way of doing things

This kind of professionalism is the Sears way of doing things. You find it in *all* departments—and in all Sears *people*, from graduate fitters to home decorators to TV repairmen. And *every* salesperson in *every* one of the 740 Sears stores.

It is their finicky attention to detail that makes Sears a "customer's store"– and lets Sears offer its famous promise *Satisfaction guaranteed or your money back*.

You'll find Sears *Charmode* bras and girdles in Sears stores and in the Sears catalog. You can't get better quality for the money. The same thing goes for girls' slips and petticoats. The slip this girl is wearing is just $1.98. Remember, you can always *charge* it at Sears.

Figure 8-21

ALCOA

CELANESE

CONTINENTAL

United Way

Bell System

WARNER COMMUNICATIONS

UNITED

LAWRYS

味の素KK

Ajinomoto Corporation Japan

    About the power of information in print Fuess added, "It's a lot more than information. People need help. And that's what this campaign is: It's help on paper." What a wonderful definition he has provided on what corporate advertising is and should be.

    Facts, faithfully presented against a human backdrop, continue to be the measure of successful major institution advertising.

Figure 8-22

How to write with style

By Kurt Vonnegut

International Paper asked Kurt Vonnegut, author of "Slaughterhouse-Five," "Breakfast of Champions" and "Cat's Cradle," to tell you how to put your own self and personality into everything you write.

Newspaper reporters and technical writers are trained to reveal almost nothing about themselves in their writings. This makes them freaks in the world of writers, since almost all of the other ink-stained wretches in that world reveal a lot about themselves to readers. We call these revelations, accidental and intentional, elements of style.

These revelations tell us as readers what sort of person it is with whom we are spending time. Does the writer sound ignorant or informed, stupid or bright, crooked or honest, humorless or playful—? And on and on.

Why should you examine your writing style with the idea of improving it? Do so as a mark of respect for your readers, whatever you're writing. If you scribble your thoughts any which way, your readers will surely feel that you care nothing about them. They will mark you down as an egomaniac or a chowderhead — or, worse, they will stop reading you.

The most damning revelation you can make about yourself is that you do not know what is interesting and what is not. Don't you yourself like or dislike writers mainly for what they choose to show you or make you think about? Did you ever admire an empty-headed writer for his or her mastery of the language? No.

So your own winning style must begin with ideas in your head.

1. Find a subject you care about

Find a subject you care about and which you in your heart feel others should care about. It is this genuine caring, and not your games with language, which will be the most compelling and seductive element in your style.

I am not urging you to write a novel, by the way — although I would not be sorry if you wrote one, provided you genuinely cared about something. A petition to the mayor about a pothole in front of your house or a love letter to the girl next door will do.

2. Do not ramble, though

I won't ramble on about that.

3. Keep it simple

As for your use of language: Remember that two great masters of language, William Shakespeare and James Joyce, wrote sentences which were almost childlike when their subjects were most profound. "To be or not to be?" asks Shakespeare's Hamlet. The longest word is three letters long. Joyce, when he was feeling more than a little playful, could put together a sentence as intricate and as glittering as a necklace for Cleopatra, but my favorite sentence in his short story "Eveline" is this one: "She was tired." At that point in the story, no other words could break the heart of a reader as those three words do.

Simplicity of language is not only reputable, but perhaps even sacred. The Bible opens with a sentence well within the writing skills of a lively fourteen-year-old: "In the beginning God created the heaven and the earth."

4. Have the guts to cut

It may be that you, too, are capable of making necklaces for Cleopatra, so to speak. But your eloquence should be the servant of the ideas in your head. Your rule might be this: If a sentence, no matter how excellent, does not illuminate your subject in some new and useful way, scratch it out.

5. Sound like yourself

The writing style which is most natural for you is bound to echo the speech you heard when a child. English was the novelist Joseph Conrad's third language, and much that seems piquant in his use of English was no doubt colored by his first language, which was Polish. And lucky indeed is the writer who has grown up in Ireland, for the English spoken there is so amusing and musical. I myself grew up in Indianapolis, where common speech sounds like a band saw cutting galvanized tin, and employs a vocabulary as unornamental as a monkey wrench.

In some of the more remote hollows of Appalachia, children still grow up hearing songs and locutions of Elizabethan times. Yes, and many Americans grow up hearing a language other than English, or an English dialect a majority of Americans cannot understand.

All these varieties of speech are beautiful, just as the varieties of butterflies are beautiful. No matter what your first language, you should treasure it all your life. If it happens not to be standard English, and if it shows itself when you write standard English, the result is usually delightful, like a very pretty girl with one eye that is green and one that is blue.

I myself find that I trust my own writing most, and others seem to trust it most, too, when I sound most like a person from Indianapolis, which is what I am. What alternatives do I have? The one most vehemently recommended by teachers has no doubt been pressed on you, as well: to write like cultivated Englishmen of a century or more ago.

6. Say what you mean to say

I used to be exaggerated by such teachers, but am no more. I understand now that all those antique essays and stories with which I was to compare my own work were not magnificent for their datedness or foreignness, but for saying precisely what their authors

Should I act upon the urgings that I feel, or remain passive and thus cease to exist?

"Keep it simple. Shakespeare did, with Hamlet's famous soliloquy."

"Be merciless on yourself. If a sentence does not illuminate your subject in some new and useful way, scratch it out."

Chapter Nine
Making the Near-Blind See

FLIPPER PROOFING

Think of all the magazines that have been launched over the past few years. Consider how the old corner newsstand has grown. Today it has a corrugated roof, air-conditioning, central heating, and a lease. And can you spot one person riding a subway, commuter train, or plane who isn't carrying some kind of printed material?

The net impression is that there must be a lot of people reading.

Observe more closely. You will discover not readers but flippers. (A flipper is to printed media what a zapper is to electronic media. A zapper mutes or tunes out TV programming via remote control.)

After some 15 years of observing readers, my "most proficient flippers" award goes to the North Jersey commuters on the old Erie-Lackawanna. I have seen the best of them polish off the *Wall Street Journal* and the *Times* before they get to Hoboken.

Flippership is a reader's response to drudgery, a zombie reaction to newsprint overdose.

Page after page of cliches, puffery, and platitudes march across the optic tract. Every day, every reader in America is exposed to about 1,800 ads. Nine out of ten are so average that they cancel themselves out.

Invisible advertising is a virus, caused by the stereotypes that invade it. I have isolated four common strains of stereotype:

1. The target audience (for example, "advertising will appeal to jolly consumptive yuppies 21–45").
2. Representation (as Mr. Hairspray, Ms. Bouffant, and little Billy Boomer).
3. Headlines. Nothing informational. Nothing offensive. Nothing controversial.
4. Layout. The Gray page: one-third headline (for the writer), one-third picture (for the art director), one-third package (for the client). Nothing for the reader.

By contrast, an ad with stopping power has:

1. One thought.
2. One major visual that is integral to that thought.
3. No client fingerprints.

These are the ads that win awards and sell like crazy.

When it comes to print, there are clients who just can't keep their hands off—who insist on a laundry list headline, cliche photos, plastic people, big box shots. And they can't stop filling in white space.

If you're a client who believes that advertising plays only a minor role in ~~. . . . .~~

1. No selling line or information.
2. Expected visual.
3. Same old models in dumb poses and situations.
4. Logos as headlines or in headlines.
5. No white space.
6. Fly-speck copy.
7. Big package stealing from or substituting for human dramatization.
8. Unreal lighting.
9. Predictable premise.
10. No sense of newness in form or in content.

I'm certain that you found many of these beasties in your own print. Just one on a page is enough to reduce its stopping power. The result is always the same: a page that says, "I'm an ad, please don't read me."

I Dare You to Flip

People out there aren't interested in your advertising. Nor do your targets approach their morning paper prepared to think strategically.

A recent study devoted to how consumers receive ads on a personal level shows "that being influenced by advertising is not something to which people will readily admit" (source: Rosenfeld, Sirowitz, Lawson). Our advertising should take this attitude into consideration.

And I may as well add, it doesn't take a critic to know what is foolish, juvenile, and simple-minded. All it takes is a selective reader.

Judging a winning ad is a lot like judging a prize fight. Bring in one of your eight-year-old kids and ask him who won. "That one," he'll say.

With this in mind I offer the following exercise: I dare you to flip.

The intention is not to lay down rules (which only entrap us) but to establish freedom from the rules.

Think of these examples as elements to look for or things to think about the next time you have to write, approve, produce, or pay for a print ad.

The flipper-proof page defies the reader to ignore it.

The flipper-proof page offers even more than an invitation—it issues a command to "notice me" through irony (Figure 9-1) or contradiction (Figure 9-2).

The flipper-proof page has been stripped of nonessentials. The effect is so riveting that it must, by necessity, stand out in the surrounding sameness.

This "I dare you to flip" campaign employs the use of heightened humanity. In this case, a familiar face that has been elevated by the ingenious molding to copy concept.

See Figure 9-3 and please flip—if you can.

Trustworthy universals *do* exist. In the following campaign, it happens to be the attractiveness of the human body. This may be the best-looking campaign running today. It is so slick it shimmers. It is vivid and intense. It's the closest thing to pure art because it makes us "see" again, and it's a perfect example of a copywriter who was smart enough to shut up.

Please flip past Figure 9-4.

If you didn't go back and flip again, perhaps you should be embalmed.

Repeat: The flipper-proof page is not dependent on principles, but on intuition and taste. It is based on a feeling for the product, not some rule. When this happens, patterns are broken, surprises are sprung with inspired leaps of imagery (Figure 9-5) and word play.

Please flip.

Although advertising is by no means literature, they both have an important common feature, staying power. This campaign (Figure 9-6), utilizing the Chivas bottle to dramatize snob appeal to justify the price, is nearly 20 years old.

On reflection you can see that the force, authority, and cumulative persuasiveness of the above campaigns derive from two elements. First, the willingness of the marketing team to be their own best judges. Not because they know so much, but because they know so little about the so-called science of the business. They haven't been spending so much time on tracking studies that they've forgotten how regular readers look at things.

Second, the fun of being involved in any of these campaigns. And by fun I don't mean "fun, fun, fun"—I mean the fun of solving tough problems. The fun of presentation. Of selling. Of knowing your advertising is helping your business grow.

When outstanding work is being done and approved on a regular basis, you can be sure there are still agencies and clients in this business that aren't afraid to have fun (see Figure 9-7).

Figure 9-1

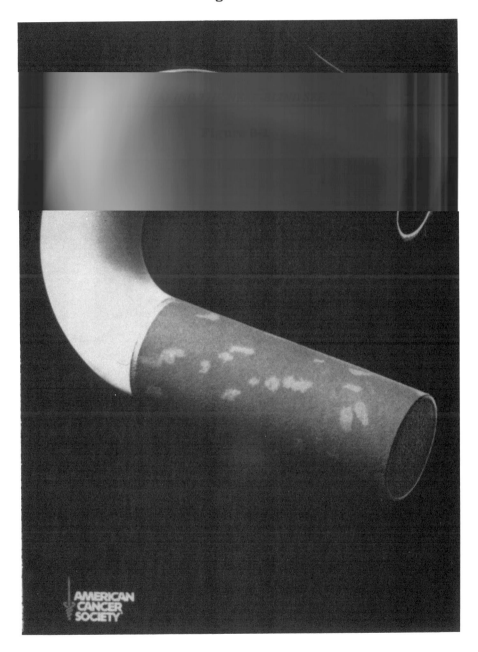

Figure 9-2

Figure 9-3

TYPE: THE TRUSTY RAZOR BLADE

I have ofttimes sat in amazement watching an art director cutting and spacing type with a razor blade, falling in love with curves and spaces.

I attributed this to the creative impulse. But I didn't have much sympathy for the exercise.

Perhaps it was my intolerance for what I thought was purely ornamental. To me, type was just another tool.

Well, I was wrong. Dead wrong. And the theoretician who said that art at a higher level is play was right.

Games can restore life. Playing with type is no exception. By playing (slicing is the art director's term), ordinary things become "extra" ordinary in an artist's

Figure 9-4

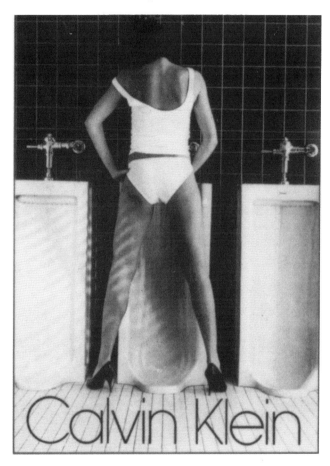

hand. If an art director's main concern is creating images that catch people's eyes, penetrate their minds, and cause them to act or feel, then I have to believe this thought provided by George Lois concerning type:

> Type is an arrangement of letters, words, and sentences by the designer to transmit a message. The true designer cuts and slices and spaces and hangs to make the reading of that message inviting, pleasurable, electric. The shape and feeling of the grouping of the words in conjunction with the architecture of the complete space, enhances and powers a good hunk of copy. So I keep slicing. For as you cut and slice, you make love to each straight line and curve and each word and letter becomes as exciting as the Parthenon.

Figure 9-5

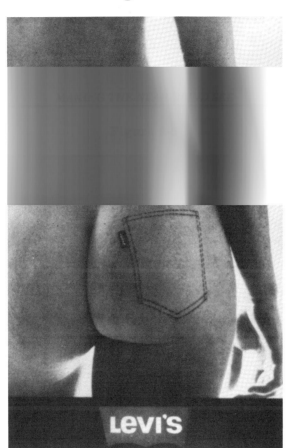

Can this really be? Even for a Greek?

Well, why not? Let's see what happens when words themselves are visualized. When the alphabet is magically transformed in word ideas that are capable of a stopping power all their own. Capable of communicating the emotion, the spirit, the tradition, the uniqueness, the competitiveness, and, yes, even the taste of the product itself.

If type on its own can be emotional, as demonstrated in Figure 9-8 by George Lois for *Esquire,* it can also be profane, as in this ad on behalf of the Holy Name Society of the Catholic Church (Figure 9-9).

Here is type as a unifying/identifying element—in the long-running and still remembered campaign for the Jamaica Tourist Board (Figure 9-10).

(Text continues on page 195.)

Figure 9-6

Figure 9-7

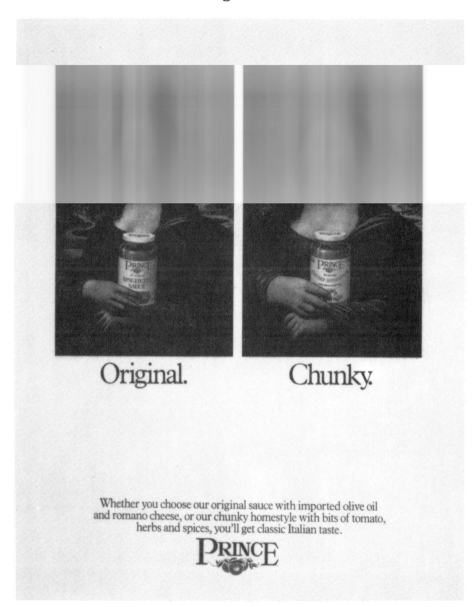

Original.   Chunky.

Whether you choose our original sauce with imported olive oil
and romano cheese, or our chunky homestyle with bits of tomato,
herbs and spices, you'll get classic Italian taste.

PRINCE

Figure 9-8

Figure 9-9

It can be uttered in prayer or in anger. The Holy Name Society needs you to keep it in prayer. Join.

Figure 9-10

If you can take your eyes off her face for a few moments, you may pick up a bargain in silk. Or perhaps even a Hasselblad.

In Jamaica, you have an excuse to stare. Faces like you've never seen before. Shades from a new spectrum. Eyes, cheekbones, skin, lips, hair — that have always belonged to different worlds. Here, together in one face.

You see a girl behind the counter of a silk shop. You wonder. How much of that loveliness is Africa? How much China? How much India? How much Europe? You can't always tell. Sometimes, Africa blends into China into India into Europe. Until the divisions are blurred, the lines of difference, lost. And what

comes out is a thing that belongs to none of them. Only to Jamaica. At its best, this new kind of beauty is fragile, dreamy, ethereal. At the very least, exciting, unexpected. So who could blame you for not paying attention to the purple silk sari she's billowing for you.

But if you *can* shift your eyes to the silk, you'll see that it's quite a buy. 60% less than the States. And French doeskin gloves. And Egyptian cottons. All 40% less.

Jamaica's duty-free prices are among the lowest in the world. Chivas Regal Scotch, $5.50 a fifth.

12-year-old Jamaican rum, $3.00. Seagram's V.O., $2.50 a fifth. Joy, Arpege, Aphrodisia, Chanel No. 5 —60% less. Professional cameras, hand-made by Jamaican George Hedley, $22.00. Hand-woven straw bags from the Victoria Crafts Market, $2.50. Leica, Canon, Nikon, and Hasselblad cameras, 45% off.

Jamaica? Among other things, it's the world's most beautiful discount house.

For more on Jamaican eyes, checkbones or rum, see your travel agent or Jamaica Tourist Board, Dept. IC, 630 Fifth Avenue, N.Y.C.

Figure 9-11

"Solid drink and good food. That's

Figure 9-12

The Charlie you kiss with.

How a lipstick makes your mouth feel is almost as important as how it makes your mouth look.

The creamy consistency of Charlie Extra-Extra-Shine Lipstick makes your mouth feel soft, creamy, moist.

The creaminess produces a luscious, glistening shine.

And the colors—37 lipsticks, 14 glosses—are as pure and distinct as they are special. And that's how it is with Charlie Lipstick.

Charlie Extra-Extra-Shine Lipstick.

REVLON

Figure 9-13

Harrings

Figure 9-14

GASP

GET ANGRY STOP POLLUTION

Let's begin with one word, in this case a proper noun: Charlie. See how the forceful and fanciful marriage of word and idea can lead to two solutions that are miles apart (Figures 9-11 and 9-12).

Perhaps you are beginning to see that type isn't something that comes along for the ride, but that newness in type counts, and that seeing something in a way

Figure 9-15

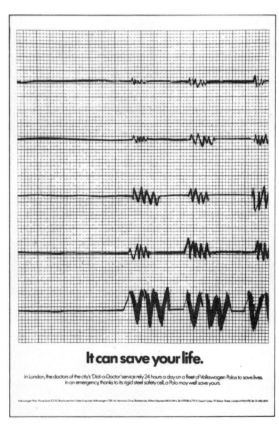

Figure 9-16

The next time you see an art director with a razor blade in hand, you'll know it's just another busybody who can't leave things alone. Who, through craft and determination, is trying to rub against the reader to stop, engage, and make an energetic sale.

From George Lois:

> The art director must have a love, not only for language, but for the *look* of language. To accomplish that, he would never go unarmed without his trusty razor blade.

PACKAGING

Recently, a new products manager asked my opinion about a new butter blend margarine. Lined up on the conference table were 20–25 competitors, including soft, light, diet, and whipped margarines. As packages, they represented the very worst in the art of gaudy overcommunication—two dozen creations from Rube Goldberg's drawing table.

Figure 9-17

There was, however, one exception. The new butter blend entry. The container was a smooth plastic crock, not a waxy cardboard box. The typeface was slightly embossed, not stamped by a machine. The character of the typeface was soft and swirly, as opposed to Las Vegas marquee. The words were set against a thin line drawing of a dairy farm scene. The brand was Shedd's. Instead of the usual hackneyed description underneath (spread, blend, and so on), the words "country crock" complemented the brand name (see Figure 9-18).

"How's this brand doing?" I asked, pointing to the package.

The new product manager gave me the facts: 8 percent share and gaining, outselling every premium, pound sales doubled last quarter, repurchase rate double the norm for a new product in the margarine category.

"It isn't fair," the manager whined.

"What isn't fair?" I asked. In a most sincere voice, he said, "That they're so smart."

It was the most inanely bizarre comment I've ever heard on any level. To him, the success of Shedd's country crock was a marketing riddle.

Shedd's was no better or no worse than any of the more established margarines. They all come from the same fats and oils technology. They all taste about the same, spread the same. The irony is that for years most established brands have been available in the same shaped container as Shedd's, only the trade called it a "tub" and it usually came in ugly yellow.

By adding "production values" (a term that should never be confined to TV) and by retooling the ordinary one-pound tub into two- and three-pound crock sizes, Shedd's doubled and sometimes tripled the "use up" rate, resulting in sales at twice the level.

I picked up the Shedd's package and put it next to the proposed butter blend product he was considering. I said, "Bob, your package is unbecoming, displeasing, distasteful. Shedd's is appealing, cultivated, tasteful. Its package looks country, smells country, feels country, almost tastes country, which gives any future advertising it does the bragging rights to key strategic words like fresh, dairy, pure, down-home, healthy, natural."

"But ours has butter in it. It tastes better," Bob said.

"It doesn't matter," I retorted. "Your package is so bad that no advertising in the world could tempt me to pick it up.

"Shedd's looks more like butter than butter. It doesn't have to say a word; all the signals are right there on the package. You'd do better ripping off its crock." (Two old names—Imperial and Mrs. Filbert's—already have.)

Was I arrogant to impose my taste on a client? You bet I was. That's what I get paid for.

Second question, who says I have any taste, anyhow? And how did I get it? Apparently "I caught it" somewhere between Pittsburgh and New York. I am living proof that Calvin Klein was right—"good taste can be learned." I try to

Figure 9-18

inflict it everywhere I can. Sneaking it into a client's work when they aren't looking. I really believe in the axiom that says: Great advertising is usually nothing more than a reflection of the tastes of the people who created it.

In spite of my arrogance, I had no luck with Bob.

Driving the cattle of his facts across my twitching face, he wore me down with the usual litany: "A new package would cost more, it would cut profit margins, besides we don't have time, we have to get out there."

We've all been to this meeting before. Good taste takes longer. That's why schlock was good enough for Bob. A product to cover his ass, out there on the shelf so he could point to it—another .01 share increment to help eke out this year's profit objective. He didn't want my opinion. He only wanted affirmation for his own lazy-brained decision.

What must be said for Bob is that in this, the decade of the entrepreneur, he was a custodian of the outhouse.

It never occurred to him that in a supermarket (particularly with package goods) customers don't first enjoy a product, they enjoy what's wrapped around it. If a product doesn't look appealing on the outside, nobody's ever going to find out what's good about it on the inside.

Dressed for Success

Over at Shedd's, his counterpart understood:

1. That the right package is not an advertising solution. It is a marketing solution that comes from a very definite strategy. And that the package itself is a reflection of that strategy.
2. That all successful products have two strengths—the quality of the product itself, and the brand images surrounding it.
3. That the more a client heightens quality the more justified the purchase (and price) of his product becomes. The absolute best strategy against generics is guilt: *If you don't buy this product, you're not providing the best for your family.* That kind of strategy is reflected up-front in the Shedd's package.

24-Hour Communication

A package is what we put out front to stop, announce, get attention. Fancy designer jeans, gold chains, expensive liquor, imported beer, tasteful cars, art, our cottages, our castles—all are packages.

Not long ago, I got one of these numerous sales calls from a financial guy. Now, nobody needs more help in this area than I do, but I always say no, 'cause I'm broke and can never afford them. This one I liked and told him to come up. After I hung up I wondered why. The answer: What he said came in a nice package—his voice.

Everything comes packaged or repackaged, from shopping bags to oysters, from art tables to garden hoses. "Sheet metal is packaging," said Helmut Krone. Remember the Ford Falcon back around 1963? Of course you don't. But a man by the name of Iacocca took most of the parts and put it in an exciting new package and called it Mustang.

A good package gives you 24-hour communication. It works uninterrupted before it's bought, even after it's bought, sitting on a kitchen or restaurant table. Packaging is the first step in the strategic positioning of your product. Don't leave the job to product engineers, package suppliers, or hacks.

Package Management

Clients coded with long-term strategies begin with package management. Today's consumers are in a hurry. Looks count. Visibility is crucial. Shelf space is precious. It's the marketer with a unified design who builds instant recognition and familiarity. The winner here is Pepperidge Farm. Stuffing, bread, snacks, cookies, I get the feeling they're everywhere.

The effect is close to what Roy Grace calls "compound interest," which he defined as "the quality of the parts getting larger and larger than it really is."

Check 'Em Out

Good package design reflects a concern for detail, fussing, and common sense. A great package is no different or easier to come by than great advertising.

In my many trips to the supermarket to research this chapter, I found it easy to spot at least a dozen or so packaging checkpoints.

Is every detail of the package well thought out?

Ready-to-eat dinners have been around for years—Morton, Swanson, Weaver, to name a few. One has left the category years behind.

The name: Le Menu. Here's sophistication with good old-fashioned snob appeal.

The marketer, Swanson, was smart enough to bury its own name. And smart enough to spend up-front on production values. Specifically, the photography, which makes an unglamorous ready-to-eat proposition downright tempting.

The heat-resistant plastic dish ready to pop into the microwave dramatizes the ease, convenience, and timeliness of the product. Le Menu is doing great. The contribution of tasteful and well thought out design cannot only be measured, it can be proved.

Is the packaging honest?

I've been watching people shop for years. Believe me, they read packages more carefully than they read the morning paper. You better be simple and up-front with your package. The winner in this category is Twinkies. The name and the clear cellophane wrapping make no bones about what it is. It's gooey. It's for kids. It's fun. Nutritionists and health nuts may hate me, but as a snack Twinkies will be around long after the granola bar bites the dust.

Is the package consistent with product personality?

The winner here is Ralston Purina.

The company must have 20 products for pups, dogs, kittens, and cats, including dry pet food that combines colors, shapes, sizes. Strong graphics capture the lovability of pets, give every package a personality.

In response to generic pet foods, which captured $160 million in sales as far back as 1982, Purina's strategy was directed to family pet owners who wanted quality. Purina is one company that understands: The better you sell a total product (in Purina's case, help for your pet to grow better and live healthier), the more positive the total share of mind.

Is the package lasting?

Is change the only way to keep pace with the changing world? In package design, sometimes the opposite is true. I refer to these as "untouchables"—under no circumstances should these packages ever be changed. My own favorite is Tabasco (see Figure 9-19). Hands-down winners are Listerine and Lysol spray. Both fight germs, odors, and potential disease. Both designs reflect functionality, strength, no nonsense. Both packages reek of efficacy. Both are untouchable leaders in their respective categories.

Does the package visualize benefit?

The winner here is Clairol's Nice 'n Easy hair coloring line. Each color and resultant shade is shown in a photo of a woman on the front of the package. In one store I counted 15 colors. That gives Nice 'n Easy 15 shelf facings. Basic rule of supermarket life: more facings, more traffic. More traffic, more volume.

Does the package reflect effort?

"A" for effort goes to Lea & Perrin's Worcestershire sauce. Its self-contained, gift-wrapped presentation separates it from all other table-embellishment brands and dramatizes the originality of the product itself. In truth, the paper package is probably much cheaper to produce than a box.

Is corny sometimes better?

If we were to sit around and wait until some art director or package

Figure 9-19

designer found a way to package Orville Redenbacher's popcorn any better than the mug shot of Orville Redenbacher himself on the front, we'd end up in the supermarket slums looking for a can of Chef Boy-Ar-Dee, the world's ugliest package.

Does the package personify?

One of the most used and useful methods of establishing a brand is through a personality—Aunt Jemima, Uncle Ben, Poppin' Fresh for Pillsbury, Speedy for Alka-Seltzer, Blue Bonnet, Mr. Peanut for Planters, the Quaker Man for Quaker Oats.

The winner for me—based on impressions, positive cumulative effect, and number of facings—is the Jolly Green Giant.

Does the combination of name and package tell me what the product is or does?

If I were introducing a new product, I would insist that the name not be a mystery. For example: Wondra. This product is both a cooking flour and a hand lotion. If I were coming out with any kind of new laundry detergent, I would not call it Dash or Dreft or Oxydol. I would approve of something like Spray N Wash. If I called my detergent Cheer, I'd qualify it, as Procter does, with All Tempa-Cheer. I've found many great name-stopping examples: Spic and Span, Mr. Clean, Mop & Glo, Wet Wipes, Cocktails for Two, Shake N' Bake, Total, Raisin Bran. Two stand-outs based on product concept and communication of concept through graphics logo and sales success are Stove Top stuffing and Lean Cuisine.

Does the package innovation match the product innovation?

The winner here is L'eggs. The whole concept capitalizes on the world's most pleasing esthetic shape—the egg. Name and product package have 100 percent integrity because each is integral to the other.

The perfume category has produced this winner: Chanel—bold, classic, unaffected.

The Package as a Delivery System

In the impressive time of less than a year, Aziza has polished off all competitors with an innovative nail color product—the Aziza Polishing Pen. The idea sounds simple. Take a pen. Take a nail color and get it to flow through the end. While Chesebrough-Pond's chemists developed the formula, it took the Pilot Pen Company in Japan to perfect the delivery system. The Polishing Pen is a breakthrough in both technology and packaging, to have the brush and polish in the same self-contained unit. It has the potential to make the 50-year-old brush and bottle business of competitors like Revlon, Max Factor, and Maybelline obsolete. Sales for 1985 were estimated to reach $30 million.

Stand Out or Be Counted Out

The elevation of the package as a strategic element expedites the sale where the sale is made—at the point of purchase.

Eighty percent of all purchases take place within that "critical :05" when the picking and choosing happens. As much as I've harped on the power of brand image, the trend toward short-term share bumps based on package, pricing, and promotion is growing.

This figures. Consumers are in a hurry; they want to get in and out of the store and make intelligent choices at the same time. If your package doesn't stand out, count it out.

THE POSTER

David Ogilvy once suggested that the poster was the only form of advertising that should be banned. Is it that Ogilvy doesn't like the sign business? Or that billboards encourage graffiti, or there just aren't enough good ones? Maybe he's just a bad doodler.

Going in the opposite direction, I would like to fling out as many arguments in favor of the poster as I can. In our constructed environment, every product, every page, every suburban mall, every city street corner has been designed, sometimes badly, sometimes well.

Within this distribution is the poster. George Lois, whose greatest impact in the graphic arts has been on the magazine cover as a poster form, believes that "The majority of truly great posters can stun the ego and add to the life and vitality of the city."

This poster (Figure 9-20) for Calvin Klein briefs resides in New York City at the corner of 45th Street and Broadway. Although there exists a certain degree

Figure 9-20

version poster to millions of passing strangers at Grand Central Station in New York City, brought its colors to Times Square. In a 30- by 50-foot niche on the facade of the Marriott Marquis hotel, a seasonal Kodak scene will be seen by 1.5 million people daily. A totally different demographic target than the 700,000 who pass the Grand Central mural, only four blocks away.

Picture Writers

Most of what we do in advertising is limited to :30.

A poster competing for attention has :01. It has to attract, explain, and sell in the blink of an eye.

This poster (Figure 9-21) is among the best in years. The written word, according to Nike, is no words. "Nike is one client who knows who they are," says writer Dan Weiden. "Our business comprises people who want to be great. Nike is no different. They pushed us to do this kind of work." The poster *is* the words. The creators have learned to "picture" their words with craft and guile.

As graphic association, the poster is the quickest way we have to reach an overburdened consumer in an overcluttered environment.

The Maximum and the Minimal

In the hands of a picture minimalist, the poster may well be the most harmonizing tool we have. A poster is a separate thing. It isn't surrounded by program matter or editorial print. A poster exists by itself, with the character of a complete thing.

A poster is the most opportunistic of all media. It takes advantage of an advertising negative—no one wants to look at it. The poster is an intrusion of a positive sort. The austerity of a well-designed poster demands the attention of the overloaded, indifferent consumer.

A poster concentrates a good idea. It forces a stripped-down interpretation.

A poster surprises—it goes beyond the routine. A poster isn't something you can fit into an interoffice envelope for approval.

Not lost in the Nike series is one of the oldest forms of advertising—the painted wall. If you're ever in the Hell's Kitchen area of New York City, look up in the air. It's a bird, it's a plane, no, it's Dwight Gooden delivering a pitch for Nike on a six-story brick billboard near the Port Authority Bus Terminal off Eighth Avenue.

"Any great ad, in any form, should warm hearts and cause people to act," says George Lois. "The greatest poster just does it in a bigger way."

Spectator Sports

Many readers will recognize the logo of the IBM Corporation and the underlined "W" on every Westinghouse product. This is the work of Paul Rand, the most influential graphic designer of our time.

206

Figure 9-21

Most heroes are anonymous.

Here's what he says about the obligation a designer has for the spectator:

> . . . because graphic design, in the end, deals with the spectator, and because it is the goal of the designer to be persuasive or at least informative, it follows that the designer's problems are twofold: to anticipate the spectator's reactions and to meet his own aesthetic needs.

What makes a good design is ultimately what you think the spectator wants.

Face to Face
Nothing is more hypnotic than the spectator seeing himself in another face.

This teenage antipregnancy campaign (Figure 9-22) for the city of New York was my first as creative director at Ketchum. It utilizes the stunning photography of Francesco Scavullo, America's foremost portraitist.

In a press conference at City Hall last summer, Harrison Golden, city comptroller, said, "I can see my own kids in these faces."

Commenting on the power of the face as a poster element, Scavullo said, "It's all in the eyes. I cast for eyes. It gives me positive pictures, not despair."

The Poster Symbol
Gene Federico of Lord, Geller, Federico, Einstein claimed that the poster was not his forte. So, I started him off on some other subjects. Finally, Federico got around to his main passion—craft as a simplifying element. He pointed to the poster. "A poster is not a means of self-expression, it's a way to convey a client's message. We're marketers first," he stressed, "not just artists."

As an example he offered the Charlie Chaplin character created for IBM. Even though he was created for TV, "He's a poster symbol."

"What's a poster symbol?" I asked.

"You can put anything down underneath that symbol and it works" (see Figure 9-23).

"As a poster symbol it carries, if you get the first grab."

Sic Transit
Here's a transit poster (Figure 9-24) that broke every advertising record for being stolen. Out of Fallon McElligott Rice, it is for the 7 South Eighth for Hair Salon in Minneapolis. The pictures themselves are from movie clip files.

This poster campaign is included in several college textbooks, and of all the exhibits I use in my own copy seminars, it's the most chuckled at and asked for.

Letting Your Eye Be Caught
Writing about posters forced me to stretch my own experience and curiosity about the subject. To a graphic artist, that's what a poster is—"push-ups for the brain" is how John Newcomb describes it.

Figure 9-22

Figure 9-23

Newcomb is the author of *The Book of Graphic Problem Solving: How to Get Visual Ideas When You Need Them.* For the young graphic arts student, this book is a rich source of instruction.

When I spoke to Newcomb directly, he elaborated: "The brain is part of the body. If you can train it to mix and match, the whole problem-solving process becomes more of a reflex."

He continued: "One exercise is going through graphic annuals, art director awards books; let your eye be caught by the visuals, then put your own selling idea to that visual."

Figure 9-24

Writing this chapter proves once again that with curiosity there is nothing that can't be captivating. Ben Shahn, the illustrious painter and poster maker, used to advise his students to do everything as long as it wasn't harmful or illegal. When approaching this poster, be prepared for unexpected results (see Figure 9-25).

211

Figure 9-25

Chapter Ten

Television and Radio

the writing and the acting. They are stunning in their visual and emotional power and carry a weight that provokes something TV doesn't usually do very well—consciousness.

Sure, it's only television. But it's where advertising has its most spontaneous and charming moments.

The best of these moments don't just entertain; they entertain ideas as well.

Speaking of the John Hancock campaign that took the 1986 Grand Prix at Cannes, director Joe Pytka commented on the Hancock formula, which flashes statistical information on the screen as the characters speak: "From a director's point of view, it eliminates all the negatives and makes the product message palatable and free of informational overkill."

Director Joe Sedelmaier's executions are so distinctive that his own peers call them "Sedelmaiers." When asked if he considers himself a director of film or a director of advertising, he said: "My success is due to the fact that I'm both. As an advertising director, at least I have something to say."

Eschewing a Hollywood education, Sedelmaier added: "Hollywood has nothing to say. In my films, entertainment's part of the message. People accept it. They smile. And my commercials sell. That's an achievement."

Just where the entertainment stops and the message begins is explained by Eddie Bianchi, DGA director of the year in 1985. We were shooting pool-outs of the Bounce campaign at the time, and he pointed to "Jump" as a good example of what he called "slipping in the product." (See Figure 10-4.)

" 'Jump' is a big musical in disguise," he said. "That's what makes the basic message so watchable."

The equation would seem to be: Emotion + Rationale = Success.

For Nike, a director would never hawk sneakers, he'd dramatize sweat and determination.

Citing the similarities between British and Japanese film, Tom McElligott

Figure 10-1

Figure 10-2

Figure 10-3

observed, "They entertain first and sell second." "They come in the back door" is how he describes it.

The balance between entertainment and product goes well beyond the legendary kitchen sink: "It's always more interesting not to know what the product is," says Steve Horn. What commercial film needs is what Willem de Kooning strove for in all his paintings: "A slipping glimpse, a lighter touch."

GETTING THERE IS ALL THE FUN

A good commercial is partly bringing an idea from the mind of the creators to the mind of the director. That's challenge enough for most directors—the fierce pleasure in creating a piece of reality that's durable and beautiful along with the irony that it has to sell something.

The making of a commercial is a three-way partnership between agency, client, and director. It can also be a three-way disaster creatively, executionally, financially. Success or failure is mutually shared. The problem is getting there.

PRODUCTION IS PREPRODUCTION

What you do during and after the filming of a commercial is often too late. This is the consensus of the creators, producers, and directors I interviewed for this chapter. It's inattentiveness *before* the camera rolls that sabotages most commercial productions.

Figure 10-4

Here are ideas that might help you approach your next project.

1. The agency and the production house should apply sharp pencils during the initial bidding stage.

2. Avoid overnight bids and unreasonable air dates. Not enough production time is the cause of most disasters. "We always seem to have time after the fact,

one the director is finishing up for someone else.

Bringing Out the Best

In advertising, no one *lets* you do anything. If it's worthwhile, you have to do battle. This includes your choice of directors. Making it different is the charge—especially when everyone is trying like hell to look alike.

When I give a storyboard over to a director, I get the feeling that the work isn't quite mine anymore. I can become a nuisance, even overprotective, of the storyboard at the expense of what I'm really after: to be different. Sometimes there are nasty little by-products in the exchange.

Sometimes, just letting go requires a delicate, sensitive process in search of mutual direction. The more democratic this process gets, the better for all. And to make it work, it's important to find and use the best director for the project.

Look for a director who is impervious to fashion, who takes every board as it comes. "How can I plus the storyboard?" asks director Joe Sedelmaier. That's the key.

There are advantages to shooting with a director who has an agency background. Such a person has an easier time differentiating between "compromise" and "collaboration." Ex-agency directors seem more attuned to the marketing problem you're trying to solve. Bianchi, ex-AD at Y&R, called his agency experience "invaluable." "It lets you know how much of a chance to take. No one wants it to flop. It's the difference between being afraid and just a little nervous."

Ally Gargano graduate Patrick Kelly, who specializes in humor, says: "To do humor you have to have experience with the form. Agency life taught me what works and what doesn't work in 30 seconds."

Frank DiGiacomo, of DiGiacomo, Travisano, says it this way: "Our roots are in the agency. Ron and I are creative partners in the strictest sense—he gives a board his visual signature and I'm the production/copy supervisor. As a production company, we don't just bid boards. The idea has to pass muster."

Ask around. Find the answers to: Is the director overbooked? Is the director a prick? There's just too many good guys for you to put up with one who is.

Looking at reels, ask yourself: Can this director tell a story in a short time? Are his people believable? Can the director create as much interest with mini-movement (Avedon for Calvin Klein) as with quick cuts or action stuff?

Check the specs with the director, not the director's rep. It's the director's visual interpretation alone that will make your idea sing.

Remember that you can't expect to tie up a top-line director for days in preproduction. So, sometimes it's advisable to work with less than a top-line director. They're just more willing to spend time on key elements like casting, which is 50 percent of any shoot. If you aren't thrilled and the account team isn't squirming, you're not there yet. "We're so conditioned to plastic that we're afraid to stand out. Yet, isn't advertising a business that's supposed to stand out? Always go against the expected faces." This is from a man who practices what he preaches, Joe Sedelmaier.

The most expensive thing in advertising is cheap film. That goes for your director, too. There are cases when it's worth it to put off the production, to wait in line for the director that *feels* right.

PREPRODUCTION

One of the few times I've ever had a problem is when the director refused to understand that it's *advertising.* Or a director who after one meeting thinks he knows more about my idea than I do. I like a director who inquires about the product he's working on. It helps to define the people on film so the viewer identifies—BMW people are "peppier" than Volvo owners; Audi and Porsche are "sportier," and so on. A director has to take the time to understand this audience.

If the shot or the reading or the framing doesn't feel right, it probably *isn't* right. Talk directly to the director. Where is it written that you must go through an interpreter? If the agency producer is strong, the director won't mind. Every time I didn't trust my instincts and let something go by, I got burned in the screening room.

Some directors like the option of having the editor save their ass. Things like "blowing it up a field," flipping scenes, repositioning, "skip framing," and the loathsome "bipacking." It's just sloppy and generally means the director has at least one bad eye.

Never rehire a director who isn't involved in at least the first cut.

When Quincy Jones was assembling rock music's greatest and largest collection of stars for his "We Are the World" video, he instructed each one to

"Check your ego at the door." This certainly applies to TV advertising—more often than not a product of creative vanity. Too bad. Ego is a terrible restriction to put on quality.

In advertising, control is no small word. In commercial production, it has become anathema.

"Most commercials are mediocre because the idea behind them is the work of a committee. Everybody hides behind one another when it comes time to make a decision. What's the attitude here? You want it realistic or new wave? Punk or Peoria? I've seen agencies take votes to decide. If directors want to get the film we want, we have to take control."

The closest to a conciliatory answer was this from an editor, who preferred to remain anonymous: "All top directors take control in their own way. And they should. What a director can add is what an agency buys. The smart producers know this—they're willing to let a director make them look good. A smart director, in turn, relies on his resources, tapping the best interior designers, choreographers, lighting people, cameramen, and crew. If you want to get to the root of the problem, I'll tell you. It's the young creative teams that some agencies let out the door to supervise commercials. It's *Romper Room* time. They have no concept of film as a whole. They fully expect you to make a cut every 36 frames. And to use every shot you make in the cut. Advertising is the only profession in the world where you're automatically an expert in a year." The editor concluded with this: "When a good director takes control, you can see it immediately in the dailies. He prevails over the amateurs."

Director Patrick Kelly has been on both sides—he doesn't see control as an issue. He delineates it according to roles. "The agency provides the idea, I give it a director's vision."

DRAWING THE LINES

I spent hours registering independent opinions by directors and agency folk concerning commercials and control. The result drew a conspicuous division (see Figure 10-5).

Again, I sought the middlemen, the editors. I asked them for their opinions

Figure 10-5

Directors' Complaints	Agencies' Complaints
Everything's a compromise.	They totally disregard the purpose of the commercial.
A let's-shoot-it-two-ways mentality.	They take over the storyboard.
Amateur night at the zoo.	They think nothing of changing script, pictorial sequence, even bidding specs.
Insecure. They twitch a lot.	More interested in reel than job.
They ruin commercials with boring casting.	All his women look like they spent their childhood in Hitler's youth camps.
Things are better in Europe. You can do anything. Breasts, french kissing, fart. Americans are scared of reality.	America versus Europe is bullshit. We're not at war between countries, we're battling for people's minds, and the way they feel about our products.
They all want to look like the other guy. If I ever had to deliver a P&G look, I'd shoot myself.	I'm suspicious of a director who has the commercial he shoots named after him.

about directors—who were the best and why. They were loose, lucid, and objective, but often repeated, "I work with these guys, so keep my name out of it." And for the most part, I have.

On *Steve Horn:*

You can't go wrong with Horn. He can make any storyboard look good.

Even his vignettes look big, and I hate vignettes.

His film has energy and upbeatness. More and more agencies are convinced this quality makes people like and buy.

Great energy, understands faster, shoots faster, yet always takes the idea where is hasn't been.

An example of Horn's work is the Don't settle for walking spot for the Honda scooter.

This commercial features a series of New York street scenes. It utilizes the music of Lou Reed ("Walk On The Wild Side"). There's no voiceover, no product shot, no logo, just the line, "Why settle for just walking?"

Only a Horn could get away with this and have the agency concur. As one editor said, "Steve is the difference between formula and magic moments."

On *Bob Giraldi:*

When you look at his rushes, they have real integrity. By that I mean Joe *sees* the film before it's shot. That helps me see the cut before I edit.

I rate Pytka high for what he gets out of the idea, the authenticity of the film, and the homework he does in preparation for the shoot.

In choosing directors for Pepsi's Archeologist spot, BBDO art director Harvey Hoffenberg recalled this about their choice:

Joe is rare, he puts work in front of business. He hasn't got a next-job mentality. We wanted *one* visionary for this spot. Joe has a great eye. His forte is working with people, the subtleties he gets. "Why do you want me for this job?" Pytka asked. We said, "We think you can do anything."

On *Stu Hagmann:*

Stu's reel is the most consistent in the business and he gets high marks for simplicity of expression.

His film solutions are uncluttered.

Stu's work is very easy on the eye.

On *Mike Cuesta:*

A perfectionist, great eye. You can tell he used to be a still photographer.

A lot of patience. He knows the agency business, understands the bullshit, and gets around it better than most.

On *Sarah Moon:*

Memorable images, nonexistent sell.

Preps well, elaborate shooting boards, knows what she's after.

Great eye, can really deliver working with a relatively small budget.

On *Joe Sedelmaier:*
By far the most controversial among editors and agency people.

The only one to go to for humor.

Joe's humor overpowers the product.

You have to put up with a lot, but you get a lot. If you want to be different and get looked at, Joe's your man.

Nerve-wracking and insulting but funny. If you're insecure, don't go to Joe.

Sedelmaier has been called odd, surreal, strange, wacko. Irked by these bad raps, I called him in Chicago. Joe gave me a message for agency people: "Agency people who don't know what they want scare the hell out of me. Have confidence in yourself and your idea. We can agree, we can arrive, but know what you want, and you'll have no trouble with Joe Sedelmaier."

On *Leslie Dektor:*

Natural, very unpolished look.

Doesn't do commercials. Captures life as it revolves around product.

Isolates people, not afraid to show their pimples.

As Dektor himself has said: "The point of my work is to capture moments that record life. People want to see themselves, not glitzy manufactured works." (See Figure 10-6.)

Comparing directors is touchy, but when the U.S. awards competitive reels are screened, a dozen or so names always pop up. One of them is Tim Newman of Trettin, Newman. Tim and I have been friends for 20 years, since our younger days at JWT. Whereas hardly anything is pure truth, I knew I'd get close with Tim. Here he offers some beautiful complaints and some grumpy insights that would suggest a course of action that might cut down the problems between agency and supplier.

Lyons: Do you consider yourself a director of film or a director of advertising?

Newman: A director of advertising has less rope to hang himself, and I don't mean length. A typical commercial is signed off on by so many levels of people that any control I could have is gone. When you get to shooting the film,

Figure 10-6

well, the junior account man could shoot it. I've done a lot of MTV lately, where I start from scratch. The vision, the storyline, is mine; I'm more of a director of film. Today, MTV is the entry level for a commercial director who wants to move to features. And because of my relative success in "video treatments," I'm starting to get nibbles to do features.

Lyons: In storyboards, what appeals to you? The idea? The vision of the board? What makes you say "I want to do that"?

Newman: Let me answer by telling you what *doesn't* appeal to me—restrictions. The most restrictions are in package goods. I avoid them, because there's always going to be less of me in the film. It gets so bad that my sole contribution is telling the agency producer what color shirt the actor should wear. Ideas? I don't come across that many compelling ideas. So, the need for vision is crucial. Execution doesn't replace ideas, but it can contribute. A board with a good idea can only make a director look good. The more good boards you get, the more good boards you get to do.

I think the word *vision* is a good description of what separates directors, because it describes a way of looking at a car, for example. I have great respect for directors like Tony Scott and Adrienne Lynne because they're masters of style; their style transcends the idea and one almost becomes the other.

Lyons: You mention Tony Scott. He's been quoted as saying that he does 30 seconds for the money. Now I see where feature directors like Friedkin,

Scorcese, Altman, and Lina Wertmuller have given the signal that they are willing to talk commercial making.

Newman: John, if you ever find yourself bidding Lina Wertmuller, it's probably to blow smoke up a client's ass, which, as we both know, is not a good reason.

Lyons: Directors take bad raps. Agencies are always pointing to obnoxious and prima-donna behavior of directors.

Newman: That's because some agencies would rather hire "sweetheart" personalities than talent. To be successful, a director has to be flexible. I'm often cited for being cynical or manipulative. I also make too many ironic jokes about the business. None of this has much to do with my work. Let people think what they want. To my friends, I'm glib. To my enemies, I'm a scumbag. Again, none of this has much to do with my work. Directors are maligned for being difficult and making too much money. But if the film I deliver is there, I never hear anyone complaining. If I'm hired, it's because of what I bring to the idea, not because I give good lunch.

Lyons: In choosing directors, all the agency has is prior experience and the director's reel. There must be a better way.

Newman: When people look at director's reels, they generally expect to find their own idea up there on the screen. I try to make my reel stand for the things I like to do. Razzle-dazzle, cinematic stuff. Every board, I want to do something I haven't done before. Film is an interpretive medium. That's what I am, an executional translator—a "circus doctor." Unfortunately, most of the people who are looking at reels don't have a vision for their own board. They're often put together badly, with no transitions, just a bunch of individual scenes framed in cardboard. They think a director is a person who puts bad story-boards together.

"I'm fundamentally a real nice person" isn't something you'd ever hear Tim Newman say. Understanding this is a great help. I meet so many other people who think they're totally charming. But if you think you're charming, you're probably not.

If not thoroughly charmed, I left Newman's apartment secure in the feeling that I had interviewed the right person.

Hiring for Respect

Film is a joint art of words and visuals. Both are put under pressure when applied to advertising. The relation of its creators, the writer, art director, director is a problem that has to be resolved every time out. My longtime friend Yael Woll of Yael Woll Productions put it this way: "If a director becomes disengaged, it is because there's no implied mutual respect."

I asked him to elaborate. "Mutual respect comes from attitude. You can spot it right away. There is an understanding and acceptance that we're trying to accomplish the same objective. When the agency dictates, the respect is destroyed and the director becomes a mechanic.

"Let's face it," Yael adds, "the committee requirements are so dull to begin

the creative team, agency producer, agency executive producer, agency cost controller, client, client producer, client TV consultant, and suppliers, including production houses and editors. It is written in production language. The assumption here is prior knowledge of the production basics.

This ad for King Kullen Markets first appeared in 1972 (see Figure 10-7). It was meant to be a humorous warning about inflation. If you have been hit by a New York-style panhandler lately, the same joke today is about half as funny.

If you are a client who has just signed off on a commercial production, you're not laughing at all. You're crying.

Since 1972, the costs of shooting, making, and finishing a 30-second commercial have increased 350 percent.

To understand production costs, we need to understand what drives the costs. So, get out your pencil and follow along. If this section isn't an eye-opener and doesn't result in saving you thousands, I'll personally refund the cost of this book.

Cost Components

Components of production costs, like those of any commodity—new car, home—move in sync with the rest of the economy. Some are dictated by union contracts. For example, scale crew rates have gone up approximately 40 percent from the beginning of 1982 to 1986. There are also material costs. A sheet of 4x8 plywood has gone up 40 percent from 1982 to 1986. Directors' fees range from a minimum of $453 to $10,000 a day for star directors. In 1968, a foot of 35mm film cost 42 cents; by 1983, 68 cents. Camera and lighting rentals are up 40 percent. Paint, wardrobe, props are outrageous. Since 1975, makeup minimums have gone from $70 to $156 per day. Not to mention overhead, contingencies, and profit margins. If a production company loses one job, it'll make it up on another.

225

Figure 10-7

What I encourage you to understand is that costs are not a subjective element of production, but rather an objective measure of what an agency and client are buying from a supplier. The agency gives specifications, and a supplier sets out to manufacture those specs.

Let's say our commercial features a toilet plunger. Let's look at how

announcer.

The difference in cost implications is obvious. The more complicated and difficult the execution, the more expensive it will be.

So, executional elements contribute to cost, but there's another driving force: production values.

Production values are the perceived quality of the film itself. The demand for these "values" is right at the top of the list of causes for driving costs up. There are reasons for this:

1. Egos. Advertising people hang out with other advertising people. They all want their commercial talked about. This goes for clients, too.
2. Demands of the competitive environment, as with high roller campaigns for soft drinks, beer, or cars.
3. The theory that adventurous techniques, like computer animation or new wave, MTV-type productions, pay big dividends. But adventure costs more.

In response to these demands, agency creative people come up with treatments and technical astonishments that have never been done before.

Even the cost of an average 30-second commercial can exceed $100,000. A lot of that comes from fees charged by star directors.

Directors and production companies fall into three basic categories— A, B, C.

A: Highest quality, star directors, very consistent work. Entrust this level with difficult executions, special production problems. Directors require a lot of support people: Broadway choreographers, award-winning set designers, lighting directors. Costs reflect this.

B: Middle level of good, very competent directors and companies. Right choice for most executions. Most bidding takes place at this level. Some at this level would be "A" with better support.

C: Lowest level, newcomers, fledgling directors being promoted by established production houses. People whose capabilities are limited by either talent, experience, or budgetary constraints. Tend to be least expensive, appropriate for low budget or "test" executions. Includes most out-of-New York production companies.

Staying Power

Production values are difficult to quantify and represent the artistic side of production. They add depth, style, texture, and give commercials visual "staying power" that keeps the viewer involved even after repeated exposure to advertising.

The residual value of emotionally felt film is the best argument for production values.

Production values can be found everywhere: in direction, camera work, casting, editing, soundtrack, detail areas like set design and dressing, use of unique locations, wardrobe, styling, use of props.

Lighting, for example, has a subtle yet powerful aesthetic effect on the viewer. I prefer "rich" lighting, which can mean back lighting or single-source lighting for drama and effect. I detest "flash" lighting where you turn on all the light switches and everything looks like a toilet.

Production values leverage visual interest. They keep the eye of the audience involved in the selling message and add audio excitement to keep the ear involved. Premise is that the more involved the audience is, the more receptive they'll be to selling messages.

However, one man's "production values" are another man's "flagrant waste of money." Many storyboards I see are elaborate cover-ups for no apparent substance. Most guilty are the young teams who have been thrown into a difficult medium when they haven't been taught basic problem-solving. That's one reason for skyrocketing production costs. Executions are replacing ideas, which are priceless by themselves. The value of producing at high levels is very subjective, very difficult to quantify.

We have seen now how the nature of the execution and the level at which it is produced are the driving forces behind the cost of a commercial. Serious attempts at really controlling costs have to focus on these issues.

What do we do with this conclusion? The reality is that on one side we have creatives—art directors, writers, producers—striving for the best, which is what clients should want them to strive for.

On the other side, we have dollar constraints and budgetary limitations. Does "best" always equal higher cost? Not if everybody does his homework.

Before the Pen Hits the Paper

I have attended many cost-cutting seminars and read dozens of articles. Some suggest that stiff competition among directors will drive costs down. Others suggest using younger, hungrier production companies. Some agencies go out of town to produce. A client I work with has a policy that eliminates the

Step 1—Framework Stage. Consider production costs even before creative work begins. This gets back to elaborate execution as one of the driving forces behind cost. Be aware, if possible, of budgetary facts of life before creative work begins. In essence, there should be a creative "cap" for each storyboard.

Many readers will see this as a creative restriction. It can also be seen as a creative stimulant. In any case, it is better to know reality up-front than try to produce a $100,000 execution for $50,000. Second consideration in the Framework Stage is production values—the other main contributor to costs. This may be less of a consideration if the commercial is to be used in a test rather than nationally. Also in this stage, you must look at what competitors are spending. Sometimes a commercial stands out *because* it's inexpensive and stark. What kind of creative clutter are we trying to cut through, and how can this help us in making our decisions regarding the nature of the execution and the level of production?

Step 2—Creative Approval Stage. Before client approval, the agency should provide a rough range price figure to shoot board. Be certain the idea can be done. Only sometimes done in the past, this should now be S.O.P. Goal up-front is agency producer involvement to flag problems. This way client isn't buying in a vacuum. Note: Client should understand that "rough" means just that.

Step 3—Prebid Stage. Be creative. Nitpick. Approved boards must be scrutinized for dramatic savings potential (as with our earlier toilet plunger example). Get into the tough area of subjective judgments. Agree before bidding on the level of director and production company, degree of "production values" needed in execution. It's amazing that this isn't always done, but it isn't. The agency should make a recommendation, but agreement should be joint.

Remember that the idea must remain intact and never be compromised. Also at prebid stage, start looking for "pooling" potential: combine with other

229

work for same client. Set appropriate time, limit number of versions or alternates. All those extra "pick-up" shots and versions take away from the main job and must be kept to minimum. All agreements in formal prebid meeting should occur with key members from the agency and client in the same room. This process is key because it eliminates the worst word in production lexicon—surprises, and it demystifies the entire film process.

Is this all complicated and time-consuming? Does it require lots of subjective judgments? Yes. But at the conclusion of these three stages, everyone knows what we are trying to buy from suppliers. We have a framework in which to evaluate costs.

Cost management requires involvement on all sides, but especially with the client, the person who had the power to say yes at the first meeting in the first stage.

Step 4—Bidding and Analysis Stage. Send bid boards with very detailed specs to suppliers at the level already agreed to. Agency people and the producer should review and scrutinize costs, submit them to cost consultant and client.

Questions to be answered at this stage: Are we getting what we asked for? Which bid is the best "value?"

Step 5—Production Stage. Reiterate all this in preproduction meeting. Make changes in estimate to reflect all versions and any extras that have accumulated. Each extra shot, angle, version will take time and money. You don't want to make the shoot race against clock.

Step 6—Post Production/Finishing Stage. All prior savings can be wasted in this stage. Several key points to remember: Get all approvals in *rough cut* form, again from the same client in the first meeting. It is an incredible waste to shoot optical and have to reshoot it. Editorial bids normally include cutting commercial, making reasonable changes for approval. Expect additional editorial labor if cutting fourth or fifth version.

In summary, a commercial is a product. Like any product, the cost is a reflection of our "manufacturing specifications." More specifically, costs are driven by execution and level of production. There is no "magic bullet" that solves the problem of commercial costs. It takes a lot of involvement, tough decisions on all sides, and a willingness to work as partners from very early on in process.

"You can't separate finished film from execution," says Phil Dusenberry. "It's essential that writers and art directors think of production as part of the creative process."

This section will mean nothing to people who resist imposed discipline. Many creative renegades will view these guidelines in much the same way they view a tightly focused strategy: right up there with bondage—not even worth considering. If you feel that way, I would ask for a little honest self-evaluation and remind you that the days of "Trust me, I'm going to the coast; you'll see the footage when I get back" are over.

I like to think of this section in this way: A good friend of mine, Rick Wysocki, sat down and did us all a favor. He wrote up a fail-safe insurance plan to cover all of our behinds. Make it your agency policy and it could save you grief

comedian comes to the footlights and says, "Ladies and gentlemen, don't look at me. I didn't write this shit."

Beautifully Believable Bergin—Hold the Flimflam

In a world of diminishing natural resources, it is always refreshing to talk with a generator of advertising's greatest resource—enthusiasm for the game. I speak of John Bergin, ex-vice chairman of McCann Erickson, longtime custodian of Coke's creative fortunes and now CEO of the John Bergin group.

If you've ever seen a nervous man passing a folded note during a meeting as if revealing a secret he wasn't quite sure of, you will always get a sense of the reverse with John Bergin. John is quite willing to "reveal the world's best-kept secrets to everyone."

John is a longtime believer in the use of people in commercials to sell people, even those who are well known when they depict believable situations. He cites Mariette Hartley and James Garner for Polaroid and Sandy Duncan for Noxzema.

"I can't tell you how much advertising needs understatement like that," he said. "The consumer is crying to see film and faces that are beautifully believable instead of just beautiful."

When I asked John to name the components of believable film, he was quick to tick off an almost biblical parade of spiritual begats.

"It's film that lets the audience forget it's watching a commercial. A moment when the consumer can actually suspend disbelief. A sense that the event or story is really taking place.

"When David Lamb caught those two farmers applauding the Olympic torch runner in that midwestern cornfield for Bud Light—that was a suspended moment in time.

231

"When we did Coke Is It, do you know we cast for that entire campaign in the local papers? We'd get 3,000 showing up the next day. None of them had learned how to act, so what we got was believable film as opposed to what a director gets by saying, 'Come on baby, smile.' "

I reminded Bergin how tough it was to convince clients that storyboards are only blueprints for the action, not the finished product. "One of the great limitations of our time," he blurted, referring to storyboards. "But only the primitives (clients) ask to bring back the board."

"Bring back the cardboard is more like it," I added. "The person who's smart enough to come up with an alternative to storyboards as a method of presentation will make a million."

Of course, I was talking to someone who had already made a million and he was nice enough to tell me how. "I usually sell without a board. I do 'key frames.' A person can present much better—that person knows what he wants on film, or should, so the creatives should be able to present their idea in the theater of his mind."

I stopped him. Are you sure you want me to print "in the theater of his mind?" John assured me that he did.

"So tell me," I asked, "how come most film is a letdown?"

"Expectation," Bergin answered. "Expectation is our biggest problem. Many times I get, 'John, your presentation was better,' from clients comparing it to the finished film.

"A lot of it is the director," he added. "A commercial isn't meant to be a medium for some director's ego; it's supposed to be a medium for a sale."

In true Bergin style, he decried young writers and art directors who are led down the "new wave" path by directors, the strong, slick ones with what he described as "production house ideas, devices, and techniques that hide the absence of a selling proposition."

We went on to discuss the hinge upon which all great film turns—production values.

"Some genius in Hollywood hit it right when he said 'you can see money on the screen,' because you can. You take shoddy and give me quality and I'll beat your socks off every time. When are clients going to learn that film quality says you care deeply about your product and what surrounds it? Production values are a statement. Quality is as important as your copy."

We finished up by talking about young people who write for TV.

"Their training is terrible," Bergin said. "They come to the agency prepared to do what they've been trained to do. Writing is virtually a lost commodity. What we have are people who claim to be writers who appear at your door, saying, 'Hey, I got this idea, like, you know, man, what if we . . .' "

What advice did he have, I asked.

"It sounds simple. Have a TV in your office or put a fake screen up on your wall. Look at the screen, put a picture there. Add another and another. Think of the process as the moviola of your mind."

John Bergin isn't one of your lightning-bolt types. He's been around quality commercial production longer and with more consistent success than most. Let's put it this way. Anybody who works as hard for such insane precision in his

idea and so little on big budgets? Not the creative director. He's too busy saving the agency's latest commercial. Not the group head. He's too busy paper-training his junior team in fundamental TV techniques. Not the media director. He's out being lunched by a rep who's pushing a Super Bowl special. Not the account people. They'd never think of reminding the client that he could produce a whole pool of radio spots for what it costs to run one second of TV time. Not even, thank God, the research department. I have yet to hear any of them suggest testing a radio commercial.

No wonder the work on radio is so good. Everybody is so intent on maintaining the high level of mediocrity on TV. In a speech delivered to the 1985 Radio Advertising Bureau convention by Ed McCabe, he offered this choice advice to the only person left, the copywriter: "Quick, do something good on radio before someone catches on and makes it as difficult as it is everywhere else."

For any number of compelling reasons, radio is truly the writer's medium. Good radio writing makes its own pictures. It tells its own story in its own style. The radio writer can't hide behind props, technique, and showbiz. In radio, there's no place to hide, nobody to blame when it's awful. Radio forces the writer to write better, to revise, to take more time with his craft. In radio, you're alone with your imagination. That's why it's such a showcase for talent.

Announcer: Every year there comes a time when a man's or woman's heart turns to hearts. Valentine's Day. And nobody has more hearts than Fortunoff, the source. Hearts come from simply platonic, to truly romantic to out-and-out lecherous. Little silver "I like you" hearts, big crystal "I adore you" hearts, teeny, tiny 14-karat gold "you're cute" hearts. And luscious sparkling diamond "run away with me" hearts. Jade, ivory, enamel, and black onyx hearts. Neck hearts, wrist hearts, finger hearts; $5 hearts, $5,000 hearts.

Hearts that say "You're wonderful." Hearts that say "I can't live without you." Even hearts that say, "My apartment or yours?"

Hearts that express everything from mild pleasure to intense crazy passion. Every kind of heart your heart desires. Fortunoff, the source. More than you can imagine, for much less than you'd expect.

This is no impostor at work. The writer is Jennifer Berne out of Martin, Landey, Arlow.

Anything TV Can Do, Radio Can Do Better

Stan Freberg, the man who once asked on radio, "Who puts eight great tomatoes in that little bitty can?" for Contadina, says that radio is his favorite medium because "It's the 'moviola' of the mind." Television, on the other hand, "can stretch people's imagination as much as 21 inches."

Slice of life, demonstration, image, humor, tugging the heart—anything TV can do, radio can do better. Radio can put money into the client's pocket quicker, because radio is the most immediate way to change consumer habits and practices, and, at the same time, demand a specific action at a specific time and place.

For example, Allerest:

Announcer: Listen to the difference between a sneeze from a cold and a sneeze from an allergy.

First, the sneeze from a cold . . . (SFX).

Now the sneeze from an allergy . . . (SFX).

Now listen to the difference between a runny nose from a cold and a runny nose from an allergy.

First the cold . . . (SFX).

Now the allergy . . . (SFX).

They sound alike, don't they? Well they look alike, too. This can be confusing, because allergies and colds are very different ailments. And a medicine that's perfect for one may not be perfect for the other.

If you have an allergy, maybe you should be taking something made specifically for allergies.

Allerest. Allerest helps relieve the runny nose, the itchy, watery eyes, and the sneezing of allergies.

Allerest comes in tablets and in time-release capsules. If you have an allergy, it's made just for what you've got.

On TV, this idea would be boring. On radio it puts consumer's eyes and ears to work to create a distinct impression of Allerest versus the competition.

Slice of Life via Radio

Most winning radio commercials have one thing in common. Humor. True, this highly successful and long-running campaign for Blue Nun is humorous, but I prefer to think of it as one of the better "slices" ever written. The creators, comedians Stiller and Meara, still keep 'em rolling in the aisles with their newer ~~successes for Shopwell's Food Emporium Supermarket and Amalgamated Bank~~

~~M: I recognized you right away.~~

S: Were you there?

M: I was dressed as a mermaid so I had to spend most of the night sitting down. Did you ever try dancing with both legs wrapped in aluminum foil?

S: No, I can't say I have. Did you order dinner yet?

M: I'm having the filet of sole.

S: Humm. The filet mignon looks good. Would you like to share a bottle of wine?

M: Terrific.

S: I noticed a little Blue Nun at the captain's table.

M: Poor thing. Maybe she's seasick.

S: No, Blue Nun is a wine. A delicious white wine.

M: Oh, we can't have a white wine if you're having meat and I'm having fish.

S: Sure we can. Blue Nun is a white wine that's correct with any dish. Your filet of sole. My filet of mignon.

M: Oh, it's so nice to meet a man who knows the finer things. You must be a gourmet?

S: No, as a matter of fact, I'm an accountant. Small firm in the city. Do a lot of tax work . . .

Voiceover: Blue Nun. The delicious white wine that's correct with any dish. Another Sichel wine imported by Schieffelin and Company, New York.

There's a much greater possibility that a good radio—as opposed to TV—commercial of yesterday is still a very good commercial today. This is because in radio the idea shines through. It can come into being without glitz or bright lights without any conditions for its production except the presence of its creators.

Consider this Molson beer commercial—Fridge.

Her: Hang on!
Him: Hello?
Her: Hello.
Him: Hi, I'm your neighbor, next-door neighbor.
Her: Yeah.
Him: I missed you when you moved in, I guess.
Her: Really?
Him: I wanted to explain that shelf in your refrigerator.
Her: The shelf? Oh, you mean the bottom shelf. The one with the whole case of Molson Golden. Boy, what a great surprise that was moving in.
Him: It was my Molson Golden, my Molson Golden.
Her: Your Molson Golden.
Him: Yeah, I had an arrangement with the person who lived here before you.
Her: Oh yeah?
Him: I sort of rented one shelf in her fridge.
Her: You don't have a refrigerator?
Him: Yeah, I'm a photographer. Mine's full of film and I needed someplace to keep my Molson Golden.
Her: Oh yeah, I see.
Him: Cool, clear, smooth. I'm sure you understand.
Her: Oh yeah, I love it. It was terrific.
Him: It was terrific?
Her: Uh-huh.
Him: What do you mean *was?*
Voiceover: Molson Golden, from North America's oldest brewery of beer and ale. The number one import from Canada. Molson makes it golden.
Her: It really was a shame you missed the party.
Him: I felt like I was there in spirit.
Voiceover: Martlet Importing Company, North Hills, New York.

Spots like these have dominated Molson's media plan for some five years. This campaign breaks the clutter of macho TV beer advertising; it includes women and gives them an equal position. Women are more than waitresses or barmaids, they're consumers in the literal sense of the word. Garrett Brown, who originated the campaign with partner Ann Winn, says, "The campaign is directed at both men and women. Sometimes in developing a spot we switch roles."

This offbeat campaign breaks ground and beer clutter with a media mix dominated by radio. Says Jim Hunter, management supervisor on the business, "The import market is easy to target with radio because radio is very segmented.

Younger audiences are difficult to reach with television, and we can't compete with the beers that are spending 50 to 60 million dollars on TV.

"The only other medium that really segments that audience," says Hunter, "is print. And we haven't until now been able to translate the strategy into print."

Richmond, Dick Orkin, Bert Burtis, Joy Golden, Stiller and Meara. Their talents are free to create without restraint. They're not stifled by demands to be deadly serious about drain clogs, lipstick, and panty shields 18 hours a day.

There's a lunatic fringe out there making radio a classic form of manic wit. How far can radio take you? I asked the leader of the pack, Joy Golden, president and creative director of Joy Radio, Inc. On the strength of her award-winning spots for Laughing Cow cheese, she's become a valuable property— valuable enough to quit the agency business and start her own commercial production company.

Here's the Valley Girl from the campaign that broke the bank for two people: the writer and the advertiser.

Valley Girl: So like, I was driving down the freeway, okay, and this totally gorgeoso highway patrolman stops me. So I said like, wow, there's wheels on your motorcycle and wheels on my car. I mean like that's really Kharmoso. He said, "You were speeding." I said, "I have to get my little round Laughing Cow in the red net bag into the fridge, okay." He said, "Where's the cow?" I said, "In the trunk, okay." He said, "You're not authorized to carry livestock." I said, "Officer, that is like really heavy. The laughing cow isn't a real cow, okay. It's cheese, okay. Mild Mini Bonbel, nippy Mini Babybel, and new Mini Gouda. You know, like really awesome and natural. Five round cheeses in little net bags. Each wrapped in wax with a cute little zip thing." He said, "Open the trunk." I said, "Okay." He said, "You need a key." I mean, like this guy was like totally brilliant, okay. I said, "You want a little laughing cow?" So he said okay. So I said okay, so he said okay, okay. So then he asked me for my license. And I said like, "When can I see you again?" He was so totally freaked, like he dropped the cheese and bit the ticket. So now it's like two weeks and he never called.

Announcer: Announcing new Mini Gouda cheese from the Laughing Cow. Big Gouda taste in a new small cheese . . .

The very quotable Golden tells the story this way: "We did five commercials. They ran for 13 weeks, over 2,000 times in ten states. Sales of Laughing Cow jumped 70 percent. And lest you think that was a New York fluke, we got the same results in L.A. and San Francisco."

After the commercials ran, D.J.'s talked about them, listeners phoned for copies, and the advertising industry showered her with awards.

"How did the idea get hatched?" I asked.

"It was a very funny visual," she replied. "Going to the store and asking for a Laughing Cow in a red net bag is a lot like the old Abbott and Costello 'Who's on first' routine."

I asked the ex-Scali, ex-Wells writer if she ever missed the agency side of the business.

"Mary Wells fired me because I was a lunatic, but all my family were lunatics. You don't get much of a chance on the agency side to be one."

"How are you doin'?" I finally asked. She gladly volunteered her take-home figure. The moral of the story—want great creative? Hire a lunatic.

Bert Burtis is quite possibly advertising's most awarded writer with 12 Clios to his credit. Bert had this to say about the specialness of radio: "When Dick (Orkin) and I started, we couldn't afford anything. We had no studio, no sound effects, no mixing equipment. The only way to do the demo was on our Wollensack. The words had to be great, the idea had to show through. There's great power and persuasion in quiet. The listener has to get closer. There's more opportunity to make a one-to-one sale. Quiet is a great tool. It's what white space is to an art director and to print. In radio, you have 60 seconds. You have the time to talk to people, to let the gags play out. In TV you're frantic. You have to announce."

I have tried to emphasize that contrary to popular perception, radio is not only the most flexible but the most highly visible medium available. In fact, I'd like to think of this section as an advertisement for radio itself.

This ad (Figure 10-8), created by Lord, Geller, Federico, Einstein on behalf of the Radio Advertising Bureau, is aimed at creators.

The theme and tagline "I saw it on the radio" highlights radio's ability to illustrate, demonstrate, and describe anything. I called Arthur Einstein and asked him if any of his own clients responded and asked for radio.

"We're quite proud of the campaigns we've already done," he said. He pointed to the agency's work for Callard & Bowser, featuring the rat-a-tat-tat voice of John Cleese.

Cleese: Look, all you American persons, it's been suggested that I urge you to go out and buy Callard & Bowser's extremely fine, rather sophisticated British candy . . . a sort of call to action. Well, frankly, the last thing you Americans need is a call to action. I've never seen such an active bunch in my life;

Figure 10-8

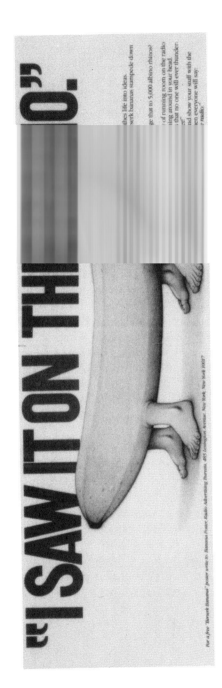

if you're not making millions or defending the free world or putting men on the moon, you're out jogging. I mean if ever there was a nation of get-up-and-go, let's-get-this-show-on-the-road, it's you U.S. persons, isn't it? You don't need a call to action. You need a call to keep still for a couple of minutes. Put your feet up, open a packet of Callard & Bowser's superior candy, and wallow in the sensual pleasure of a bit of toffee or butterscotch or even juicy jellies. Trouble is, two minutes of that sort of pleasure you'd all feel guilty and have to rush back to work and start slaving away again—the old American work ethic. So to help you, we've made Callard & Bowser candy jolly tricky for you to find. You may have to comb the streets to find a shop that stocks it. And then, it may be jolly tough discovering where it's hidden. But when you do find it, you'll have expended enough blood, sweat, and toil to be able to really enjoy it . . . clever bit of marketing, really, isn't it?

"Cleese has a way of making fun of a product and yet make it endearing and acceptable to the customer." Einstein went on to cite two unsuspected benefits derived from the campaign. "One of the stations we used was WQXR. Many gourmet food stores use this station as background instead of canned Musak. Cleese's voice was piped directly into the store at the point of purchase to precisely the people who were most likely to buy our candy.

"Additionally, Cleese draws attention from D.J.'s around town who would take off on the commercials." This resulted in what Einstein referred to as "add-ons"—more media time for no charge.

No Funny Hats, Only a Voice
That "no funny hats" quote is from Joy Golden describing the magic of radio. To a writer, radio is a matter of throwing your voice out and listening to it. Seeing how different it is from the voice with which you usually speak. Sure, there's plenty about that voice that you recognize, but the amazement comes from the realization of how many compelling voices you actually have.

Can you live with control, yet create free of restraint? Radio gives you your best shot. It was August Strindberg who declared that few people are "lucky enough to be capable of madness." I thought of all the people who helped me with the background for this section. It became clear that in order to be saved in this business, one has to be certifiably nuts.

Chapter Eleven

Techniques

phy, million dollar shills.

Why bother to beat your brains out trying to break new creative ground, when you can go to England and have a real technician execute it for you?

"If you haven't been to England in this business, you're not even *in* it anymore and that's a tragedy," laments John Bergin.

At issue in this chapter is the question—do you get attention only with visual and verbal gimmicks, or at the expense of simplicity and directness?

A review of techniques—not canoeing or flipping an omelette but advertising techniques—can help distinguish what is borrowed and what is relevant. It can help you learn at the planning stage what is best for the idea, assuming there is one. Note: Technique alone is never enough and it is likely that the more you rely on techniques, the more energy you steal from the idea.

HUMOR—OUR MOST PRECIOUS TREASURE

The world likes humor, but relatively few American humorists have been famous. "We decorate our serious artists with laurels and our wags with brussels sprouts," quips E.B. White.

In advertising, the reverse is true. We praise and raise our humorists. The list embraces not only today's top-notch talent but the heroes of our adolescence—Bernbach, Freberg, Tinker.

These entrepreneurs accelerated the idea that humor in advertising was worthwhile. If advertising was absurd, it was because of the preposterous claims it made: Art steps in when nature fails (from a nineteenth-century corset ad). If advertising was gray, it was because the fraternity boys were taking themselves too seriously.

In the 1960s, humor gave advertising distance and perspective. Humor came out of the closet and gave creative elbow room. One product, Alka-Seltzer, set the standards for the use of humor in advertising. Phrases like "I can't believe I ate the whole thing" and "Plop, plop, fizz, fizz" became part of our lingo. And a jingle written to an early Alka-Seltzer classic, "No matter what shape your stomach's in," climbed the record charts as a hit single.

Doyle Dane's "spicy meatball" commercial-within-a-commercial in which an actor gets sicker and sicker as he does endless retakes eating "Mama Magadini's" meatballs was named the best-written commercial ever by International Broadcast Awards (see Figure 11-1).

And "the pie-eating contest" where the seasoned veteran offers a latter-day Refrigerator Perry "what the guys who overeat for a living take for relief." All of this started at Jack Tinker Associates where life without humor was unthinkable.

Being an Alka-Seltzer nut, I was delighted to talk to Charlie Ewell, who wrote my all-time favorite Alka-Seltzer spot. It featured George Raft as an inmate leading prisoners in a banging chorus of tin cups demanding "Alka-Seltzer, Alka-Seltzer" after another bad meal.

"Tinker in those days was an anarchy. That's why the work was so good. The Raft idea came from a Cagney movie, *White Heat*. But instead of Cagney yelling for his mother, we had George Raft yelling for Alka-Seltzer."

On humor, Ewell says this: "Humor is the projection of personality. If you're ingratiating, it buys you a competitive edge when you haven't any."

Figure 11-1

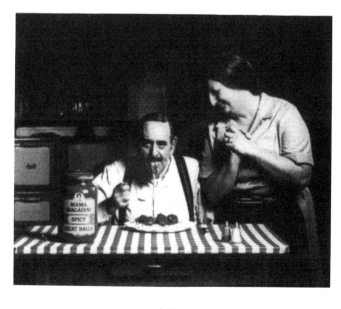

Humor in advertising reached out in many directions. We got the outrageous from Stan Freberg for Sunsweet prunes.

And we got the off-beat and human from Bob Gage for Cracker Jack (see Figure 11-2).

"Everybody remembers childhood. They remember Cracker Jack in their

Figure 11-2

Creators like Gage proved that you could put money into an advertiser's pocket by eliciting a smile.

Gage relates, "Demand was so great that the factory couldn't handle it. The people at the plant were actually preparing Cracker Jack ingredients themselves. A pinch of this, a pinch of that. It was a sight out of Rube Goldberg."

Did all this make adland's gray suits sweat? Of course it did, and in the process it toppled the Harvard Business School adage that says you can't force distribution with advertising.

The Putdown

"Humor collections are scarce, pale, and ill-selling. And serious writers suggest it would hurt their reputations to be connected with anything flippant or funny." So says E.B. White. Again, in advertising the reverse is true. A sense of humor is still worth gold in the trophy case and in the pocket of the seasoned advertising practitioner.

See Figure 11-3 for advertising's most decorated film in 1986. BBDO's art director Harvey Hoffenberg analyzed its success. "This was truly a one-joke commercial. All of the prior action is a setup for the perfect end line. We had another line, I don't even remember it, but it was wise ass, not subtle; it betrayed the character. When the professor who knows everything is asked what Coke is and says 'I have no idea,' that's the ultimate putdown."

When humor fails, there's no noisier thud. When it works, there's no more memorable advertising.

Figure 11-3

Director Patrick Kelly, a prime contributor to the original Federal Express series created at Ally Gargano, says this: "If my comedy succeeds, it's because humor has always been a personal means of expression." Admitting to a set of rules, Kelly said: "Yes, there are rules. Hundreds. Starting with a history— Keaton, Chaplin, Lloyd. Humor is a science. There's structure, timing, charac-

funny bone. To laugh is one of our most compelling needs. Laughter, used as an advertising tool, works when the product, not the humor, emerges as the star.

Fattening on Trouble
"Humorists have always made trouble pay," E.B. White says. Nothing has served creators of advertising humor better than life's down moments. Like the frustration of a wayward package (Figure 11–4).

Certainly there is nothing ridiculous about a man making a will, but humor is achieved in this funeral spot for Volkswagen as a billionaire leaves nothing to his spendthrift wife and partner but everything to his practical, Volkswagen-driving nephew (Figure 11-5).

"I was looking for a relevant situation for a car, when I saw this funeral pass by. How could I put a Volkswagen into that scene? (This is Roy Grace, author of Funeral, speaking.) There's a certain irreverence in good commercial humor, taking something logical to its illogical conclusion."

Rising to the sparkling surface of these commercials is the product that in some small way counters human woes. At the top of their form, these commercials remain in complete touch with the source of our material: ourselves.

Humor with Heart
There is little hysteria in advertising humor. It won't stand much pushing. It has a certain fragility. Humor is the observation of oneself in microcosm. What could be more interesting than that—observing our own awkwardness? Human failings usually provide our resident funnymen with all the material they need.

When Marvin Honig's fiancee decided to impress him with her cooking skills, Honig in turn had to put as much effort into eating it ("She put a lot of effort into it—I had to pretend that it was terrific"). Groom's First Meal for Alka-Seltzer was born. It portrayed Alka-Seltzer as the hero and a perfect solution for another of life's unsettling moments. The empathy was there, the response was

245

Figure 11-4

Figure 11-5

there. *TV Guide* even ran a recipe for a heart-shaped meatloaf in memory of that almost fatal meal.

Humor with heart is humor that rubs that funnybone.

Say It Like It Is

~~In a phone interview, Joe Sedelmaier, the art~~ ~~g~~ works exclusively in comedy, put it in perspective: "I used Clara Peller long before anybody ever noticed her. You know what some agency genius did? He went back and redubbed her voice to sound like a genteel old lady. Then I cast her in the Where's The Beef? series. I needed a tough customer. Do you think for a minute anybody would have heard 'Where's the beef' if Clara sounded like a little old lady?" (See Figure 11-6.)

Despite the bad rap that Sedelmaier's characters take from agency types—that they're "spacey, wacko, and look like they've been dug up from the set of *The*

Figure 11-6

Village of the Damned"—people on the street relate to them on a gut level. "They work, they sell, and sell well," says Sedelmaier.

Additionally, there's the dialect school that oozes with humor. An iconoclastic type of backwoodsiness that even Mark Twain might have approved. A case in point is from Bartles & Jaymes, the wine cooler entry from Gallo (see Figure 11-7).

Exaggeration

The comic poster effect of the idea. This is the theater of exaggeration. Sedelmaier is the most conspicuous humorist we have today of all the directors who shoot commercials for a living. His work is instantly recognizable. His commercials have been called surreal, odd, strange. They have also been called the best. As noted earlier, Sedelmaier has continually taken bad raps by agency people—"he's a dictator," an anarchist, difficult, out of control, insulting. "Once Joe gets the job the only time he asks you about anything is 'what kind of donut do you want with your coffee,' " says one agency producer.

Before any criticism of Sedelmaier, one must objectively look at his work. I see an absolute fidelity to one idea. His humor is always used to advance that idea to solve one problem or to make one specific selling point. Jartran rents trucks of all sizes. You won't get treated haphazardly on Alaska Airlines. If it has to be there overnight, Federal Express. I also see the work of a visual stylist: that insurmountable torrent of paperwork terrorizing your office is dramatized by

Figure 11-7

the "paper blob." When the quality of Dunkin' Donuts is questioned, he gives us a group of eccentric old ladies to debunk it.

"He isn't an advertising director, he's a hyperbolist" is a quote from an accountoid I work with.

Replies Sedelmaier: "My first duty is to get the message noticed, to enter-

would probably end up to be my Clio (see Figure 11-8).

The Convert

"Hello, Room Service? Send me up a room."

Welcome to the chicken soup of American laughter, the stand-up comedian of the Borscht Belt.

Dozens who have stomped the Catskills have also played Madison Avenue: Henny Youngman, Rodney Dangerfield, Buddy Hackett, George Burns, Bob Hope, Jonathan Winters, Red Buttons, Rich Little, Will Jordon.

But it was a Broadway Danny Rose character who ended up as advertising's most endearing and enduring humorist.

His name was Jack Eagle, but you know him as Brother Dominick, pictured here with Steve Penchina in the It's a miracle series for the Xerox 9200 copier/duplicator (Figure 11-9).

This commercial covers all the territory:

Based on an amazing fact, it offers an amazing benefit.
It's human and humorous.
It demonstrates.
It creates its own star.
It positions Xerox as the company that understands office management problems and the people who have to solve them.

The creator of this commercial was Steve Penchina, then of Needham, Harper, Steers, now costarring at Penchina-Selkowitz. It started with a tough advertising problem. "Everybody at Needham had tried to solve it," Steve recalled when I spoke to him on the phone.

"The Xerox 9200 was a very complicated, very expensive copier. It pro-

249

Figure 11-8

Figure 11-9

duced an incredible number of copies at an incredible speed. The obvious executional solution was high tech or computer animation. But my partner, Alan Kay, and I were looking for something human. The solution came out of hard work and directly out of the product. We boiled it down to the fact that this copier just didn't make stacks of paper, it made booklets because of its sorting capabilities. We thought up situations where that might apply—playbooks for coaches, scripts for actors, and so on. Then one day the word *manuscript* popped up in conversation. This led us to caligraphy and the monks who pushed and perfected it to an art. The minute we saw Jack Eagle, who was a Borscht Belt comedian, there was empathy, even in the first casting session. Here's this poor guy working forever to make something perfect; to his boss it was terrific, but not good enough. Our hearts went out to him, and the cameras weren't even rolling yet. I remember we had a funnier line, but it wasn't related to the product. I woke up in the middle of the night with the It's a miracle line. Through investigation, we had distilled the creative solution down to three words."

Religion, humor, and advertising are always a touchy mix. I asked Steve about this.

"Yes, we had some doubters. I have to credit one person, Wally Oleson at Xerox, for fighting it through. It was *his* baby. Every winning idea needs to be somebody's baby."

Steve Penchina assured me that he is not a born humorist. He's is just like any other writer who thinks, waits for thoughts. If he stays awake, his patience will be rewarded. While involuntary, the humor was a by-product of digging— still the most useful method of hunting for advertising magic. In this case, an advertising miracle.

It's Okay To Laugh

There are tangible standards on music, art, drama. But humor is whatever makes you laugh. Humor delivers us from solemnity, brings us closer to common sense, and strengthens attachments to your brand. How can advertising possibly be creative when it has to pitch a product? Try serving it up with a laugh. It's a wonderful way of dealing with the difficult stuff and smiling the system apart.

One caution: While almost anything in modern life may be comic, that does not necessarily make it humorous.

MUSIC

"Everybody must get stoned," wrote Bob Dylan. His lyrics could well work in a parody of the song overdose sweeping Madison Avenue. As a form of what *Forbes* magazine calls "emotional shorthand," popular music as a marketing tool is sending several dominant messages. One, parodies are ascending, but jingles are by no means a spent force. Two, music marketing, the marriage of a product to a musical performer, is a thriving business. Three, rock and roll is as mainstream in the 1980s as Double Your Pleasure, Double Your Fun With Double Good, Double Good Doublemint Gum was in the late 1950s.

Assimilated Rockers

In the mid-1970s, it would have been unthinkable for Procter & Gamble or Ford to use rebel music with outspoken lyrics that flirted with revolution, drugs, and sex. Rock and roll was the voice of a new generation. Today, it serves as a nostalgic hook for the hooked, the assimilated, and the baby boomers. Songs like "Help," "Be My Baby," and "Proud Mary" for Lincoln-Mercury signal conscious strategic and demographic shifts. Rock 'n' Weave rhythms like those of Marvin

Gaye's "Ain't No Mountain High Enough" appeal to younger consumers because they take them back to better times. In turn, these good feelings are transferred to the product, in this case a Cougar or a Topaz. Pop music isn't kids' stuff anymore. It's big stuff and big business. The same MBA types who run advertising run the Rolling Stones.

happier times and sunnier places. To some, this campaign might be verbal strutting, even hedonistic. To others it's the ideal.

Implicit in the long-term success of this campaign is the integrity of the arrangement itself. It's so well done that the younger audience actually thinks that Sunkist got the Beach Boys to write a song for a soda pop.

Integrity means you don't screw up someone's favorite song. When that happens, and it happens a lot in parody music, you don't win a customer. You lose one.

Ex-rock popper Don Danneman (Cyrkle of Red Rubber Balloon fame), president of Mega Music, had this to say about parodies: "I'm comfortable doing parodies. I know a lot of composers aren't. But we were all kids once; in a parody I get to play the song I loved growing up. Doing a parody is a musical education. It doesn't matter if it's the Beatles or Mozart, a composer has to take each musical part of the instrumentation and build it again, layer upon layer, as true to the master's image as he can."

Painting Pictures

All music has a unique pull on our emotions. Certain words and melodies are linked forever in our personal image banks. I can't hear Mancini's "Moon River" without thinking of an 18-year-old Thunderbird spot. I can't listen to these lyrics by Cole Porter—"There's no love song finer, but how strange the change from major to minor, every time we say goodbye"—without hearing Ray Charles and Betty Carter sing them. And who can hear the theme from *Now Voyager* without seeing Paul Henreid perform his famous two-cigarette gesture for Bette Davis?

How can the marriage of music and emotion be successfully integrated into advertising and play a strategic part in the success of a marketing plan? There are three widely accepted methods:

Marriage of product to a jingle.
Marriage of product to parody.
Marriage of product to musical performer.

Let's take a closer look at each one.

The Jingle

The jingle is original music and lyrics composed for a product. Of all "musical marriages," the jingle offers: the most instant recognition for the money; the greatest potential for long-term good feelings for your product; less risk of disaster than going the parody route, and most flexibility at initial creative stage: original music, underscore, new arrangement, vocal or instrumental.

The problem with most jingles is that they sound like the word itself—light, tinny, trivial, accessorized. When I pointed this out to Don Danneman, president of Mega Music, he recalled an incident involving choreographer and spokesman, Geoffrey Holder.

"When we were introduced on a job I said I'm Don Danneman, I'm the jingle writer. In his most resonant, approaching-God voice, Holder replied, 'You mean you're not a real composer?' "

The lesson here for Don and for all of us—always classify yourself at the highest level of what you do. Consequently, I never go to a jingle house, I go to a musician. That way, I never have to say, *don't* give me a jingle. They understand what I'm looking for.

1. An elevating melody.
2. A differentiating and distinguished musical logo for a special set of words.
3. A creative orchestral solution.

Top-rate music suppliers are melodists first who happen to apply their craft to commercials. For example, I use George Grant of GNU music a lot. George does all the WCOKE stuff for Coke.

Last year, I gave George an impossible set of lyric specs for a Fleischmann's oil jingle—words like "no cholesterol," "saturated fats," "not greasy." His solution was a Gilbert-Sullivan takeoff where the words seem sung and said at the same time. It made the client happy because they heard all the words, and I was happy because I had a disarming yet totally listenable piece of music. Says George: "The Gilbert-Sullivan lyrics don't take themselves so seriously. It was a format that fit the assignment without being ludicrous."

Music is dressing for your advertising. A Mickey Mouse piece of music can cause as much damage to a product as a leisure suit to a gigolo. Music is out there in front. No kind of glitz can substitute for substance. Bill Backer of Backer

Spielvogel helped compose such golden oldies as "It's the Real Thing" for Coke and "When You've Got the Time, We've Got the Beer" for Miller. He had this to say when he appeared in print in the ongoing *Wall Street Journal* series on ad greats: "We don't take a jingle to a client until we've played the tune with one finger. People don't hum chords and rhythms. There has to be a melody and

Schaefer is the one beer to have when you're having more than one.

A jingle can get inside a little kid's head:

I wish I were an Oscar Mayer weiner, that is what I'd truly like to be,
'Cause if I were an Oscar Mayer weiner, everyone would be in love with me.
Oh, I'm glad I'm not an Oscar Mayer weiner, this is what I'd never like to be,
'Cause if I were an Oscar Mayer weiner, there would soon be nothing left of me.

A jingle can build a world brand. As if it were something new, global advertising is an overtalked subject. In 1971, 500 students of every nationality stood on a hill and sang "I'd like to buy the world a Coke." It ran in 25 countries, conveying the spirit of partnership, harmony, and understanding. You want to talk about "world brand advertising," talk to Coke. They've been doing it for a quarter of a century.

When I asked Backer, "What gives a piece of music integrity?" he said, "The idea it's based on. Fifty to sixty percent of the music done today is a substitute for an idea. 'I'd like to buy the world a Coke' had a point of view—the brand itself. It was something only Coke could say. It was entirely credible."

The right musical expression can transform the personality of a whole company. GE makes everything from ice boxes to tune boxes. Included in that range are a lot of products, a lot of competitors, and multiple demographics. With the rousing jingle, "We bring good things to living, we bring good things to life," GE has neatly shifted consumer attitudes. No longer a stamped-out processor of appliances, GE has moved into the company of its space-age competitors, Sanyo, Sony, and Panasonic. GE sells power. That's their product. The power of its "good things to life" theme linked to the stories they tell so

255

warmly on TV (buying your mother a refrigerator for Christmas) is an example of the difference between a jingle and a musical property.

The 60-year life-span. The oldest known jingle was recorded in the 1920s for Wheaties—"Have you tried Wheaties, they're whole wheat with all of the bran." I don't think the product has changed a bit and its "wholesome" strategy remains intact. Only the dressing has changed. Today, utilizing an energetic musical face-lift, Wheaties is "What the big boys eat."

Don Danneman again: "If I didn't believe that emotion could be transferred, we wouldn't be in this business." The "we" is Don and his partner/wife Eileen, who, in one of the more cosmic moments in this book, "has heard the angels sing." Of all the commercial musicians I spoke with, they were the only company to offer a working philosophy.

Says Danneman, "Whatever the emotion, we say 'do it.' By 'do it' I mean a 100 percent commitment to the expression of that emotion in music."

The Parody

A parody is an existing piece of music that's been lifted, abridged, or rewritten to accommodate a product or a campaign.

The use of parodies by major league advertisers is a growing epidemic. In a recent and well-documented piece in *Madison Avenue,* reporter Michele Conklin lists the songs that have made "the commercial charts." It includes songs by the Beatles, the Beach Boys, Dolly Parton, the Pointer Sisters, Carly Simon, Lou Reed, Cole Porter, Elton John, Arlo Guthrie, and Stevie Wonder.

Ripping off somebody's favorite song might sound easy and wonderful to the copy team, and it gives the client that "I'm so excited" feeling, but as a creative solution, parodies aren't always musical magic and most times are troublesome and dangerous.

My old friend from the Thompson days, Sid Woloshin of Sid Woloshin Inc., bristles at the thought: "So many parodies serve as substitutes for an idea, an unnatural grafting that doesn't grow out of the product. After a few months, all a client's left with is a six-figure invoice."

Talking to Woloshin and other commercial musicians, the list of raps against parodies is a long one:

> They're an open admission that you don't have an idea.
>
> A bad parody pushes a product, not an emotion, and that defeats the purpose of music.
>
> They're not kidding anybody. Parodies test better immediately, but they don't have any lasting impact.

Building on that is this from an anonymous contributor: "Procter & Gamble's translation of 'Love and Marriage' into the words 'crispy, chewy' for Duncan

Hines cookies is detestable. It's typical Procter. Money can buy Procter a lot, but it can't buy an emotion. What does love and marriage have to do with chocolate chip cookies, anyhow?"

Curiously enough, the same music writer cited Nestle's "Cure for the Summertime Blues" for Toll House Morsels as an example that goes into the

lyric becomes pitiful. In some cases, parodies *do* work. That happens when the idea doesn't take backseat status but works in conjunction with music that drives the idea home.

When does it work? When Doyle Dane used Carly Simon's "Anticipation" as a dramatic "release" for Heinz ketchup escaping from a bottle into a juicy hamburger, they were tongue-in-cheeking the long-standing, thick, slow-pouring differentiating property of Heinz ketchup. For me, it is easily one of the best uses of a parody. For immediate impact, Sprint, the long-distance telephone service, featured the Stevie Wonder hit "I Just Called to Say I Love You." Sales out of Sprint's telemarketing center rose 25 percent in the first three days.

Six months after we broke our campaign for P&G's fabric softener Bounce, featuring the Pointer Sisters' "Jump," the product's share went up two points and is still inching up.

In describing this commercial, *Forbes* magazine says: "The P&G message is clear: 'Bounce is hip, Bounce is in, Bounce is bouncy.'" But the real message is strategic: It leverages a solid benefit—"Clothes you can't wait to jump into." Michael Zager (Zager Productions), arranger for "Jump" and for many gold albums, says, "It's very clear why people respond: the authenticity, the association directly with the record. The same title and selling idea go hand in hand. It's melodic in every way, as opposed to a slick jingle. It's got a true record sound. The commercial doesn't sound *like* the song, it *is* the song."

Another example cited by Sid Woloshin is Honda—"Honda is very good with music. Take their new campaign, 'What will be, will be.' The implication of the line is that Honda is always on the leading edge. But they took the old Doris Day tune, 'Que Sera' and arranged it in a contemporary way. And they were smart enough to tag their commercial with their old two-note logo, Hon-Da."

It's hard not to mention two other winners in this category. Citizen Watch offers scintillating metropolitan types getting ready to take on the town as Al

257

Jolson sings "About a Quarter to Nine." (See Figure 11-10.) And then there's Young & Rubicam for Lincoln Mercury. They're very careful in maintaining the sound of the original songs: the Beatles' "Good Day Sunshine," the Temptations' "Get Ready," Rod Stewart's "Passion."

Does it work? Well, in the past years the average age of a Cougar owner has dropped ten years to 35, and market share is up to 6.5 from 5.5. With big ticket sales like that, nobody's complaining about the $100,000 price per song that an agency might be charged.

Matching Product to Performer

The Rolling Stones never started out as part of a marketing plan, but recently they ended up in one for Jovan, the perfume. As part of a promotion,

Figure 11-10

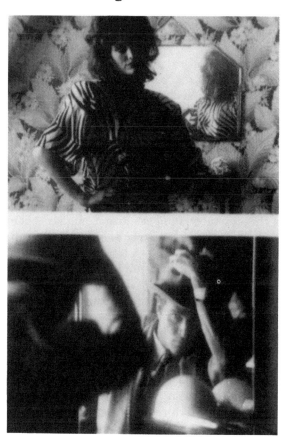

Jovan accompanied the 32-city Rolling Stones tour in the form of a Rolling Stones American tour poster, a $5 value that sold for a buck to anyone who purchased $5 worth of Jovan products.

Contrasting Jovan's 1981 sales with the cities where the Stones appeared showed a 12 percent sales gain attributed directly to the Jovan/Stones promo-

Steve Winn of the Golden Nugget Casino in Atlantic City. High visibility rollers like Sinatra and Kenny Rogers are used without chirping a note.

Loyalty to a performer can transfer to loyalty to a product when his or her music fits the dreams, aspirations, and values of the consumer. *Matchup* is the key word: The right song, the right group at the right time and place, implemented into a marketing strategy, not only gains instant prestige and sales but long-term goodwill, good feeling, and good vibrations for your product.

Sid Woloshin is the generalissimo of commercial musicians. His career spans 20 years and his work includes such original jingles as Like a Good Neighbor (State Farm), You Deserve a Break Today and You, You're the One (McDonald's), and Come to Think of It, I'll Have a Heineken. Avoiding actuarial tables and the swings and sways of this business, he remains at the top of his craft. I asked him a handful of questions as a kind of summation to what has turned into a Ulysses-length section.

Lyons: What do ad agencies have to understand about advertising music?

Woloshin: To relinquish control. Stop competing with me. Stop hiring me as an expert and treating me like a fool.

Lyons: How does this happen?

Woloshin: The decision-making process inside agencies is very confusing. Either you have some autocrat who makes a subjective decision based on what's relevant to him alone or it becomes a participatory thing where the agency democratically takes votes. In the "you deserve a break today" days, it was Keith Reinhard and myself in conjunction with the client who had the power of approval. Today, McDonald's has 200 MBA's, not two.

Lyons: What did that kind of music do for McDonald's?

Woloshin: It took a successfully run business and gave it visibility. It was frosting on an already beautiful cake. McDonald's has grown from $6 million to $500 million in advertising billing alone.

Lyons: With a jingle?

After an awesome pause, he answered: "A jingle that was untouched by sweaty hands. Somewhere it's said that the average person holds 3,000 melodies in his memory bank. There are lots of jingles in that bank—it's still the most effective form of musical shorthand there is. When it comes to establishing an emotion, there's no better economy than a jingle."

Bruce Springsteen's latest songs have been passionately topical and deeply felt. His songs look at things and find both gloom and hope. The same can be said for the wild extremes we find in commercial music—when it's right it can indeed be an emotional source of strength for pride and product. Although passion is the goal, toe-tapping is acceptable.

Star Advertising

"What's happenin', baby?" To find out, just visit any agency casting department.

Negotiations. Retainers. Contracts. Trips to the coast to seal the deal. What's happening is that more and more clients are asking for stars and celebrity talent as spokesman or voiceover.

Zap-resistant and audience-holding, the million dollar-a-minute business of the celebrity pitchman is king of the advertising techniques. Nobody can deny that a star can buy your product attention.

Say you have an honest story, like Cliff Robertson tells for AT&T, or you want to create awareness for a low-interest product, like Jim Palmer did for Jockey shorts. An authoritative spokesman can help.

On the other hand, overkill can be murder. A case in point is hawker supreme John Houseman. Even a money-moron like yours truly can relate to Houseman's esteemed mug and his heavily cultured voice telling investors that Smith-Barney makes "money the old fashioned way, they earn it."

Here we have one institution creating another. The Smith-Barney/Houseman matchup is perfect. While Houseman's attributes as a credible person help set Smith-Barney apart from the pack, it's the compelling importance that Houseman gives to the idea that carries the message: a no-nonsense approach to hard work and the rewards of money that the ordinary person can buy into. After five years, his credentials are stronger than ever. No one approaches the majestic Houseman as the epitome of celebrity endorsers.

However, Houseman also represents the hazards that await clients who hitch their fate to a rising star. Houseman has used commercials to become an industry unto himself as a hawker of cars (Chrysler), cooking oil (Puritan), hamburgers (McDonald's), condos in Florida, and a car dealer who advertises on cable TV. According to a *Madison Avenue* article playfully entitled "Would you buy a burger from this man? A car? Some stocks?" the other corporate efforts to capitalize on Houseman's fame haven't fared well. Chrysler hasn't renewed, McDonald's was a classic mismatch, and Procter is out.

And how do the folks at Smith-Barney feel about this? "People have felt a

IBM's innovative use of a Charlie Chaplin lookalike to explain its personal computer is a perfect example:

1. It humanizes the company.
2. The use of pantomime to demonstrate features and advantages helps reduce the complexity of a wordy explanation.
3. The tone is unsomber and brings a lofty company down to the average man.
4. The use of Gary Merrill as voiceover adds class to the whole presentation.

The agency, LGFE, used its imagination and saved its client a ton of residuals, not to mention the long-term serviceability of the character itself.

Before you consider using a celebrity, here are some general principles culled from talent negotiators inside advertising and out:

Is it a good celebrity-product matchup? Joe Namath for Brut is, Joe Namath for anything else is not. If the product, presenter, and audience fit, it can work. And it all must be based on a sound idea.

Don't use celebrity pitchers for me-too ideas and me-too products. They only accelerate a quick fade and fall for product and star.

Don't hire for popularity. It can backfire. It also robs you of the persuasion that comes from believability. Conversely, look for talent agents who have a knack for spotting rising stars in the arts or sports. This allows you to sign them at a fraction of the price. "We have to be more accountable," says Peter Kelly of William Morris. "We don't get paid unless other people work." Media darling of 1986, Refrigerator Perry went from practically nothing to $100,000 a shot. It got so bad that his Bear teammates call him Mr. Endorser. As of this writing (just a year later), Perry is more an overweight villain than a darling.

Don't go in cold. Get on the phone with the artist or celebrity. Discuss the idea and the script. Explain why it's good for them and for your product. Ask whether the star uses the product. How would the star realistically integrate the product into his life? Take script suggestions related to style, delivery, habits, vernacular. And don't let the business affairs person tell you that they'll handle the call. You, the creator, should handle it.

Don't let the same department squelch a deal. If they can't get a deal, hand the negotiations over to an outside professional. Your casting people are smart, but they're not as smart as negotiators who've been at it for years.

If you're considering a star, consider the dangers, too. (1) Cost. (2) Fading stars—last year's star is this year's bum. (3) Overpowering the message—remember, this isn't the movies. Advertising is essentially message-oriented. (4) Overbooking—only Bill Cosby gets away with it. (5) Value threats—look what happened when Miss America, Vanessa Williams, was caught in the buff. A lot of contracts and ideas had to be ripped up. Drug scandals in the sports arena haven't stopped clients entirely. If you're on the agency side, include a "morals clause" in the contract, although "a morality clause is hardly do-able today" says Kelly. There's just too many kinds. To some clients, "farting in public is immoral." (6) Death or injury—Add a clause covering this to the contract.

How about creating your own star? Charlie the Tuna is one of the most successful and trustworthy presenters in the annals of stardom. For fame, prestige, and sheer seniority, the characters we create ourselves have made the very best company representatives. The Campbell Kids, Speedy Alka-Seltzer, Buster Brown and his dog Tige, Nauga, Mr. Clean, the Ty-D-Bol man, the Marlboro man, the Maytag man, the Pillsbury Doughboy, the Fruit of the Loom guys, and those cool raisins decked out in shades for California raisins (see Figure 11-11). Someone could make a killing with a poster or a calendar starring all those.

Bert Lahr for Frito-Lay potato chips is, in my opinion, the all-time winner in the advertising celebrity sweepstakes. This award-winning campaign featured Lahr, the lovable but cowardly lion in *The Wizard of Oz* (see Figure 11-12). Lahr, so identified with that role, is tempted by the devil (also played by Lahr), "Bet you can't eat just one." He still lives on every package of Frito-Lay chips, but when Lahr died, so did the campaign. He was an impossible act to follow.

Many stars have appeared in commercials *before* acting fame. Sandy Duncan for Noxzema, Louise Lasser for Nyquil, Mariette Hartley, who made the popular Polaroid series with James Garner—all were relatively unknown. So was John Moschitta, the fast-talking star of those Federal Express commercials.

For 20 years, Dick Wilson as Charmin's Mr. Whipple has challenged Yul Brynner's "King" for the title of most enduring role. It all started, so the story around Benton & Bowles goes, when Wilson got a call from his agent.

"What do you think of toilet paper?" he was asked.

Figure 11-11

"I think everybody should use it," replied Wilson.

For 20 years, consumers have been claiming that they "love Mr. Whipple, but hate those commercials."

"I *am* the commercials," says Wilson in reply.

In contrast is Wendy's Where's the Beef? campaign. It made Clara Peller an instant celebrity, but only for an instant. Whereas Clara was a great idea for a commercial, Whipple was a great idea for a campaign.

Finally, there's the nonrecognizable celebrity—the whole idea behind the American Express Don't leave home campaign. Status as personified by the celebrities is a strategic element and serves to make the card more desirable. The man or woman in the crowd can identify with a celebrity who himself is invisible.

What doesn't work? As an actor, an adoring public might be attracted to a name on a marquee and say this is a talented man who does good work, I'll pay to see him. Yet, when a consumer sees the likes of Sir Laurence Olivier for Polaroid in the 1970s or John Wayne for a pain reliever or more recently, Burt Lancaster for MCI or Kirk Douglas for Sperry or George C. Scott for Renault or Alan Alda for Atari, the jump isn't so easy.

Figure 11-12

I'll just eat one... I'll just eat one... I'll just eat one... I'll ju

"Look who I got to do my commercial" might be enough for a client—but to the savvy consumer, appropriateness seems to matter more.

What about crossover roles? Credibility can emerge from a TV role. In this case, TV celebrities work better than movie stars:

They're less removed.
You're used to having them in your living room.
They're family.

When Karl Malden, who played a San Francisco TV detective, talks about lost or stolen American Express cards, that's a credible fit. In her role as Alexis

Carrington, Joan Collins plays a bitch. In a couple of new and very funny spots for Sanyo kitchen appliances, she plays off of that role—as a sex object in her fifties who doesn't even know how "to melt food" or "fully bronze turkey." Collins brings a certain purity to the role. In one spot she calls meat loaf "that long garlic muffin." Another ends with Collins saying, "Who says I don't know my way

company, a sinking city (Detroit), and a country that had lost its pride in the way it makes things. The actor is saying, "Take that, Japan." It takes a winner to get up on behalf of someone who's down. The role is that of an underdog more than a star.

That's a little different from, say, razor mogul Victor Kiam touting a guarantee for one of his Remingtons. Who cares about a self-promoting man who buys a razor company so he can play Iacocca on TV? Likewise Leona Helmsley, who acts like a self-appointed madame. The idea of turning your client into a star should, in most cases, be resisted. If your client insists, take a good look at him. Ask: Does he look like what he's selling? Does he look like he could run the kind of business he runs? Frank Perdue, when he talks about chickens, fits. When he talks about entertaining "chicks"—he doesn't.

If you are the president of a tie-clip company or one that manufactures bleach, no one cares. If your company offers a personalized service like enter-tainment, airlines, restaurants, I think I'd like to meet you. Thumbs up to Steve Winn, who personifies his own Golden Nugget Casino.

Thumbs down to the sanitized helicopter-hopping Frank Brennan of First Jersey Securities. You don't get to me, Frank, and no, I won't come grow with you.

Thumbs up to the hungry banker for Midlantic.

The next time you're thinking about turning your client into a star, remem-ber—if he doesn't look like a chicken or have the qualities of an eagle scout, forget it.

Match or mismatch? Demographic association, honesty, and attractiveness are useful guidelines to measure the stopping power of a star. The wrong star can be a momentary hero who can save the copy team from having a legitimate idea. The right personality can be a natural expression of the total marketing mix.

What this chapter has attempted to stress is *valid connection*. Are we playing celebrity match or celebrity mismatch?

On sports: Jim Palmer is sexy, John Madden is personable, Air Jorden electrifying, and John McMahon is outrageously effective for Kraft mayonnaise. In truth, sheer ineptitude wins the Miller Lite troup a campaign based on a solid product and premise, featuring lovable incompetents like Bob Uecker, Marv Throneberry, John Madden, and group. Which points to the fact that sports figures are more valuable *after* they retire (see Figure 11-13).

On the tough, the gruff, the obnoxious: Tough dandruff, tough beards, tough trucks, guys who chew snuff. Jack Elam, Jack Palance, Claude Akins, Mr. T., Hulk Hogan, Deacon Jones, Butkus, Garrison, Alzado, Connors, Nastase, McEnroe, Martin. Against this nail-chewing group of nasties is the tough guy with sensitivity—Merlin Olsen for FTD and Mean Joe Greene in the Coke classic—who give the advertising top spin and twist.

On the voice as star: Remember when the voices out of Hollywood were as

Figure 11-13

distinct as the faces? Bankhead, Edward G., Bogey, Bacall, Karloff, Andy Devine, Judy Holliday. The voice was such an integral part of the personality.

In commercial advertising, the voice itself is the star. Listeners react because they know (or think they know) the sound; they recognize the voice as a "somebody." Distinctive voices draw attention. Orson Welles for Taylor wine and Eastern, the gritty Tammy Grimes, the screechy Arnold Stang, the austere

Geoffrey Holder, I love. He could make an Easter egg hunt on the White House lawn sound like the invasion of Normandy.

I've always wanted to use David Wayne, who does the voiceover for the consistently convincing United Fund "Thanks to You, It's Working" campaign, for the NFL. The best announcer's announcer is Joe Sirola, who captures the essence of a script faster and better than most.

The most creative use of a voice award goes to Memorex, which has used the power and range of Ella Fitzgerald's voice to demonstrate the true fidelity of its tape.

I find it impossible to write a piece of commercial copy without hearing a certain voice delivering it. This only helps to develop an added element of character to your writing—to make it more than what it is. There's a writer's expression "learning to see again." With the right voice, the consumer can learn to listen again.

On super tykes: "The smaller, the cuter, the older they get, the more you love to hate them." This from casting director Ruth DiPasquale, now of B&B, ex-BBDO, who spent months trying to recast adland's most famous and successful kid—Mikey, the adorable patsy for Quaker's Life cereal. "Mikey is now 18 years old and they're still looking," says DiPasquale.

"There's a puppy dog quality you look for, big eyes, fat face, a nose that's grown just a little too fast for the rest of him. And always shoot tight, big fat close-ups. You can't lose with the right kid. Kids and dogs—there isn't a casting department in New York that isn't looking for a Mikey or Alex (Stroh's beer) for one of their clients."

On those you love to hate: Sometimes consumers go out of their way *not* to buy a product simply because of the choice of star.

Most cited in this category are Dick Van Patten, Ed McMahon, and, surprisingly, the much-loved Arnold Palmer. In his earlier work for Lanier business products, Palmer matched up well. The target was serious management types bent on function and efficiency. Palmer was perceived to represent all of these. He was serious, well respected, professional, and well liked. But his more recent work, particularly for Hertz, gets reviews like this from a casting director—"You have to be pretty hard up to play straight man for O.J. Simpson."

On real people: I can hear my client readers now—how could I forget real people?

Whereas "Candid Camera" stuff gratifies most clients, the executional form has become an overused technique. It's just a lazy way to solve a creative problem. Real people are generally unconvincing because it's a convenient format for clients to force-feed a litany of copy points. Wooden people and wooden deliveries are what they get.

I can think of two notable exceptions.

Dannon Yogurt used real geriatrics from Soviet Georgia as experts on the art of living the long life (see Figure 11-14). For me, they qualified as spokesmen for a disarming and arresting campaign. And Tylenol's use of real people was a potent device in helping the product recover from the damaging press received from the Tylenol kills in 1982. A lot of people thought the product was done for. But the frankness and trusting manner of these commercials and the willingness of Johnson & Johnson to spend money on tamperproof packaging to restore the good faith of its customers is a classic case of advertising and public relations at

Figure 11-14

their very best. And response to the campaign demonstrates the ultimate fairness of the American consumer.

Deciding on the right technique is no different than deciding on the right idea. You gotta go through the crap until you get to the point when you say "that's it."

I'm just trying to find a villain.

Is it ridiculous to think sex doesn't matter? Yes. Sex in advertising, any kind—exploitive, neutral, explicit, implicit, relevant, or irrelevant—plays a growing role in advertising today.

Some women might think this Soloflex ad (Figure 11-15) for body-building equipment isn't fair play, but it's aimed at men who have responded to the tune of a 20 percent sales gain since it started running. Says Jerry Wilson, Soloflex's president, "There's no way I can sell the product without selling sex."

Some observers find this (Figure 11-16) terribly romantic, others, too hunky. The fact is, it constitutes a breakthrough for the category and the agency, Ogilvy & Mather. According to David Ogilvy, "It was the most risqué copy I have ever seen." But he didn't stop the copy from running, and today you can hardly stop the sales: up 25 percent in the first year.

And Figure 11-17 is something you don't regularly see every day in *Good Housekeeping*.

Is it relevant? Well, the photo was taken with an Olympus camera and was featured in the gallery exhibition entitled Big Nudes. She sure looks relevant to me. What's startling about the ad is . . . it's British. "Sex is not something the British have been very good at," says Don White, an ex-Benton & Bowles London creative chief. "While the French smoulder, the Italians steam, and the Americans analyze," he says, "the fact is sex is all in the mind, and that's where the British do it best." White's No sex please, we're British, and other pertinent articles on the subject can be found in *AD's* Second Annual Look at Sex issue.

Does It Fit?

What some American critics call "blatant" sex, others call an attitude of the user. What some practitioners call "bottoms up" advertising is plainly a man's adoration of a woman's rear (see Figure 11-18).

The truth is, society sets trends. Advertising only follows. Clients are acutely

  (Text continues on page 274.)

Figure 11-15

To unlock your body's potential, we proudly offer Soloflex. Twenty-four traditional iron pumping exercises, each correct in form and balance. All on a simple machine that fits in a corner of your home.
For a free Soloflex brochure, call anytime 1·800·453·9000. VHS Video Brochure™ available upon request.

BODY BY SOLOFLEX®

©1986 SOLOFLEX, INC. HILLSBORO, OREGON 97124

Figure 11-16

Figure 11-17

Figure 11-18

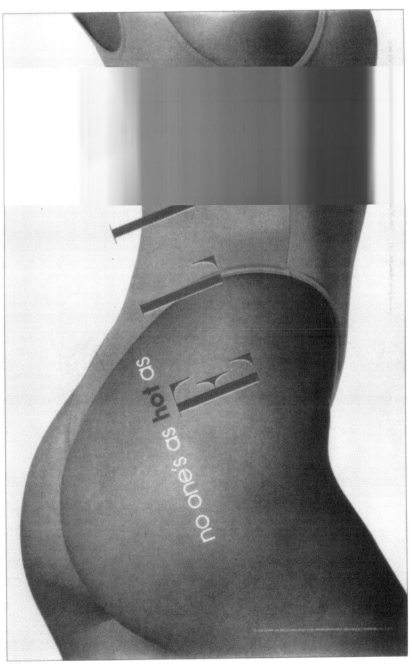

sensitive to public reaction. All a client needs is a bag full of negative letters and the "offensive" advertising stops. I never regard the sexy ads I see as good taste, bad taste, or quasi-pornographic. And I never ask whether it's moral or aesthetic. For me, the use of sex is appropriate if it's sensual or hot; it's striking; it *fits* the product.

To fashion a more definitive explanation of the use of sex in advertising, I went to the art director who designed America's "hottest" advertising for Calvin Klein (see Figure 11-19).

Her name is Rochelle Udell. The people she's worked with read like advertising's "Who's Who": Milton Glaser, Alex Liberman, Calvin Klein, Richard Avedon, Jerry Della Femina. Her credits include stints as creative director on magazines like *Gentleman's Quarterly, Self,* and *Vogue.* More recently, she was advertising director at C.R.K. Advertising, Calvin Klein's in-house shop, where she created her hottest work.

Udell was about three months into her new job as Della Femina's senior VP, executive art director when I spoke to her by phone. It was the day after Thanksgiving, a day off. She was in the office with her two children, flooded with work, energetically reminding me that "life is seven days a week" and saying that she doesn't need much sleep.

Figure 11-19

Calvin Klein Underwear

Lyons: I'd like to talk about sex as a way of selling a product. Is there such a thing as sex as a strategic element? And did you and Calvin have a strategy?

Udell: Fashion is a visceral business. The turn-over in trends is tremendous. We wanted to transcend trends. We didn't have the luxury of sitting down and writing a strategy. *What Calvin knows, is about Calvin.* That's as close to a strategy as we ever got. Calvin's body-conscious person. He works out. His

Udell: As far as Calvin's concerned, both genders are hot. That's what sex is all about.

Lyons: Sometimes you can't avoid being called bad names. Prudes think you're disgusting. Feminists think you've sold out.

Udell: Just call me a feminist with a sense of humor.

Lyons: What critics call blatant sex, advertisers call attitude of the user.

Udell: The most active form of communication is clothes. The user picks the clothes—the observer responds . . . the communication is complete.

Lyons: A transmitter needs a receiver.

Udell: Right. You have to ask yourself—do you want to be an active part of things or an impassive observer? Calvin's clothes aren't for voyeurs.

Lyons: Some advertisers think the use of sex is an opportunity. Others think it's a risk.

Udell: When there's a natural marriage, sex is a powerful tool. People are sexual objects. Sex is part of what they are, not exclusive to what they are. For frozen french fries, sex is not appropriate. For Calvin, it is. Consumers aren't dumb. If you use sex in a wrong-headed way, they get bugged. If Apple Computer did that, it would be upsetting. Not because it's sexual; it just wouldn't fit. When one doesn't fit, that means it's imposed. That isn't bad taste; it's bad advertising.

Lyons: How do you feel about your underwear man beating the Marlboro man as America's most noticed symbol?

Udell: It feels great. Of course, the subject matter is infinitely more interesting than a cigarette.

Lyons: I know the subject is sex, but I detect another note of high passion in your life—work.

Udell: I could say I have a ton of problems and I don't know where to start. But that's where the kicks are, solving them. I'm not one for excuses. I

275

think creative people are victims of the conversations we have in our own heads about how overworked we are. You and I both know somehow we get it done.

Lyons: Heroes? Do you have any?

Udell: Anwar Sadat, Solzhenitsyn.

Lyons: Mentors?

Udell: Mentors are different. Jerry Della Femina and Louise McNamee are marketing geniuses.

Lyons: What makes them geniuses?

Udell: Insight and optimism.

When I asked Rochelle Udell to sum up her talent, she said, "My talent doesn't fall into slots. It's a set of skills I take and apply to the problems I'm working on."

Her colleagues describe Udell's influence as inspirational. I concur. I was prepared to buy myself *Dr. Ruth's Game of Good Sex* for Christmas. I think I'll buy some Calvin Klein underwear (small) instead.

DEMOS

A good idea announces itself. A bell rings. But that's just the beginning. An idea needs a stage.

TV, advertising's most conspicuous venue, provides eight basic ways to stage an idea: slice of life, exaggerated graphic, animation, vignette, personality, testimonial, talking head, and demonstration. The very best of these is demonstration.

According to a Greek philosopher, with a long enough lever, you can move the world. I could say the same about a good demo. Only in this case I would be moving inventory. Nothing leverages a product's superiority or benefit better and turns it into a sale faster.

A convincing demo never has to argue; it shows. "Don't tell me, *show* me that it works." We hear this all the time in focus groups.

A good demo doesn't confine itself to a "selected target audience." It makes immediate sense to everyone.

Demos are hardly ever beautiful. They are functional and invariably cost less to produce.

Consider the following three classics. Each uses the fragile, agile egg in a powerful, telegraphic way.

Johnson & Johnson told the world that Band-Aid had "stickability." To prove it they showed an egg in boiling water being lifted out by a Band-Aid.

And Volvo demonstrated the fragility of a body when thrown from a seat without a seat belt around it (Figure 11-20).

Figure 11-20

And Figure 11-21 demonstrates the flexibility and comfort of a new pair of Hickey Freeman shoes. I spoke with the art director, Norm Tannen, about the shoe commercial. "The idea was inspired by a print ad done by Paccione (then a crazy art director, now a serious photographer). It seemed a natural. The commercial cost $6,000 and a lot of eggs. Demos are funny. When you come up with one," he continued, "you never know if it's going to work. This one, I really have my doubts. But when it works, you feel like cheering."

Whereas it is easy to send mixed communication in words, this is hardly possible with a good demo.

Take the Polaroid Land camera introduction. It could have been long-winded, brag copy heralding the breakthrough that the instant camera really was. They could have gotten wrapped up in their own technology. Instead, they demonstrated the benefit, not the attribute.

As noted earlier, Bob Gage, DDB's first art director, says: "We weren't selling cameras, we were selling love" (see Figure 11-22).

The Polaroid campaign proves one thing—you can demonstrate anything, including an emotion.

A good demo is straightforward. If it's different enough, the consumer thinks you're spending far more than you actually are (see Figure 11-23). This is extremely important to a small advertiser. Just because the competition has twice your money doesn't make them twice as smart.

A good demo can dramatize anything the naked eye can see. It can even dramatize what can't be seen very well (see Figure 11-24).

There are demonstrations that can save you work or save your life.

Demos can be simply unbelievable (see Figure 11-25) or unbelievably simple (see Figure 11-26).

And when you think you've run out of good demos, you could always try a gorilla (Figure 11-27), or an elephant (Figure 11-28), or a wind-up toy (Figure 11-29).

Demonstrations are worthy of an entire book. I am flabbergasted by the number of truly great ones. And nowhere is a great demo prized more than in the area of packaged goods. It is in this category, where there is little difference between competing products, that a demonstration can make a huge difference in terms of perceived product superiority.

Dawn is a dishwashing detergent with a true difference (see Figure 11-30). It actually separates the grease from the water, which leads directly to its unique strategic position: "Dawn takes grease out of your way."

Tide put one sock inside another and both came out of the washer clean, thus dramatizing that "Dirt can't hide from intensified Tide."

And Pampers built a mega-dollar business with baby bottoms that were drier than the competition.

To demonstrate the softening attributes of Procter & Gamble's Downy fabric

Figure 11-21

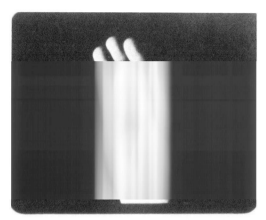

Figure 11-22

softener, diapers were cut out of burlap bags. After the diapers were soaked in Downy, babies paraded on TV in their burlap diapers without scratching or showing any signs of irritation. From Grey Advertising and great.

A good demo is the only "proof-sale" there is.

Which leads to my all-time favorite demo (see Figure 11-31). The televised ketchup race, which Heinz loses because it's slower (thicker) than the rest, is the work of Bert Steinhauser. He says: "They called me Mr. Demo at Doyle Dane. Other people were doing Volkswagen and Polaroid. I was doing my demos. Pink pads versus big blue (Brillo versus S.O.S.), ketchup races, you name it.

"A demo has to be entertaining. It can't be tricky. A demo has to be the whole idea, the whole commercial.

"I remember when we got the account, we went to the Heinz plant. Bernbach was there, Bob Levenson, too. I wandered into a room where I saw two plates. One plate was Heinz. The other was dripping and running. I asked the research guy what he was doing. 'I'm testing viscosity,' he said.

(Text continues on page 284.)

Figure 11-23

ANNCR (VO): Here's what you could be getting into when
   you buy a pair of work boots. This is a $45 boot
   after 3 hours in water.

(SFX)

This, a $60 boot.

This, an $80 boot.

While this is a Timberland work boot. Timberland,
waterproof, insulated boots start at about $60. So if
you're spending $45 or more and not getting work
boots as good as Timberlands, your feet aren't the
only thing getting soaked.

281

Figure 11-24

There are two cars here.
The one you can see is a
Mercedes-Benz.

Since a car is an amalgam of some 10,000 separate components, attention to little things can mean a lot.

No car manufacturer perceives this more clearly than Mercedes-Benz.

The tail light on a Mercedes car quite literally illuminates the Mercedes-Benz commitment to detail.

Ridges have been designed into the face to ensure the light is visible even in the most adverse circumstances.

With the car on the left above, enough dirt has splattered the rear lights to make the car virtually unreadable from the rear.

In the same conditions the recessed sections of the Mercedes-Benz rear light have remained dirt-free. The car remains visible.

A fact that increases the safety of the occupants and of those travelling behind it.

Closer inspection will show further evidence of Mercedes-Benz attention to detail.

Deflectors on the front roof pillars keep dirt and water away from side windows. A rain runnel above the rear window keeps the rear view clear.

Though seemingly unimportant, features such as these can have a major influence on safety.

To see, or be seen, in time is critically important on the road. The milliseconds of reaction time they can buy for the driver of a Mercedes-Benz could be the most important milliseconds of his life.

Mercedes-Benz.
Engineered like no other car in the world

Figure 11-25

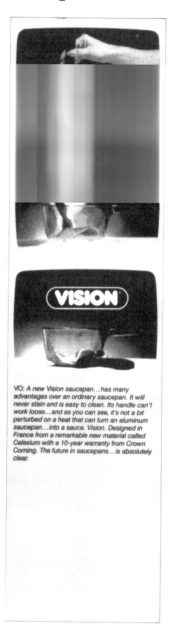

VO: A new Vision saucepan…has many advantages over an ordinary saucepan. It will never stain and is easy to clean. Its handle can't work loose…and as you can see, it's not a bit perturbed on a heat that can turn an aluminum saucepan…into a sauce. Vision. Designed in France from a remarkable new material called Calexium with a 10-year warranty from Crown Corning. The future in saucepans…is absolutely clear.

Figure 11-26

"I asked how long he'd been doing that, and he replied, 'About 30 years.' That's how the whole idea was born."

"Mr. Demo" went on: "Heinz had a 23 percent share then. They were set to close the Pittsburgh factory. After about a year, the Heinz share was about 39 percent. It was the greatest supermarket turnaround of all time."

There's no single advertising format that has been parodied more than the demonstration. Ernie Kovacs. Johnny Carson. On "Saturday Night Live" and "The Honeymooners." Think of all the takeoffs on collapsible fishing poles, Vegematics, and Oriental bamboo steamers. You're not the only one who's laughing. The manufacturers are laughing, too. All the way to the bank.

Figure 11-27

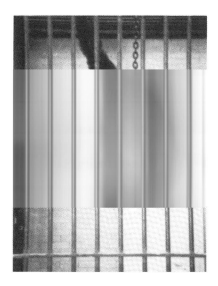

Figure 11-28

Figure 11-29

1. *Video:* Two batteries being mounted onto a toy fireman; it starts climbing step by step.
Audio: Clicking sound at each step on the ladder.

2. Music in step with rhythm.

3. MVO: "National's new Hi-Top is climbing this skyscraper."

4. Background music.

5. Aircraft noise, background music.

6. Background music stops.

7. Sound of fire being extinguished.

8. MVO: "Now you've seen the power and endurance of these batteries. – New National Hi-Top."

Figure 11-30

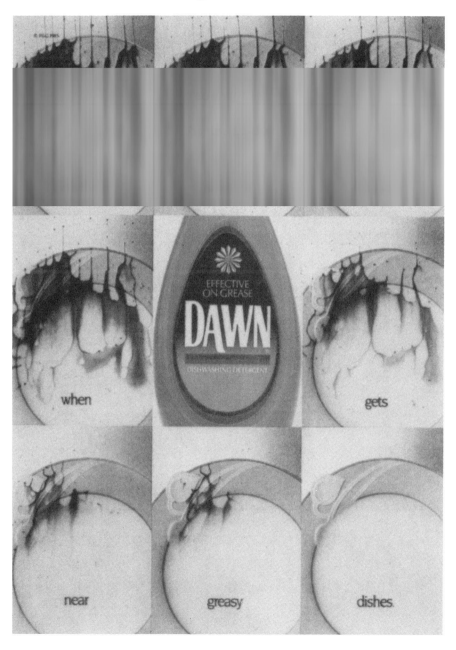

Figure 11-31

C'mon Jonno. We're gonna have a ketchup race.

SFX.

You're never gonna get it out.

Heinz . . . It's too thick and rich to run.

Chapter Twelve

On Responsibility

The O'Toole quote puts advertising people a cut below labor union leaders, but a cut above used car salesmen. In the same piece, he recounts this from the *Wall Street Journal:* "In its early years, *Who's Who* barred athletes, criminals, ad agency executives, and celebrities of dubious morality." O'Toole cannot believe "that considerable and mounting negative attitudes about advertising will not eventually reduce the effectiveness of each individual advertisement." He adds, "I cannot believe that it will not inevitably erode our efforts to attract the most brilliant and creative and ethical people into our business."

Worked up and worried, O'Toole poses a final question: "What are we going to do about it?"

My first inclination was to ignore the question entirely. Even if I were guilty of ad mischief, it would be improper for me to examine my own conscience. For one thing, I wouldn't know how to get in; for another, I wouldn't know what to do when I got there; and for a third, I wouldn't let me in in the first place.

My attitude is this: When every plumber, mechanic, repairman, politician, lawyer, oil company executive, insurance agent, public utilities worker, and Pentagon contractor finds it necessary to defend his profession, I'll start defending mine.

So why don't I just stop? Because the sudden stop would kill me. And because I'm looking for a fight. This is an equal opportunity book; why not go after the critics? Before I did, I called John O'Toole. John is in Washington these days, as executive vice president of the 4A's. He's advertising's "representative at large."

John O'Toole didn't agree with me. "I'll tell you why," he said. "We do have a responsibility because there is not a vast amount of *mis*information out there about plumbers and lawyers. We have the obligation to promote what's real about our profession rather than what's false. That's why I'm in Washington. That's why I want people like you to use me."

289

Thanks to John O'Toole, I'm seeing things differently. Given the chaotic state of advertising, it's understandable how we're all fair game for detractors.

John O'Toole is an openly admitted lobbyist. He is a high-caliber advocate and has an intense faith in advertising as a profession. He has been there. He knows all the angles.

O'Toole notwithstanding, I have my own hypothesis: The picture of an advertising professional as one part sleaze and one part slick is claptrap from outsiders who are dropouts or pushed-outs themselves who couldn't make it in the business, misread advertising, and take their self-serving claims (which usually come from quacks with professional stakes in psychology) too seriously.

Being responsible is not something we in advertising consciously are. We do not arrive at work sporting a "Have you hugged a consumer today?" button. On a day-to-day basis, responsibility in advertising can be better understood if looked at as two words—*response* and *ability.* Said another way, responsibility emerges from our ability to respond.

As communicators, we exchange information. Therefore, we must be honest and sensitive to the people we want to reach. If we don't respect people, we don't belong in advertising. If we are arrogantly smart, we only become cynical about the intelligence of others. Nothing betrays advertising faster than manipulative, insulting advertising. Yet, pick up most books about advertising written from the outside and you'll see advertising depicted as the great manipulator. Here's one: *The Image Makers* by William Meyers, who contends that advertisers reign "as the creators and controllers of our consumer culture" with the power "virtually to dictate buying habits."

In reality, it's the other way around. Effective advertising responds to needs and trends. A *real* sale is made on the consumer's terms, not ours. Advertising is a reflection of a person's mood. If we capture and captivate that mood and hook it to a reasonable benefit, we haven't manipulated anybody. We've created a customer. We've made somebody's life a little better or easier.

Says Lois Korey: "We're advocates, really, just like lawyers. But we argue our client's cases in public. And we have to put them in the language of the people. We're a link between the manufacturer who knows so much about his product that he can't look at it objectively, and the consumer who doesn't care how it's made, only what it will do."

ADVERTISING FOR KIDS

Slime Time

At the risk of seeming to weaken my own case, let's turn to one body of work that may justify John O'Toole's remarks. This is the advertising on kids' Saturday morning TV—slime time—where every hero solves his problems with violence and mayhem. This is the closest advertising ever comes to brainwashing.

As a father of four boys, I didn't have many rules for my kids. "Good morning," "Thanks, Mom," "Excuse me," "Don't get up, I'll do that"—these aren't so much rules, but indications that thoughtfulness and everyday polite-

50 figures.

Today your kids can wage galactic chaos from every room of your house. They can learn anew the gunfighter's principle: The only way to resolve any conflict is with a weapon.

In kid advertising, nothing pays off faster than violence. The effect on a Saturday morning sitting in front of the scooby doo tube, if not brainwashing, is brain-damaging. Voltron, Defenders of the Universe, Gobots, and the Masters of the Universe featuring such characters as He-Man and Skeletor. "He-Man." The expression strikes me as repulsive and terminally harmful to a young boy. To be a he-man means to grow up dumb, insensitive, soldierly, and never daring to think without an order. What a pathetic ambition it is to grow up with the intention of being a he-man. Think of what he misses; Mark Twain, Christopher Robin, Charles Dickens, and Abe Lincoln (who had nothing on a Saturday morning but his books). He also stands a good chance of "finding women a riddle and a nuisance" for the rest of his life (words from Paul Theroux writing about our insistence on a man being a man).

Don't think for a minute that violence isn't big business: "Masters of the Universe" did $350 million and when you throw in all the licensed gear, it bumps to $1 billion in business for 1985.

Says Peggy Charron, founding head of Action for Children's Television, "Mattel created that program solely to sell toys. That may be good for advertising, but it's terrible for children. Too often today, for Mattel and Hasbro and the rest of them, the whole program is a commercial. The same companies are designing the programs that pay for the commercials on those programs. And they're only subtle in the sense that they won't put commercials for Masters of the Universe toys on the 'Masters of the Universe' show. So, instead, you put My Little Pony toy commercials on 'Masters of the Universe,' and vice versa."

Obviously you have to do your homework to keep up with all the he-men on

291

the board of directors of toy companies. Whatever vision is dancing in children's heads at Christmas, it's likely to include a battery that propels a violent weapon.

Maybe if I played with the Rambo doll (the runaway toy of 1985), I'd turn into one myself. I'm not sure what I would go after first—toy companies who pollute kids' brains, or chemical companies ideally situated next to a body of water. I certainly wouldn't go it alone. I would probably invite She-Ra (that's He-Man's sister) to come along.

On the record, advertising has a lousy record when it comes to self-regulation in such an important matter as our kids. The Children's Advertising Review Unit (CARU), established in 1974, has published a ten-page booklet entitled "Self-Regulatory Guidelines for Children's Advertising."

CARU lists five basic principles that should be considered before we create advertising directed to kids. I have condensed them below:

1. Don't exploit age. Young people have a limited concept of what is credible and what isn't.
2. Don't exploit the imagination.
3. Be truthful and accurate. Give nonhype information.
4. Commercials should aim to influence social action that's positive and healthy, not destructive and violent.
5. Advertising should never enlist kids to pressure parents for what is advertised.

Cleaning Up Our Act

Are things getting better? Peggy Charron again: "It is getting better, however slowly. There's more advertising for nonsugared cereals, which is definitely a good trend."

If pugnacity and hostility aren't sufficient provocation for making things better faster, I offer the following list as canny suggestions as to how you and your kids—as consumers—can help advertising clean up its act.

1. Resist cereals named after monsters or cartoon characters. Resist anything that insinuates that it's made with fruit when it isn't.
2. Be wary of little girl doll commercials shot through pink and green filters and little boy doll commercials shot with Star Wars visuals. (Ever wonder why you always see two boys together? Or two girls together? Because boys sell to boys. And girls sell to girls. Tricky, huh?)
3. Beware of toy figures shot at severe angles that distort the scale and make a tiny toy appear huge. Watch out for toys shot in bunches, as in a phalanx of G.I. Joes. Your kid will never spot the mice-type super reading "sold separately," and will be disappointed when he gets only one.

4. Avoid, out of principle, all stores that begin advertising for Christmas on my birthday (Halloween). Radio Shack is the perennial culprit.
5. Scorn any product whose commercial even hints that you're a rotten parent if you don't buy the product for your kid . . . or makes one kid look "out of it" to his peers if he doesn't have the toy.

think there's anything more divisive, defeating, or heartbreaking than a poor kid looking at a young, sallow-faced yuppie on TV with a steam locomotive circling his living room on a track.

A book I've always wanted to write is a parent-to-parent guide to buying toys. The working title would be *25 Toys That Won't Get Thrown Out with the*

Figure 12-1

Christmas Tree. Now, I'm not a consumer psychologist. I never attended a baby expo, or deprived my kids of their lullaby lamps, so maybe this book is a little old-school. But old school can be beautiful, and when it comes to fun, memories, and imagination, it beats the buy, buy, buy for baby school most of the time.

My list of suggestions would begin with a pet. Preferably a dog. Not the kind created by Walt Disney, but more like a James Thurber dog.

If not a dog, any barnyard animal will do. A weanling pig, for example . . . one who lives quietly and doesn't end up violently. If not a real pig, a book about one, the theme of which is that pig is saved by a spider—a book that would end on this note:

> Wilbur [the pig] never forgot Charlotte [the spider]. Although he loved her children and grandchildren dearly, none of the new spiders ever quite took her place in his heart. She was in a class by herself. It is not often that someone comes along who is a true friend and a good writer. Charlotte was both.

Now that is my idea of a "he-man."

Celebrating Our Gifts

Admittedly, creativity in the cause of kid consumers is open to serious questioning.

I could go on and review the perennial good guys. Let's just tip our caps to them: Lego, Fisher-Price (Figure 12-1), Keds, McDonalds, Matchbox, Jell-O, Health-Tex.

We could also go on about the $700,000,000 of media money donated to campaigns created pro bono by hundreds of agencies. The responsibility here is to treat clients who don't pay you the same way as the ones who do.

Advertising doesn't save. It doesn't corrupt either. It's merely a wonderful venue for turning personal responsibility into a celebration of one's own gifts.

The following story, reported by Phil Dougherty, advertising editor of *The New York Times,* appeared under the title: "The Only Gift He Could Give." The ad described in the story is shown in Figure 12-2 on page 296.

> This time last year Frank M's family prepared for the Christmas of 1983 as if they were zombies. The heart had gone out of them that summer when the sickness that had their youngest child coughing continually was finally diagnosed as cystic fibrosis, an almost sure killer.
>
> Frank, the head of the house, went about his art director's job at Ally Gargano/MCA like an automaton wanting to strike out at something but not knowing what to do for his little girl.
>
> This year, with the child now seven years old and doing better than her parents had expected her to do, things are looking slightly better. And Frank has done something and learned something.

He created an ad, a controversial, hard-hitting ad that he feels has educated a lot of people about the horrors of the genetic disease. And he learned that he had some real friends in the business.

Frank is not the father's real name. Not only does he not want publicity for himself in this matter, but he is especially concerned that if his neighbors and the little girl's school chums know the truth, they will treat her differ-

national organization declined.

Yesterday, Robert K. Dresing, president of that Washington-based foundation, explained his reaction to the ad. First, he is opposed to dealing a blow like that to the psyche of young victims. Second, that negative an approach, he believes, would have a bad impact on contributors. "People want to be on a winning team," he said.

But there is something to the story of our Frank M. that reminds me of the Christmas tale of the ragged juggler performing before a creche in a darkened, empty church because that was the only gift he could give. Frank makes ads—good ads judging from the Clio and One Show awards crowding one shelf in his office. So, although the local office of the foundation proffered volunteer jobs, he was not satisfied until his gut-wrenching ad got an audience.

And it got one, thanks not only to his drive but also the voluntary help of Jerry Cailor, a photographer with Cailor-Resnick; the photo retouchers at Spano/Rocconova; the modeling company and all 16 kids who are professional models; two type houses and an engraver. All worked gratis.

Then between August and October, Frank raised $24,000 by calling or writing only 45 friends and associates, including Silas Rhodes of the School of Visual Arts, from which he graduated, and Della Femina, Travisano and Partners, where he used to work.

The money was not to pay for the space, but now that the ads have brought enough to pay for themselves, the extra money will be given for research.

"I had to do something," he said at one point. "How could I not do an ad? I do an ad for anything else that comes around the corner."

Figure 12-2

Chapter Thirteen

Heroes

Someone who doesn't *tell* you how to do it, but who makes you want to do it.
In a word, a hero.

My own early hero was a sculptor, a painter, a poet, an architect—Michelangelo.

When he started working in the Sistine Chapel, five of his painting peers came over to assist and advise him on fresco techniques.

The quality of their work was not what he desired. So, he threw them out, locked the chapel doors, and spent the next four years alone on the scaffold.

To me, this is a lesson in what it takes to make quality *and the cost*. And what helped make Michelangelo one of the greatest, if not *the* greatest of all artists.

I saw that proficiency and improvement came with sweat. Sweat we must, or the genius is wasted.

As a young copywriter I was also influenced by the fact that Michelangelo never said, "I don't do ceilings."

THE PROMISED LAND

I needed someone closer to the street. A patron saint, as it were, of mavericks and misfits.

I needed a voice with the sound of conviction that left no doubt about his respect for the creative mind. This was in the 1960s. So, I suppose there was no way of avoiding Bill Bernbach.

Bernbach was a submerged thread running through most of the great work at that time. States Ed McCabe: "If you were really good and couldn't get a job at DDB, you had to start your own agency."

Bernbach was more than style or structure. His advertising had always the sound of one person talking to another. An intimate transaction—that's what advertising was in Bernbach's hands.

Once an ad had this voice, a consumer could care about it and think of it not so much as a call of the wild as a call of his own kind. An ultimately human ad.

At DDB an ad was never finished if you could make it better. (Even if the client had bought it, even if it was running.)

I remember a speech I heard him give at the United Nations. (I was taking notes like a schoolboy cramming for a test. I suppose even then I knew someday I would write this book, because I saved everything I ever found instructive about the business.)

The following are some of my scribbles from that Bernbach talk.

"Advertising," he said, "is no different from any good writing. The first headline written is probably awful. But the writer and art director think it's clever—they're both having a good time. It's the reader who gets the work. The true test of every ad is when the reader gets the kick and all the copywriter and art director get is hard work."

Never leave the consumer confused, cheated. That was one of Bernbach's guiding principles. And make sure the magic comes directly from reality, not make-believe.

CONNECTING UNLIKELY THINGS

There are countless examples of how Bernbach applied this realism to his ads.

A slice of bread with teeth marks representing a bite. A black boy, an Indian, a nun enjoying Jewish rye bread.

A box of Barton's candies after it had been raided by a chocolate lover (see Figure 13-1).

Another slice of bread with the center ripped out, and the headline: "That's where the Fairmont butter was."

An ad for Fairmont frozen strawberries created by a literal-minded agency might have read "At Fairmont, every frozen strawberry is whole." The picture used by every other agency would have been a whole strawberry. At Doyle Dane, it was always the unfamiliar. In this case, a lonely stem. The headline read: "This is all we have to cut away."

Because of Bernbach, writers and art directors became equal partners—a team.

Writers stepped over the line; they did thumbnails, picked type, and forced themselves to think visually.

Art directors who previously would find typewritten scripts under their doors in the morning began to think long before the copywriter ever began to write.

They began to stray from their drawing boards. Together with the writer they began to have a voice in product strategy. This meant more control over the work, and it meant long-range rather than short-range solutions.

Figure 13-1

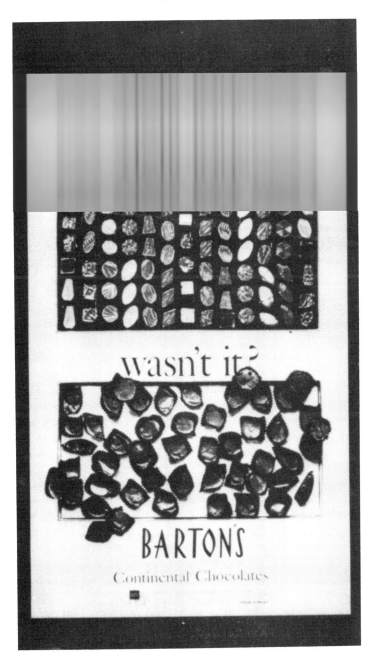

The team concept was revolutionary at the time. "First you make a revolution, then you figure out why," mused Helmut Krone. It gave DDB its special raffishness and drew talent from everywhere.

It was Bernbach who re-educated the creative team to take control of the creative product. If it has anything to do with your idea, be there. Even if you have to break down doors to do it. That means at the client level, too. Get to know the client. Learn to act and think like a proprietor. Clients can sense it and put more value on it than anything else you'll ever do. The clients start asking for you. It'll scare the hell out of the managers—but it's the best way for a creative person to beat them all to a seat on the board of directors and into the final yes or no position.

Bill Bernbach died October 11, 1982. At the U.N. chapel memorial service, Bob Levenson, longtime friend and protege, offered this tribute: "So much of our work was delivered as a love offering. We loved him and we wanted to please him very much."

Levenson summed up in those two sentences the essence of DDB's corporate culture and the way it motivated creative talents through the past more than quarter-century. "The best words any of us could hear was 'Bill loved your ad.' The worst words were 'He hated it.' We wanted him to eat it up. And we were thrilled when he did. And we tried harder and harder until we did."

When I interviewed Levenson, he had just taken the creative reins at Compton. In a touching moment, he took a framed birthday memento with a handwritten note from Bernbach down off the wall.

"You can't use this," Levenson said, " 'Cause someday I'm going to write my own book about Bill."

But in the next sentence, he kind of paraphrased it for me: "Bill didn't bribe people. There were no such things as spot raises and field promotions. But you knew he was always watching. He always led us to believe that he knew and cared about what we were doing."

Trapped into Being Interested

The National Federation of Coffee Growers of Colombia campaign is 1980's version of pure Bernbach. He always preferred photographs in advertising because he considered illustration or cartoon a cop-out. His objective was always to make the advertising more realistic and also more honest, more dramatic, more involving, more surprising, springing a trap for the reader so he hardly recognized it as an ad. Bernbach believed that a photograph gave you more options. A photograph can be enlarged, reduced, cut apart, silhouetted, matted, strobed, screened.

Consider poor Teddy, that's the burro (Figure 13-2). The guy on the couch is the registered trademark, Juan Valdez.

Teddy was hacked up, flipped on his back, had his legs and neck recon-

Figure 13-2

Fame has its price.

structed. Another donkey's tail was added and his nose retouched. Not exactly the life of a first-class ass, but it is a job.

"It wasn't strange for me to shoot the job in parts," says Larry Robbins, the photographer. "I do that all the time, even when I'm not shooting components. I don't go out and find pictures. I make them."

And this from Doyle Dane's art director Mark Hughes: "The client intended to increase its budget, yet retain the same old face. We had an already existing face in Juan Valdez (created by Helmut Krone). Our objective was to disarm. To say to the trade: 'Here's Juan and his mule busting their butts in media. We want you guys to go and sell.'

"We ran seven ads. Trade inventories increased 290 percent from a campaign that was never asked for but we knew was right."

One of the oldtimers at DDB once said, "Some of Bill's best ads were done without him ever having to pick up a pencil." It seems legitimate to give Bernbach the credit for this one.

Postmortem
The merger of DDB and Needham Harper Worldwide signals, for many, a sad postscript to the Bernbach era.

301

No one doubts that the new agency will do fine work. That is not the prevailing fear that grips Madison Avenue. The fear is echoed in Bernbach's own words: "I fear all the sins we create in the name of creativity. I fear we may be entering the age of phonies." (See the photo of Bernbach in Figure 13-3.)

HE WOULDN'T PLAY THE GAME

Saul Grubstein was my art director at SSCB over a three-year period in the mid-1970s. We served as a kind of song-and-dance team for clients. We wanted them to get the impression that, along with the squares, the agency had its odd-balls, too.

When I first met Saul, I said to myself, "Here is a man truly in trouble. He's set in his ways and he looks like his name." When Dostoevski's underground man says, "I'm a sick man, an unattractive man, a destructive man," he could have been describing Saul.

Yet the longer I worked with Saul, the more I recognized him as the only pure one among us.

He filtered out all contrivances, pretensions, and distractions. Client hand-holding, creative reviews, and focus groups in cities where, according to Saul, "nobody seems to live," made him sick.

Figure 13-3

Bill Bernbach

He never fell into the "trappings" trap. He conserved his energy for the most important things: ideas and his craft.

His life in advertising was bound to that craft. He applied an element of stubborn simplicity to everything he did.

I remember, in particular, an assignment for the Menley James client. They made Contac and had just introduced Love cosmetics for women via Wells, Rich,

is doing it successfully.

At the point-of-sale we wanted to give the consumer the opportunity to buy the entire line of four products as a big-ticket gift item or to buy a single product, one at a time.

So the product had to be displayed both ways. Saul designed four packages featuring individual parts of a man's body. A big face for the antiwrinkle product, a torso for the cologne, and so on. He numbered them one, two, three, four. Saul was insistent that the package be photography. He almost went crazy trying to find the perfect piece of swipe to use for the mock-up for the package. He finally found it. When he was finished cropping and cutting, not only did each package work individually, but when you put them together, they actually formed the whole figure of the man, as if it had never been cut up at all.

I thought it was so brilliant that I wanted to trademark the idea and give it some bullshit name like "sequential unit packaging." Saul said, "No, let's just call it picture puzzle packaging, 'cause that's where I got the idea: in the picture puzzle department at Lamston's Five and Ten."

Like every creative team, we had lots of marketable ideas that we never did anything with.

It verifies a sad truth: Most creative people are great at having ideas and absolute dumbbells when it comes to implementing and cashing in on them. No wonder we're always broke two days before payday.

In these times, it may be that true simplicity is impossible, but for Saul the task and the glory of advertising came from being gloriously simple.

He would spend hours trying to avoid a needless "cut" in a commercial. "The best commercials are little stories told in a single take," he would insist.

His storyboard people resembled charming toads, but they always illustrated clearly the storyline, action, and idea. He never allowed his assistants to color a board—a practice I preach even today. "A storyboard should indicate action. I'm making a film, not a hallmark," he would say.

His vision for the film ultimately resulted in some really great screenings, but the agency and the client never knew what to do with our work. Eventually it would come to no good end—mauled in a suburban shopping center at the hands of a ruthless focus group. Saul and I were there viewing from the other side of the glass in a darkened room, munching the egg rolls provided by a motherly research director. Witnesses to advertising's own grisly version of the executioner's song.

Once we were working on Rise shave cream, which is thicker and moister than its competition. It gives your face better protection against cuts and nicks.

In my typical digging fashion, I found out that a razor travels up to speeds of 40–50 miles per second over a man's face. We had so many fake starts on a visual for that fact that eventually I got bored and dropped it. A few days later, Saul came up to me and said: "We'll shoot this guy's face real tight like we're on a race course; we'll crank up the razor speed and have race noises in the background. They'll be so scared, they'll have to use Rise. I got an end line for you, too: 'Rise. It'll make your morning drive a lot less hairy.' "

Separate Paths, Same Destination

Saul and I used to nudge each other a great deal about God. I believed; he didn't. But usually at the end of a discussion (he on one road, I on another), we would arrive at the same place. We were after the same thing. It was a unique kind of synthesis that taught me as much about solving problems as it did about the Almighty.

Saul always gave a sort of dignity to the art of art direction. He was convinced that art could meet life in advertising.

He didn't give up. It was a combination of the right ideals at the wrong agency, diabetes, and eventual blindness that forced him out of the business.

Golden Days

I talked to Saul not long back from his Park Slope limestone. I told him about the book. "You're in the book," I said, "under heroes."

He was touched and reflective. At times his voice was full of pain. But when we started talking about the business of advertising, his voice became resolute and resounding, like he'd never been away.

"Other art directors used to come in and watch you work," I said. "You were always cropping, snipping, blowing things up. Where did you learn to work that way?"

"I wanted to be a fine artist, but I didn't want to starve," he said. "I got a job at *The New York Times* scaling and cropping photos. Bill Golden at CBS saw my work and hired me. He taught me most of everything I know. For Golden, there was always an answer. I would do 20 sketches—he would never criticize, never tell me what to do. He'd just mumble. That was a sign that there was something more I could do. I learned to dig from my insides. Even when I'd done everything and there was no more to do, there was still a better answer.

idea look good."

I asked him, "If people never left Golden, why did you?"

"I was always walking away from opportunities and bigger jobs. It was because I was basically insecure. Even when Golden liked something I did, I always thought maybe it was an accident.

"There's a Jewish superstition that says 'do yourself praise and God will take it away.' I was just scared, that's all."

"We're all scared," I said. "Maybe that's what drives us to do better. What made you jump to the agency side? Wasn't that a big transition?"

"No," he replied. "There's no difference in my mind between fine art and commercial art. Because you're using the same principles. You analyze a problem and solve it. I never knew how to act like an art director. That's what killed me—I never worked from preconceived formulas. Every idea should come directly from the problem, and every problem is unique."

"Do you have any advice for young people in the business?"

"When I was at Cooper Union, a classmate was critical of one of my designs. He said it looked too much like Paul Rand. My teacher said, 'No, no, no, that's all right—when you're young, you have to know who the quality people are and who the hacks are. Eventually you'll break away.'

"And keep it simple. All the great ones knew when to stop."

"You have every right to be bitter," I said. "Are you?"

"Not really. I just could never understand them—the ones that told you they wanted quality work but wouldn't let you do it. Like us at SSCB. It was like ripping up roses and planting them in a desert. The climate was all wrong. The environment was too stifling."

Saul thanked me for the opportunity to talk about one of the loves of his life, advertising.

He still keeps busy. On Sundays, his wife, Marylyn, reads him *The New York Times*. He listens to his extensive collection of classical music, and he's surrounded by the largest collection of Picasso books outside of Rizzoli's.

"I even art-directed my little Susie's graduation invitation (Cooper Union, of course). Everybody loved it."

In one way or another, Saul will always keep entering my life.

I was watching a rerun of *Broadway Danny Rose*. Woody Allen plays a down-on-his-luck agent. One of his clients is a parrot who sings "I Gotta Be Me."

I thought of Saul.

Chapter Fourteen

Starting Out

To quality, you need only be a sociologist, psychologist, logician, tactician, and sometimes magician who is keenly aware of trends and preferences and is able to read the future with uncanny accuracy.

And it helps if you're a rebel, a risk-taker with talent who has the courage to get it down on paper. Someone who never stops saying "it could be better" and who has the persistence to make sure that talent comes through against sometimes impossible odds.

If you're willing to make that kind of commitment, you'll be happy in advertising. If you can't, you'll find advertising a miserable place to work.

ON ASPIRATIONS

I come in contact with a great number of young business people. Although they are bright, energetic, and ambitious, many are victims of their business school training. They overrely on analysis. They seem to want everything to be "just right."

When things go smoothly, its their own analytical skills. When things go wrong, it's the system.

At a quality agency, you'll be measured solely by the level of your thought/ idea leadership, that is, the effect your ideas have in driving the client's business forward.

Advertising is action-based. It's an I-want-it-yesterday business. In an occupation whose main work is meeting emergencies, we can't stop for "safety first" practitioners who have nothing more on their minds than formulas that guarantee personal success. In advertising, FORMULA = RUT.

The emphasis is in doing: "Do something" as long as you believe it's constructive. As a recent client said, "If you're going to save my business, start this weekend."

Advertising recognizes the importance of instinct—the right message to the right person at the right time—as a starting point.

The question is, does it feel right? Not, can I prove it right?

Educators might bristle, but the problem with many graduates today is that they seem to be devoid of playfulness, innovation, and surprise.

I'm not sugggesting that business schools exist as farm systems for advertising, but candidates should at least know coming in that great work is the result of trying anything and everything.

Any agency can train a hack. Let's not start them out as one.

How Advertising Differs

Advertising is unlike any other business I know on three counts.

One: With every problem, the solution is given. It resides in the product itself. Learn early to immerse yourself in the product. Dig hard for the magic and, above all, love, honor, and obey the consumer.

Two: Advertising is a collection of positive thinkers with uncommon creative ability. You'll find talent everywhere. In advertising, to create is an unalienable right. N.W. Ayer president Jerry Siano concurs: "No other business lets you use your head in so many ways. I've been at it for 30 years. I've been bugged, but never bored."

Three: Nothing stays the same. States Burt Manning, "Nothing stays status long; you keep happy not by maintenance but by staying ahead." With every new ad comes the opportunity to be different. To be happy in advertising is to take pleasure in being different.

Four: If you're a root creative, nothing is impossible. Decide what it is you want to do. Act, have 24-hour belief, and you will achieve it.

If this sounds like a lecture, it is. I wish someone had given it to me when I was starting out.

How to Begin

There is always the chance that your career will be better served by *not* starting out with an agency. In fact, some of the giants of our business had other jobs before they joined agencies.

Claude Hopkins, one of advertising's most successful copywriters, started with Bissell carpet sweeper.

Bill Bernbach, founder of Doyle, Dane, Bernbach, who brought his unique style of sensitivity, humor, and soft sell to advertising, started in the mail room at Schenley liquors and later worked for Paul Rand, a refugee from the Bauhaus School of Design.

Before she answered an ad for a writing job at the Jack Tinker Agency, Lois Korey, creative head of Needham, Harper, Steers, wrote TV comedy for Steve Allen, Ernie Kovaks, and George Gobel.

Reva Korda, creative head at Ogilvy, worked at Gimbels, and later "for a handsome increase of $10 more per week," she went to Macy's. One day she

worked as a shipping clerk, messenger, and menswear salesman at Macy's. "I was a one-man recession," he says. "But the streets of New York are a big, tough campus. You learn what people think, what they want, how they talk, why they buy. What better training for a writer?"

Hal Riney started as a junior account executive, found out what they were, decided he didn't want to be one, and became an art director.

As for myself, I got my basic training at Hubbard's fruit and vegetable store in Pittsburgh. To Mr. Hubbard, bad produce was a personal insult. He made this sign: Please touch the merchandise. He'd think nothing of hacking open a tomato or apple or pickle from the barrel to show a customer how fresh and juicy it was inside. Customers who had no intention of buying tomatoes or pickles would walk out with pounds of the stuff.

"Let 'em touch it, and you're halfway home to a sale," he would say.

It was a lesson I never forgot. Go to the merchandise. Touch it, feel it, squeeze it, eat it. Then go write about it the same way you would talk to a friend. A bright friend. Be specific and energetic and give lots of useful information.

It taught me that each one of us *is* the customer. I remember every summer, Mr. Hubbard would sell corn on the cob, "a Hubbard dozen" for 40 cents. That meant every customer got 13. "It keeps them coming back. When they come back, I know I have a customer for good." What he was saying was: A real sale begins *after* the sale. I couldn't have started with a better first job.

PICKING THE RIGHT AGENCY

When the time comes to hook up with an agency, think of it as a school you want to attend. If your work has any merit at all, it will be purified of its defects by the standards that the agency demands. Such standards come from the personality and character of the agency's leader.

On the one hand, there's Bernbach and Leo Burnett. They were magnificent teachers in the sense that they never told you how to do things, but instead opened windows and exposed you to a world of ideas.

On the other side are the doers—McCabe, Riney, Korey, McElligott—who inspire by the work they do themselves. They never let you lose your enthusiasm for your work. They never, as Jerry Siano notes, "let you see gray."

Try to match the agency's personality to your own. Look for people within the agency who like what you like and whose style enhances your style. The agency that lets you express your personality best is always the best choice.

Remember, what you are interested in is not nearly as important as what you're really good at. Find out what your abilities and talents are. Are you a free thinker? Are you good at numbers? Are you logical? Do you have good people skills?

Getting a job isn't the goal—matching abilities to tasks is.

HOW TO GET IN

Think of yourself as a new product. Give your letter or résumé some drama. Consider long and hard what you want to include. Remember, you're an unknown and want to get noticed. Your personality has to stand out before your work does.

Your letter, book, and résumé are a reflection of how single-minded you are. Determination is the appropriate tonality. Your voice must say, "I really want this." I always wrote my résumé in the third person. That way I could get it all on one page. It avoided what I hate about résumés—the boring look of chronology and graduation dates. It also gave me the opportunity to demonstrate two essentials in advertising: expression and compression.

Also include something of a personal nature: "John enjoys playing poker and drinking beer in the bleachers at Fenway. His son claims that it's impossible to stump him on a sports question." I don't think an interview ever went by without someone trying to stump me (and occasionally someone did).

Once I got into the business, I organized my résumé into case histories using a problem, solution, result form. It demonstrated the effectiveness of my work. I used call reports (written recaps of client presentations) and quotes from my client's work.

In one case history (Ford truck), I used quote after quote from Lee Iacocca, Ford's general manager then.

When I was interviewing at Grey, they had just won the Ford corporate account. I know my reference to Iacocca helped to get me the job.

Make your introductory letter "pointedly personal." Quote the person you're writing to, refer to a campaign they did or a speech they gave. If it takes a little ego-stroking, stroke away.

How to Get Names

If you admire a certain agency or campaign and want to find out the people involved, get a copy of *The One Show Book* or the *Art Directors' Annual.* All the big winners are in there.

The Interview

Just as there are no formulas for a great ad, there are no hard and fast rules for a successful job interview. Today's man and woman must have an intuitive knowledge of how to sell any product—including themselves. Your concern is not only getting looked at and listened to, but getting *believed.* It is in that spirit that I offer the following don'ts.

1. *Don't be an "eegot."* (overfriendly, one who openly worships success).

2. *Don't be too earnest.* To the hardened advertising pro, overplaying earnest is always ludicrous.

3. *Don't bend forward* as if you are wearing a hearing device.

4. *Don't bob your head up and down* in an affirmative manner. You will give the impression of a gooneybird whose only function is to take deep breaths between gulps of water.

5. As one whose taste in language has always run toward the declarative sentence, I beg you to *shun psychobabble* (verbal formalities that blunt the communication they pretend to promote).

I can recall one such psychobabble exchange. An account supervisor called and asked me to see an MBA recruit. Here is the entire transcript of that interview:

Lyons: "So what makes you think you'd like advertising?"
Recruit: "I've prioritized my goals. Career-wise, advertising offers the best way to maximize them."
Lyons: "Ize don't like it. Ize thinks you should try another field."

"Ize" was not very nice that day.

Now for some do's:

1. *Be curious.* When I ask "do you have any questions?" 80 percent of the people I interview say no. It's the one who says "I have a hundred" who gets the job.

2. *Know ahead of time what the agency's products are.* Mention campaigns that you like or don't like, and why.

3. *Know about the business.* Read books, such as Ogilvy's *Confessions of an Advertising Man,* and *Leo,* a wonderful little gem containing the wisdom of Leo Burnett. It was put together by Burnett people as a tribute and a token of respect and love. Also, a book I was introduced to at J. Walter Thompson, *The Techniques of Producing Ideas* by Jim Young.

4. *Have a point of view about current commercials* and what you might do to improve them. A favorite question of mine as an interviewer is, "What campaigns do you wish you had worked on?" The answer tells me if the applicant knows the difference between what is interesting and what is not.

5. *Have a vision.* I always ask, "Where do you see yourself two years from now?" The answer is a good gauge of your determination, confidence, and commitment.

6. *By all means, have a sense of humor.* I was interviewing a young graduate from Northwestern. I really loved her book. Halfway through it, I knew she could think through a problem and give it a twist. We chatted for about an hour, but never once did she mention money. Finally, I said, "Why haven't you mentioned money?" "An act of faith," she said. I hired her on the spot.

And Post-Interview

Always follow up an interview with another letter. Don't tell me *that* you want to work with me. Tell me *why.* Be specific. Pick up something from the interview itself that sparked you. Refer to it in the letter. Remember, you're knocking on somebody's door. And you can only knock once. Person-to-person on a human level is your main concern.

FAME AND FORTUNE

As a beginner in advertising, you will be competing with a group of highly individualistic people. For reasons of simplicity, I have broken them down into two main groups. Advertising-as-a-serious-profession group. Advertising-as-a-get-rich-quick-way-to-success group.

It is never hard to tell one group from another. The first ends up reasonably happy, rich, and well dressed. Group two ends up in a studio apartment using Hamburger Helper. Making personal success a number one priority is operating on a shallow level. Success in advertising is a by-product of hard work. Note: Credit is never given for wearing the right suit to work.

Certainly a great career hangs on great talent. But much of what is necessary for professional success has little to do with talent at all. If this is true, what then makes up the rest? Three things: ambition, toughness, savvy.

announce to everyone that you're working 12 hours a day. Warning: All is not lost if you smile.

2. Forget tomorrow. Concentrate on where you want to be a year from now.
3. Build support on the way up. Everybody needs a rabbi.
4. Love what you do. Attach yourself to people who feel the same way. Nothing is more destructive than working with people who bitch or badmouth the agency or business.
5. Get to know your agency. Who the key players are and what it expects from its people. If the person who gets you stats isn't as professional as your supervisor, change agencies. Ordinary people doing extraordinary work is what distinguishes agencies.
6. Demonstrate to people who are in decision positions that you want the next level. On key issues when you want a definite yes or no, trade up. Call the person on the next level.
7. Ideas. Get assigned to a worthwhile product. Then dig. The ideas will come.

Toughness

1. Persevere. There's a big difference between saying "I think I want to be a supervisor" and "I'm going to be a supervisor."
2. Don't feel guilty about working hard. And if you're a woman, don't ever apologize to any man for it.
3. Don't worry about rejection. There isn't a profession anywhere that pays you more for revising your own stupidity.
4. Consider the fact that you're dissatisfied with everything you do as a positive. Keep at it. Advancement comes from one word: tenacity.

313

Savvy

1. It's not what you learn that counts; it's what you can contribute from that learning.
2. Break down problems into components. Get the snags out. Isolate, then define the problem. That's a 50 percent of any battle.
3. Make sure every suggestion you make is actionable. It only eliminates saying dumb things.
4. Understand the difference between E.Q.—energy quotient—and I.Q.

And remember, be nice. Advertising is a very small business.

Plus Curiosity

One day you'll wake up at age 65 and wonder how you got there. That's how fast it goes in advertising. Make every moment count. Have a passionate curiosity and never fear where nosiness might take you. To illustrate, following is a true story.

A young copywriter was assigned to a new account, a midwestern meat company. He visited the client's factory. The operation was clean and efficient. No scraps on the floor, no blood on the aprons. The employees had a deep-boned commitment to quality.

He was fascinated with their almost corny love for cold cuts. He wondered, is there some hidden beauty in a slice of salami?

Near the end of his tour, he noticed a woman in a white sanitary apron gingerly adding spices, condiments, and peppers to a recipe that was one of the company's best-sellers: olive loaf sandwich meat. The copywriter wanted to know if spices were used for all cold cuts. The answer was, "Yes, spices can be added to any kind of cold cut according to taste. But since most cold cuts are made for kids, most of our recipes go light on spices."

The copywriter couldn't wait to get back to New York. Out of that experience would come a unique new line of sandwich meats. He would position the product directly for adults. The recipes would be hotter and spicier. The taste would accommodate the trend toward spicier foods.

His first ad would announce an exciting new name for America's shopping lists: *Introducing Hot Cuts, the adult cold cut with zip.*

Here was an idea that had all the ingredients for success:

1. It conformed to consumer need.
2. It shook up a sleeping category.
3. It found a unique niche in the market.
4. It could be implemented by the manufacturer at little extra cost.

The moral of the story is this: The people you meet in advertising aren't at all like those in fiction, where the characters seem restricted by the author's lack of imagination and experience. In real advertising life, experience only serves to stretch the imagination. Every experience is an opportunity to bring new ideas to the client's business that will knock the socks off his competition. As a

In advertising, happy endings aren't the exception. I know an enormous number of happy pros. They stay happy because their passion for work hasn't been muffled by compromise. It's what we lose through compromise that makes us so weary. As Burt Manning says, "No one can stay happy in advertising gutlessly."

Use all your energy to better your work, not defend it or whine that the client made you do it. Do this, and you'll discover what the good ones have discovered—you don't get into advertising, advertising gets into you.

AFTERWORD

room and finding all your boyhood heroes there waiting to say hello.

The characters I met became more than sources of quotes, they became my support system. When the book bit me like a mad dog, when it wanted to go one way and I another, or when it landed in the garbage (which happened more than once), I'd ring up the likes of a Jerry Siano, who would invariably come through with something like "I'm jealous as hell, sounds like the kind of book we've all wanted to write."

Rummaging through my notebooks the names keep coming: Jim Johnston, who started me off in the right direction. The gracious Keith Reinhard (who got me four typewritten pages plus a copy of Paul Harper's *Working the Territory* overnight). Joe Seidelmaier kept me laughing and Rochelle Udell floored me with her dead-centered answers. Nor was I amazed to find the *doers* in our business at their desks at lunch. Tom McElligott and Bob Gage both picked up their own phones.

In these mega-days when agencies are making way for holding companies, I wanted to know how to keep happy. From Minneapolis I got this: "I only do what I like. That includes clients" (Nancy Rice, Rice & Rice). From Portland, Oregon this: "We stay happy by doing ads, keeping it small and unpolitical, and working with clients who want to be great" (Dan Weiden, Weiden & Kennedy). From New York this: "Happiness is realizing that our ability is in our originality to create customers for our clients" (Mal MacDougall). And from Raleigh, North Carolina this: "Find an agency that honestly believes in something. Make sure your beliefs are the same and every now and again remind yourself there's more to life than advertising." (Charles McKinney, CEO of McKinney, Silver, who had every reason to be happy. He had just returned from a press conference. His agency had just won the Stephen Kelly Award honoring the year's best print.)

It is good news to report that the majority of the people on these pages are still wide-eyed enthusiasts, permanently fastened to the dream of creating yet another great ad for their clients. They perceive advertising as a game much like any game: Ecstasy when you soar, agony when you don't. It's when you go outside your comfort zone that the game becomes a form of high art as sure as dance or drama.

"It's only when I get up there, do I know what I'm going to do." Even though I'm 5′7″ I understand what Michael Jordan means.